A STUDY OF OMBUDSMAN SYSTEM IN INDIA WITH SPECIAL REFERENCE TO LOKAYUKTA IN MAHARASHTRA

A STUDY OF OMBUDSMAN SYSTEM IN INDIA WITH SPECIAL REFERENCE TO LOKAYUKTA IN MAHARASHTRA

Preeti Dilip Pohekar

GYAN

The publication of this book was financially supported by ICSSR and the responsibility for the facts stated, opinions expressed or conclusions reached are entirely that of the author and ICSSR accepts no responsibility for them.

ICSSR Consultant

[Dr. V.N. Alok, Associate Professor (Public Finance) I.I.P.A., New Delhi]

A Study of Ombudsman System in India with Special Reference to Lokayukta in Maharashtra

ISBN: 978-81-212-1055-3

Published in 2010 in India by
Gyan Publishing House,
5, Ansari Road, Darya Ganj,
New Delhi-110002
Phones : 23282060, 23261060
Fax : 011-23285914
E-mail: books@gyanbooks.com
Website: www.gyanbooks.com

Lasser Type Setting by: Quick Media, Delhi
Printed at : G. Print Process,Delhi

Contents

List of Tables

List of Graphs

List of Chart

Foreword

Dr. Preeti Dilip Pohekar has come out with a very useful book on one important aspect of governance in the country today. This is a study of Ombudsman system in India with a special reference to Lokayukta in Maharashtra, that she undertook as a part of her PhD studies. The need for good governance is now universally recognised as a key factor to ensure development of a country whether it is in terms of social justice, elimination of poverty or creation of employment and economical advancement. The book contains very valuable information on the institution of Ombudsmen in different countries and the efforts made in India to create institutions to remove public grievances in general and corruption in particular.

The institution of Ombudsman is incidentally more than two centuries old. It started in Sweden and it is no coincidence that Sweden and the Nordic countries are rated even today among the least corrupt and well governed countries in the world. These countries seem to have done well, not only in terms of the parameters for economic development but also in terms of human development index. The concept of the Ombudsmen as an instrument for ensuring that a public organisation perform its function properly and effectively delivers the services to the citizens is a key institution that ensures good governance in a country.

The book mentions that according to Caiden, "Ombudsman is institutionalised public conscience-the essence of what the government ought to do, that is to cultivate the well being of the citizens and the preservation of individual liberty and equitable treatment of all citizens by the public bureaucracy."

It comes as a surprise to learn that out of the 200 and odd countries in the world today, nearly 150 have got Ombudsmen or Ombudsmen like institutions. They are known by different names in different countries as Defensor del Pueblo, in Spain, Argentina and Colombia. Parliamentary Commissioner for Administration in Sri Lanka and UK, Me Diateur de la Reapublique in France, Japan, Mauritania, Senegal, Public Protector in South Africa, Protector de Citoyen in Quebec and so on. One perennial problem faced in governance is the relationship between the state as instrument of governance and citizens who are the governed. The forms of government may vary but the quality of governance depends upon the extent to which it is able to come up to the expectations of citizens and perform basic functions like maintenance of law and order, providing rule of law, giving opportunities for every individual to raise to his full potential. Although the quality of governance varies very much among the countries, the fact that the institution of Ombudsman appears to be more common shows that at least the basic urge to ensure that the state has some mechanism for redressal of the grievances of the citizens is more or less universal.

Against the background of the institution of Ombudsman, the book focuses on the specific institutions that have evolved in our country for tackling the issue of public grievances in general and corruption in particular. The Central Vigilance Commission was set up in the government of India as a result of the recommendation of the Santhanam Committee in 1964. It acquired its enhanced power and a statutory position after the 1997 judgement of the Supreme Court in the Vineet Narain case. Along with the introduction of the Central Vigilance Commission, in the states the move was made also for setting up Lokayuktas as agencies which will look in to the grievances of the public and also tackle the problem of corruption.

The Book examines the relative success and failure of these institutions. So far as the Lokayukta is concerned, the observations may some times appear to be contradictory. On page 146 is an observation, 'though Lokayukta is successful at the state level, yet there is a need for impartial, independent and public oriented machinery. After going through the articles in the newspapers, i.e. Times of India, Indian Express, The Hindu in the states, it seems that it is working successfully. But all the institutions have teething troubles'. But the overall impression one gets after going through the book is that the Lokayuktas are pleading for more powers and feel themselves constrained in their operations.

The book brings out more tellingly the ongoing effort for introducing the Lokpal which is focused on tackling the issue of corruption at the political level. The Lokayukta deals with the corruption at the bureaucratic level and the CVC does the same so far as the government of India is concerned. But when it comes to political corruption, there is a mass reluctance, as the author says, lack of political will among others, in introducing any legislation that will check corruption. The author has done a valuable service for a more informed debate about the efforts made for cleansing public life by documenting meticulously the history and the vicissitudes of the efforts to introduce the Lokpal Bill for the past four decades unsuccessfully.

The basic fact to remember is that the root cause of public grievances and poor governance ultimately is corruption. Corruption is lack of integrity. This could be intellectual integrity, financial integrity or moral integrity. But when it comes to public life, it is financial integrity that dominates. The sad fact is that over the years, Indian political system has become a prisoner of the money power and muscle power. Even the Election Commission conceded after 2009 elections that while the Commission could do something about controlling violence and malpractices like booth capturing, against money power they were helpless. It is in this context that serious discussion about the possibility of controlling political corruption through instruments like Lokpal becomes matter of urgent priority for all thinking and concerned citizens. And in tracing the history of Ombudsman all over the world and the experience in India in the context of Lokpal and CVC, the author has rendered a valuable service.

Political will in our country is exercised only under a two conditions. The first condition is the TINA factor (There Is No Alternative). The second factor is that the powers that be realise that the measure would be popular with the voters. Our past experience in different areas show that political will gets exercised when there is the TINA factor. Mr. Narasimha Rao, the former Prime Minister of India who used to say that not taking a decision was in itself a decision was forced to introduce the economic liberalisation programs because of the TINA factor created on the foreign exchange front in 1991. Similarly, the Emergency and its consequences led to a situation where the leaders who came to power after emergency tried to protect themselves by making the invocation of President's Rule under Article 356 more difficult by amending the Constitution.

The TINA factor sometimes is also created by institutions which are difficult to be ignored. The Judiciary and the Election Commission are two such institutions. For instance the public interest litigation filed by Prof. Chockar and Prof. Trilochan Shastri, two professors from IIM, Ahmedabad, finally led to the landmark 2004 judgement of the Supreme Court which made it mandatory for the candidates in elections to declare their criminal records, assets and educational qualifications by filing an affidavit. This is a major step which can introduce a degree of transparency in the political process. Transparency ultimately is the best anti dote for corruption. Malpractices flourish only when there is a lack of transparency. The emergence of information technology and its increasing application in governance is a very welcome step. The development of technology especially of the mobile phones with camera is eminently welcome. It is one instrument that in the hands of every citizen empowers him to act as a whistle blower and call the bluff of the corrupt through the sting operations. After all, in the 14th Lok Sabha, 11 members of parliament were expelled because a TINA factor was created by the sting operations where they were exposed demanding money for asking questions in parliament.

The most important challenge before every citizen is whether a TINA factor can be created for cleansing the political process through the Lokpal BilL.

As mentioned earlier judiciary.is one institution that can create the TINA factor. The second one is the Election Commission, which excersising its powers for conducting elections in free and fair manner, can bring a degree of discipline and transparency in the political process. These institutions combined with information technology, can create the environment for moving towards greater cleanliness in public life. Nevertheless success will ultimately depend a lot on the educated and empowered citizens. As it is rightly said, a people get the government they deserve.

The government incidentally must be congratulated for enacting the Right to Information Act, 2005 which is still in its early stages of implementation. The RTI Act can prove to be a powerful tool in the hands of activists and NGOs to educate the public about their rights and bringing greater transparency in decision making process of governance and there by check to great extent corruption in different aspects of governance.

In the ultimate analysis, the quality of governance depends on the two factors. The first is the people, who are in charge of governance. The second factor is the institutions, through which they operate. Sweden and the Nordic countries has been systematically ranked as among the least corrupt and better governed countries under many parameters. This is not surprising when we recall that Ombudsman as an institution serving as a public conscience of the country evolved in Sweden, that too nearly two centuries ago. A healthy tradition creates a powerful dynamics of its own. The development of effective instruments for government like Ombudsmen is the first step in achieving success and equally important is the type of people who would be selected to govern them. The quality of the people who come to operate these institutions can be ensured by the very process of selection which must be transparent^! n addition it must be particularly ensured that the individuals considered for the office are also people of integrity and command universal respect.

In short this study of the Ombudsman system in India with special reference to Lokayukta in Maharastra, is a very useful source of all relevant information in the context of evolving the right type of institutions for governance and operating them. It must attract the attention of all right thinking concerned citizens of our country.

I wish the author and the book all success.

N. VITTAL I.A.S. (Rtd.)
Ex. Vigliance Commissioner

Preface

On this page, I would like to jot down all words, which are an expressions of my feelings that I have gathered in my heart during my research work. These are the heartfelt words, which I would like to pour on this page.

I was working on the Lokayukta office, that is situated in Mumbai. Obviously, it required me to visit the office various times. After all, I thought that it is a government office. Even though it is not as like another government offices, whether the officials would be co-operative with me or not was my doubt. And surprisingly, right from my first visit to the office, the functionaries made me frank with them and so kindly interested with my research work. I am very thankful to the functionaries in Maharashtra Lokayukta and Upa-Lokayukta office.

Secondly, I am thankto the Director, Regional Branch, Indian Council for Social Science Research, (ICSSR) Mumbai for conferring on me a study grant award for my research project.

I am immensely grateful to Prof. Vasant Limaye without whose co-operation this work would not have taken shape in which it is today. His helpful memories cast a spell over me.

I am thankful to Prof. Dr. Paras Bora Sir for his direct and indirect guidance. On this page I would like to thank to my friends and colleagues—Dr. Lena Kulkarni, Dr. Yugandhara Topre, Mrs. Jaydevi Swami, Dr. Shayesta Talat, Mr. Sandeep Yeole and Mrs. Lata Iyyer.

I am also thankful to the Librarian IIPA, New Delhi, the Librarian, ICSSR, Mumbai. The Librarian, IIPA, Regional Branch, Mumbai, Maharashtra, The Librarian, Kalina University, Mumbai, The Librarian, Institute of Local Self Government, Mumbai, The Librarian, S.B. Art's & Commerce College, Aurangabad.

How can I express my gratitudes towards Dr. Ramesh Dhoble, Dr. Prem Prakash Pandey and Mr. N. Vittal ? I pray God to create one Ramesh Dhoble (my guide) in each and every educational institute so that education sector should be more qualitative. I request God to cultivate one Prem Prakash Pandey (Deputy Director ICSSR, New Delhi) in each and every governmental office so that administration would be more transparent, efficient and effective. A person like N. Vittal (who enclosed his foreword to this book without any hesitation or expectation) is every administrative system so that would not be subjected like this which I focused. I am also grateful to Dr. V.N. Alok who examine my thesis for granting financial assistance.

Last but not least I must convey my gratitude towards my family without whose co-operation this search work would have been absolutely impossible, my father Dr. Dilip Pohekar, my husband Mr. Datta Mahajan, my grand mother Smt. Radhabai, my mother-in-law Smt. Kamalabai and Smt. Yashodhara, my beloved brother Sojwal and my loving son Malhar, my sisters, Dr. Swati, Mrs. Dhanashri, Mrs. Rajeshwri.

It is my duty to pay gratitude to Gyan Publishing House for a timely publication of this book.

I hope, this book will prove a milestone in the studies on Lokayukta and Ombudsman system in India.

Preeti Dilip Pohekar

1

Ombudsman : Origin, Meaning and Development

1.1 INTRODUCTION

This introductory chapter is divided into three sections. The first section covers the problem formulation and importance of the subject which is necessary for going to the second chapter; i.e., Lokpal in India. Rising corruption is at the root of Ombudsman system world over including India. Hence, the second section discusses on the basic concept of corruption and maladministration in Indian scenario in the ancient and modern days. It also provides the list of Corruption Perception Index published by Transparency International. The third section makes a review of the worldwide Ombudsman system.

SECTION 1

1.2 PROBLEM FORMULATION

Corruption is all-pervading. No society is above corruption and no political system is immune to it. It is said that corruption is deeply rooted in human nature. Since time immemorial efforts have been made to curb and control corruption. The saints, the prophets all over the world preached virtues, preventing misconduct, irregularity so as to strengthen honesty, sincerity and integrity in administration. However, all such efforts seem to have gone in vain. Society without corruption has remained a distant dream. In such a situation the only alternative is that of building up more and more institutions like Ombudsman.

As many as 15 States in India have adopted 'Lokayukta' – a public grievances redressal institution formed on the basis of Swedish Ombudsman. There has been considerable delay in this country to evolve the institution of Lokpal at national level. The politicians, academicians have time and again expressed their doubts on the jurisdiction and functioning of Lokpal. The nation has witnessed hot debates on the floor of the House about the vital areas concerning the institution, such as should the Prime Minister be under the purview of the Lokpal? As a result, it happens in respect of other issues, the Lokpal Bill has become a toy in the hands of the politicians. It could not be passed for the last 35 years. As against the merits of the Bill and the institution, party politics and petty considerations always prevailed and the result is that country has remained without Lokpal on the eve of the 21st century. It's a matter of deep concern as to why the bill is delayed? What would be the rightful jurisdiction and the framework of the working of the proposed Lokpal? Taking into consideration the allegations made against the Prime Minister in recent period, the question of inclusion or non-inclusion of the Prime Minister within the purview of proposed Lokpal has become very sensitive. In the prevailing atmosphere can Lokpal work independently and free-from executive control?

To establish Ombudsman is one thing and its effective functioning is something different. We have Lokayuktas appointed in as many as 15 States and they have been functioning for the last 2 to 3 decades. Hence, over a period of time, many vital issues have come up. This book goes into some of these issues in general and pertaining to Lokayukta in Maharashtra in particular.

The vital question is to what an extent Lokayuktas have been able to control corruption and curb maladministration in the states? What types of cases the Lokayukta in Maharashtra deal with? There is lot many factors that do not appear in the formal reports of the Lokayuktas submitted to State Legislatures such as the response of the departments, attitudes of the functionaries, etc. The complainants are at receiving end and the fate of the disposal of their complaints largely depends upon the co-operation of the concerned departments. Here, the aggrieved persons come across many odds and difficulties, such as non-payment of compensation for lands acquired by government, delay in fixation of pay, delay in pension, non-receipt of medical allowances, bribe for getting the bills sanctioned, etc. There is always a scope for probing into such matters.

The effectiveness of Lokayukta has its bearing on the relationship of the Lokayukta and functionaries in the Mantralaya including the Chief Minister and the Ministers concerned. Therefore, the question is, whether the government is positive about the working of Lokayukta in Maharashtra? Could we get the impression that the office of the Lokayukta is strengthened due to active help and proper response by the ministers and bureaucrats.

In European countries, Ombudsman feels confident about its independent and impartial working similar is the case in respect of Lokayukta in Indian states.

1.3 IMPORTANCE OF SUBJECT

In the light of such experience, efforts have been made in this study to analyze how far Lokayukta is successful in controlling corruption and ventilating the grievances of citizens in the state for corruption free democratic society.

It is significant to note that there has been hardly any effort made so far to review the working of institution of Lokayukta in Maharashtra for research. For academic study the institution has not attracted the attention of scholars, academician or media also. It seems, as a matter of fact, Maharahtra is the first state establishing the office of Lokayukta. Hence, there is a dire need to undertake such a study which may fulfill by present research. This study has critically focused on the jurisdiction, functions and limitations of the Lokayukta, as well as his role in curbing corruption and preventing maladministration. It can be humbly said that this is the first effort to focus the Lokayukta institution in Maharashtra academically. It attempts to know how far Lokayukta is a good redressal of public grievances. It can also be considered as the part of administrative reforms taking place for last 30 years in the country. The overall purpose of the study is also to know the confidence and trust of the people towards Lokayukta on the background of European countries.

In European countries, people have confidence in Ombudsman, which represents the participatory administration. Further study of Lokayukta in Maharashtra will help to create awareness among the people and the government departments towards the sensitive issues of controlling corruption and curbing maladministration by the Lokayukta. A common man faces many administrative problems in his daily life. Besides these, due to bribery, favoritism, nepotism he is trapped further and hardly gets a prompt and quick administrative reply. On the other hand, the administrative officers come across many difficulties while working with those who hold power. On this background, it is important to understand the role of Lokayukta to help the common man. Hence, this study will prove useful.

As it is said, power corrupts and absolute power corrupts absolutely. In such a situation, an honest functionary cannot function effectively. The obvious result is the nexus between corrupt politicians and corrupt bureaucrats. It is therefore, important to study the function and role of the Lokayukta in view of such nexus.

1.4 OBJECTIVES OF STUDY

This research tries to understand the old problem in a new way i.e. corruption is an old problem and Lokpal/Lokayukta is a new way. The subject is important considering the hurdles in the way of establishing Lokpal at the center and effective functioning of the Lokayuktas at the state level. Following are the objectives of the study:

It attempts:

1. To understand the need and working of the institution of Ombudsman.
2. To go into analysis of the reasons as to why an appointment of Lokpal at the center has been delayed.
3. To examine the proposed Lokpal bill with Lokpal as

the sentry of democracy in the context of citizen's grievances against administration as well as their charges against those who hold power and authority.

4. To examine the role of the proposed Lokpal in handling the growing corruption.
5. To review the emergence and working of Lokayukta in Maharashtra.
6. To review the jurisdiction as stated in the Act as well as in practice analyze the cases of corruption which could not be considered by Lokayukta in Maharashtra.
7. To understand the relationship between the Lokayukta and the Cabinet, the Lokayukta and the Legislature, the Lokayukta and Judiciary in Maharashtra.
8. To evaluate the overall role of Lokayukta in administrative structure of Maharashtra as a safeguard and protector of citizens.

With these objectives, a humble effort will be made to give a few suggestions for the sound and effective functioning of Lokayukta in Maharashtra.

Efforts will be made to realize these objectives in the light of the findings of the study. Efforts will also be made to bring out the weaknesses and limitations of the institution of Ombudsman if any in Indian situation.

1.5 HYPOTHESES

In order to fulfill these objectives, a few workable hypotheses are presented-

1. More effective the Lokayukta is greater is the possibility of reaching at the deep roots of corruption with a view to overcome the problem of corruption.
2. It is only through the appointment of impartial person of integrity as Lokayukta, the purpose of reducing corruption and ventilation of citizen's grievances will be fulfilled.

3. The degree of success of Lokayukta is directly related to the availability of adequate investigation officers at his disposal and required response from the Government in this regards.
4. It can be pleaded that greater the number of complaints, citizens lodge to the Lokayukta, fuller will be utility of this office.
5. The effectiveness of Lokayukta depends upon timely adequate information supplied to it by the government departments.
6. Straining relationship between executives and Lokayukta, leads to obstacle in the way of his functioning whereas sound relationship results into speedy and effective results.

1.6 REVIEW OF LITERATURE

To get an overall picture of the Lokpal institution and to clear the concept and its scope, it is proposed to survey the literature on related subjects in general and Maharashtra Lokayukta in particular.

1.6.1 Literature on Ombudsman

Ombudsman is a worldwide experience. Nearly, 152 countries are the members of 'International Ombudsman Institute'. It means, nearly 152 countries have adopted Ombudsmanship. There are some books available on this subject.

1.6.1.1 Books on Ombudsman

'Ombudsman and Others' by Walter Gelhorn is a classic. Gelhorn, a distinguished lawyer and authority on public administration presents his thorough observations of the research on Ombudsman institute in 9 countries that reduced conflicts between citizens and administration. Those 9 countries are Sweden, Finland, Denmark, New Zealand, Norway, Japan, Poland, USSR and Yugoslavia. The findings of Gelhorn in this regard are:

1. Ombudsman is a bold guardian of citizens.
2. Ombudsman system in these Scandinavian countries resulted in reducing corruption so much so that there are few occasions of corrupt incidents there.
3. In Sweden, Ombudsman's annual reports are presented in an edition of 3,400 copies and are made available to the scholars, libraries, journalist, judges and administrators. But the readership is a very few. The reports are not read widely.

Finally, he noted that one of the Ombudsman's important accomplishments is achieving uniformity.[1]

One of the important works done by Frank Stacy on British Ombudsman is notable. He studied and observed the working of 4 years of British Ombudsman in his study entitled. 'The British Ombudsman'.

According to him, the Parliamentary Commissioner (British Ombudsman) had solved the problems of maladministration. However, he criticized that many cases left unresolved also[2]. This is a major drawback of British Ombudsman according to the author.

Rowat Donald, an expert in Public Administration wrote two books: one is 'Ombudsman' and another is 'The Judicial Ombudsman'. He pointed out that Ombudsman can arouse the confidence of the people in the democratic government.[3] He supported Ombudsman system as the safeguard against the individuals engaged in corruption and irregularities. Executive is under Ombudsman's control in several countries; but how to control judiciary remains. In Alaska, courts are under Ombudsman's purview. Ombudsman's Annual Report in Alaska reveal that in 1990- out of 7600 cases loaded to him, 120 dealt with the courts alone.[4] It means, nearly 2% cases per year are dealt with the courts. In Sweden and Finland, Ombudsman can directly supervise the behavior and procedure followed by the Judges. Of course, should the courts be under Ombudsman's purview or not is still a controversial issue there.

These are some of the books available on world

Ombudsmanship. Besides these, in some national and international journals, there are some articles on this subject.

1.6.1.2 Ombudsman as Presented in Articles of Journals

Gerald Caiden in the 'International Review of Administrative Science' noted that Israeli Ombudsmen did a good job to humanize the citizen's relations with impersonal government authority.[5] According to him, Israeli Ombudsman insists powerfully on public rights and asks him to stand against politicians and officials. Israeli Ombudsmen are proud of their work; whereas, Nigerian Ombudsman is a unique experience[6]. In Nigeria, there are no limitations on how complaints are lodged with the Ombudsman. Ladipo Adamlokan noted in his article, 'The Nigerian Ombudsman'.

> "...its structure of a Chief Commissioner at the national level co-ordinating with the work of Commissioners at the state level, is a response not only to the federal nature of the country, but also to the extensive scope of responsibility covering public and private organizations throughout the country."[7]

Another notable feature is that Nigerian Ombudsmen themselves as well as the students of 'Ombudsmen Institution' give an adequate publicity of their functioning so that potential beneficiaries might know existence and the achievements of the institution, overall world experience of Ombudsman by every account has increased public confidence towards administration.

> "... The Ombudsman has to make officialdom and the government meaningfully, respond effectively."[8] —

is a suggestion made by Rowat Donald in an article. 'Maladministration : Issue For The Ombudsman,' in 'The Australian Journal of Public Administration'. So far as the reports and recommendations of the Ombudsmen are concerned, major limitation of the institution is its reports are recommendatory rather than mandatory. Further limitation can be pointed the types of cases the Ombudsmen deal with.

Yardley in article 'Ombudsman in UK' published in IJPA says,

> " ...the majority of Ombudsman cases are concerned with comparatively minor matters such as delay in assessing tax liability, failure of repair a council, flat adequately, normal procedure in dealing with planning application..."[9]

Thus, the material on Ombudsman available in different books and journals throw light on both positive and negative aspects on the working of the Ombudsman.

1.6.1.3 Websites on Ombudsman

There are some Web pages launched on Ombudsman in various countries. The entries and notes are important as the latest information on worldwide Ombudsman experience.

In Finland, the least corrupt country in the index of 'Transparency International', Ombudsman is an autonomous administrative unit attached to the Parliament.[10] It is supported by the logistical service of Parliament. In Finland, Ombudsman can observe the administration of justice also. Its powers are extended to the purview of the President. In Sweden, Ombudsman is a Legislative Commissioner for investigating citizens' complaints of bureaucratic abuse.[11] It is independent, impartial and arbiter between government and the individual. In Greece, the Ombudsman was established in 1996. The period of 6 to 7 years, it exercises real control over the administration and proved its importance as well as protection to citizen's rights.[12] It is accountable to the citizens in Greece.

In New Zealand, Ombudsman is accountable to the Parliament.[13] In European countries, there are some private Ombudsmen, local Ombudsmen and Ombudsmen for the departments.

In the USA, there are several types of Ombudsmen. For example, Colorado, Chicago, Texas, Kansas Universities have Educational Ombudsman. The Chicago University is the first that introduced the Educational Ombudsman. The Students Ombudsman is salaried-part time official.[14] The Students Ombudsman is selected from the students only. He works with the students and administrators or faculty members.[15] His main purpose is to bring attention to injustices done or abuse of discretion. In Kansas University, Ombudsman can consider all sides of a issue in an impartial and objective manner in order to resolve it and concerns raised by any member of the University Community.[16] There is a provision for Ombudsman in 'University Senate Rules and Regulations' of Kansas. The Ombudsman for Education is the channel of student's satisfaction.[17] It is strongly committed to maintain confidentiality. In Colorado University, Ombudsman is the third party who assists faculty, staff, administrators and students.[18] Besides these Educational Ombudsman, there are other Ombudsmen in the USA. The Crime Victims Ombudsman is to attempt and ensure that all crime victims are served justly, equitably by Carolina's Criminal Justice Organizations.[19] Crime Victim Ombudsman is neither an advocate nor a defender of bureaucracy. Detroit city in the USA has its Local Ombudsman. It is an independent city agency.[20] It evaluates both sides of citizen and government. Michigan state has Legislative Correction Ombudsman. It is an agency of the Michigan Legislative Council to provide the Michigan Legislature with oversight of the Michigan Department of Corrections.[21] There is also the Funeral Ombudsman which was introduced in the USA in May, 2000. The Long Term Care Ombudsman is to advocate for Nursing Home Residents and others who receive Long-Term care services. Its programme is mandated by the 'Older Americans Act, 1971'.[22] It deals with the people who live in nursing homes. The city Kentucky has Small Business Ombudsman. It provides Public information and education about the free services available in small business.[23] Like the USA, the UK also has several types of Ombudsmen. The Police Ombudsman is an independent police complaints system for the public and police.[24] The Prison and Probation Ombudsman office is for prison services ad national probation services. [25] There is Ombudsman for Pension in UK. There are also the Local Government Ombudsmen...they not only deal with complaints but also issue an advice to the local government in any matter.[26] In England, there are 3 local government Ombudsmen. The UK also has Funeral Ombudsman like the

USA. He is a solicitor with wide experience in the consumer field as a consultant to a variety of organizations.[27] The Insurance Ombudsman which is also called 'Financial Ombudsman[28] resolves the unresolved disputes and complaints concerning endowment mortgages. The Ombudsman for Estate Agent is devised to address disputes between member agencies and consumers who are actual or potential buyers or sellers of residential property of the UK.[29] The Banking Ombudsman deals with banking matters. The Pensions Ombudsman deals with the disputes in the pension schemes. The sale and marketing of pension scheme is the main area of working of Pension Ombudsman.[30] Its decisions are always final and binding on all parties. There is a Dental Ombudsman in South Africa. It deals with the practitioners and patients.[31] Australia has Mining Ombudsman who deals with Australian Mining Industry. It tries to prevent human rights abuses in mining industries.[32] It has the capacity to investigate the complaints of mining companies operating overseas. Germany has the office of Ombudsman for Disability. It works to achieve the general objectives of disability policy. It aims at full participation and equality for people with disabilities. In Sweden, Children Ombudsman is to safeguard the rights and interests of children.[33] Its activities focus on UN Rights of child information, implementation and application. Korean government has set-up Ombudsman for Investment by the enactment of the Foreign Direct Investment Promotion Act, 1998.[34] It resolves the difficulties of foreign companies that invested in Korean Companies. European countries lead Ombudsman not only in the government sector but also in the private.

India doesn't have Ombudsman in the government sector at the Central level. But, Reserve Bank of India and Life Insurance Corporation have their own Ombudsmen. The Ombudsman in RBI deals with the banking matter under the banks of RBI only.[35]

Customer's problems such as saving accounts, loans, etc. are dealt with by this Banking Ombudsman. Insurance Ombudsman in LIC deals with the problems related to the insurance policy matters.

To compare with the European countries, Indian Ombudsman i.e.; Lokayukta in the states are not quite popular. There is a constant demand for Ombudsman at the central level i.e.; Lokpal but is in vain since last 35 years. At the state level, 15 States have implemented the Lokayukta system. [It is discussed in chapter II]

All the above said countries are the members of IOI and some are of EOI. European Ombudsman Institute (EOI) aims to promote and disseminate the concept of Ombudsman in the European countries.[36] It is a non-profit making scientific organization. In the European countries International Ombudsman Institute (IOI) promotes the Ombudsman system throughout the world. The members of the IOI are bound by the ethics of the institutions.[37] The IOI makes it compulsory that the person holding a chair of Ombudsman must be impartial. It tries for the independence, flexibility, accessibility and credibility of the Ombudsmen.[38] The institute organizes workshops, conferences and seminars.

This is a survey of literature available through books, journals and web pages on Ombudsman is concluded as below:

1. Ombudsman is an unique experience in the Scandinavian, European, African and Australian countries.
2. Ombudsman is effective in those countries in the government as well as private sectors also.
3. Ombudsman affects a whole life from Children Ombudsman and Funeral Ombudsman.
4. International Ombudsman Institution (IOI) as well as European Ombudsman Institution (EOI) are trying best to popularize the Ombudsman institute.

1.6.2 Writings on Proposed Lokpal in India

Though there is Ombudsman in Banks and Insurance Sector in India as well as Lokayukta in States, there is no Ombudsman machinery at the central level in India. The issue of establishment of Lokpal has been under consideration for the last 40 years and so. Whenever the Bill is discussed in the

Lokasabha or Rajyasabha, media gives a wide publicity to the discussion. Otherwise, the issue is almost forgotten. There is a very little discussion on the Lokpal and also a scanty literature is available on the issue. However, some of the books and articles those are available, are discussed here.

1.6.2.1 Books on Proposed Indian Ombudsman

When 'Lokpal Bill' had been passed in the Loksabha it was put up before Rajyasabha in 1969. M.P. Jain, a scholar in Public Administration published his study namely 'Lokpal : Ombudsman In India' in 1970. He referred to the growth of the idea of Ombudsman in India. He examined the report of the Administrative Reforms Commission on this issue[39]. His observations on the Ombudsman machinery are:

1. Ombudsman can give relief on many more grounds than the courts can do.
2. A person who is appointed as the Ombudsman must command confidence of both the ruling party and the opposition party.
3. Ombudsman is required to be politically neutral.

D.R. Saxena examined the Lokayukta in 12 Indian states and published a book 'Ombudsman : A Redress Of Citizen's Grievances'.

He observed that this Ombudsman like institution has become neither popular nor effective in all the states. He raised a doubt, whether the states should continue the institution or not.[40] His is a very remarkable and important observation in this study. Girdhar B. Sharma is one of the scholars who studied on Ombudsman plan in India. He wrote a book 'Implementation of Ombudsman Plan In India'. He critically examined the concept of Ombudsman in addition to the Lokpal Bill, 1971 and 1977.[41]

Some of the suggestions he made are include:

1. Lokpal should be given constitutional status.
2. Ombudsman system should be obligatory for center as well as for all states.

3. Ombudsman should not be mere formality but an instrument of democratic working and safeguard for citizens' rights.

Giridhar B. Sharma finally argued in bringing Ombudsman in India.

'Citizen Administration And Lokpal' by Jagadham and Makhija is a systematic study of Lokpal in India. The authors strategically pointed out the establishment of Lokpal.[42] For a speedy and satisfactory redressal of citizen's grievances, Lokpal is recommended. R.K. Dhawan in his book 'Public Grievances And Lokpal' also stressed on the same.

'Ombudsmen' edited by IIPA is a collection of the Colloquium on the topic which was jointly organized by the British Council Division and the Indian Institute of Public Administration. All the above said studies are old except this one.

1.6.2.2 Articles in Journals on Proposed Lokpal

Corruption is everywhere. In Malaysia, South Asia, Japan, Indonesia and Thailand bribery is on a large scale and it has developed certain pattern. The bribe-taker is reasonable, even refunding the pay off if he fails to deliver.

In India, Social ethics are conveniently set aside when incidents of corruption and bribery take place, is an observation noted in the editorial article of "The Southern Economist'. Josseph Ponnoly wrote in CBI Bulletin,

> "..The Judiciary itself has now stepped into stem the tide of corruption which has become wide-spread an unquestioned way of life for the politicians and the officials in every field of public administration" [43]

It includes the absence of independent grievance redressal machinery in India and it is high time for our country to have its own Ombudsman. Some scholars suggested changes in the Lokpal bill. One of the changes suggested in the editorial of 'Radical humanist' is that, the Lokpal must have its own investigating machinery [44]. The Lokayukta in some states does not have investigating agency. P.K. Gopinath has also suggested that the Lokpal should have legal powers to prosecute an accused to the minister.[45] S.S. Tiwana in an article in 'Administrative Change' criticized that not any government in India is serious on this issue.[46] But, there is a continuous demand for Lokpal. According to an article published in the Journal of 'National Academy of Administrative Science', the launching of the institution of the Lokpal is a great experiment of the organized society by attempting to humanize administration.[47] It is suggested by experts that the Ombudsman system should be two-tired in India. S.S. Singh suggested that the Lokpal Bill can be 'Permanent Commission on Political Corruption'.[48] He published an article in Indian Journal of Public Administration on the Lokpal. In India, such a watchdog is necessary. U.C. Agrawal in his article in Indian Journal of Public Administration suggested that the success of Lokpal depends on the caliber, character and competence of the person to run it.[49] V.M. Sinha in his article published in 'The Journal of Political Science Review' emphasizes on the need for introducing Lokpal in India. He noted his expectation that Ombudsman should be a representative of the parliament to supervise the observance of laws and status.[50] He points out the role of proposed Lokpal and his constant efforts to see that the people get a good and satisfactory government.

Lokpal in India has been criticized theoretically and practically. The objectives of Ombudsman device are to make administration free from corruption and maladministration. Haridwar Rai and S.P. Singh stressed on the objectives and to make it responsive to the wishes of people in an article in 'Indian Journal of Political Science'.[51] But it is difficult in Indian scenario. Partisan spirit is so dominant in the Indian political system. The politicians and their supporters among the public will not react positively to the presentation of the facts laid by the Ombudsman involving in legal administrative injustice is an observation made by Shanthinaoy Shail in the 'Calcutta Journal of Political Science'.[52]

There is an article on corruption in ancient India in 'The Journal of Parliamentary Information'. The author points out,

"...the idea of check on the excess or misuse of power by

officers of the state had not only germinated but had blossomed in ancient India, centuries before the Christian era."[53]

The author has visualized the functionary similar to modern Lokpal institution in India. Hence, one can say that the concept of Lokpal is totally not new for the Indians. Ombudsman is located in some cities of India. It acts as an overseer and a regulatory body.[54] These are a few articles on Lokpal in India published in the journals and magazines.

1.6.2.3 Webpages on Lokpal in India

Very few web pages are available on the Indian Lokpal.

On occasion of election in 1999 Bhartiya Janata Party launched various web pages. One of them is on Lokpal issue. The government of Mr. Vajpai introduced the 'Lokpal Bill' in 1999 and declared that he himself wanted the Prime Minister under Lokpal's purview.[55] But it was not materialized in his tenure.

Union Home Minister argued (Aug.18, 1969) that the real authority for the removal of the Prime Minister is Parliament so neither Lokpal nor Lokayukta have authority in this sense.[56]

This issue of inclusion of Prime Minister under Lokpal's purview is in a hot debate even today. On September 13, 1996, S.R. Balsubramniyam, the then Minister of Parliamentary Affairs put it in the Loksabha with the support of inclusion of the Prime Minister.[57] But Again, it was not passed.

Mr. Devegoda, the then Prime Minister also promised to strengthen Indian anti-corruption agencies through Lokpal.[58] Besides the promises of all the Prime Minister, the Lokpal bill is not yet passed.

But the Banking Ombudsman in Reserve Bank of India and Insurance Ombudsman in LIC are established. The Banking Ombudsman have been appointed to receive the complaints relating to provision of banking services.[59]

These are some web pages on the proposed Lokpal in India. The Loksabha debates 1969, 1996, 1971, 1974, 1979, 1985, 1996, 1998, 2001 as well as the report by the Joint Select Committee provided important information relating to Lokpal Bill. All the information available on this issue makes a loud outcry on the formation of Lokayukta.

Thus, a very scanty literature is available on Lokpal in India.

1.6.3 Literature on Lokayukta in Indian States

India has Lokayukta in 15 States. Some notable literature relating to them got available for this study.

1.6.3.1 Books on Lokayukta

There is only one study on this issue made by Dr. Mary Parmar on Lokayukta in Himachal Pradesh. The cases handled by the Lokaykta imitate the administration in Himachal Pradesh. It bring the cases of allegation in the eyes of public.[60] Though the Lokayukta in Himachal Pradesh has positive features, it also have weaknesses. The Himachal Pradesh Lokayukta needs more authority in respect of personnel policies of his office.

K.S. Shukla and S.S. Singh make one more study. This book covered Lokayukta in 10 states in India. The study discovers that the institution has not been as effective as was expected and recommends various measures to strengthen it.[61]

These are books available on Lokayukta in the states in India.

1.6.3.2 Articles in Journals on Lokayukta

There are the articles in journals which focused on the Lokayukta in the Indian states. In Kerala, Ombudsman for Local Government constituted as per 'Kerala Panchayat Raj Act.'[62] Ombudsman can take care of ordinary Citizens in Kerala. It provides a flexible and largely informal method of obtaining judicial remedies without the need of formal and often-expensive procedural wrangles in the court process.[63]

One more article published by Mary Parmar in Indian Journal of Public Administration which is a paraphrase of her above-said book on Himachal Pradesh Lokayukta.

Thus, the number of articles published on Lokpal in journals is very less.

1.6.3.4 Articles in Newspapers on Lokayukta

The news, features and articles in the daily newspapers are also very useful to throw light on functioning of Lokayuktas with their weaknesses and positive points. The institution of Lokayukta in Punjab was caught in the crossfire between two political parties in 1992 when it reported against 3 ministers.[63]

In Karnataka, MLAs are not under Lokayukta's purview. S.M. Krishna, Lokayukta, Karnataka wished to bring it up.[64] According to him, Lokayukta in Karnataka needs to be set its functioning. In Andhra Pradesh, All India Civil Services are excluded from Lokayukta's purview 75% of the petitions are related only to abuses of power, etc.[65]

A few articles are published on Lokayukta in Maharashtra. 'The Hindu', 'The Times of India' and 'The Indian Express' have published some of them. However, regional newspapers have not covered matters on Maharashtra Lokayukta largely. May be they are unaware of the importance of this institution. There are also some websites on Maharashtra Lokayukta. But it is simply the collection of newspaper articles / news. Internet is one of the main sources of collecting information on Ombudsman but there is no information available on Lokayukta on web pages.

Thus, the literature on Maharashtra Lokayukta is scanty. Hence, this study is mainly based on primary data; i.e. government documents and the information provided by the Lokayukta office.

The debates in the Legislative Assembly on Lokayukta Bill provides important data. The Lokayukta Bill was presented in the Assembly in 1971 and was passed. The Maharashtra Lokayukta and Upa-Lokayukta Act, 1971 is a squeezed literature in this study. The rules and regulations on the appointment, removal, tenure, salary, staff, position, jurisdiction, functions, etc. are given in the Act.

The Annual Consolidated Reports constitute another important source for this study. Actual information of the office, its working and limitations are revealed from such information. The annual budget of government of Maharashtra for 1999, 2000, 2001 also proved important for this study.

Due to the secrecy followed in the office of Lokayukta, the addresses of the complainants which are useful for the study could not be obtained.

Thus, while reviewing the literature on the study, it is clear that a lot of web pages are available on Ombudsman but a very few books, articles in newspapers, journals and periodicals are available. This study of Lokayukta in Maharashtra is based largely on primary data.

1.6.4 Other Readings

For this study, the co-related literature on topic such as corruption is equally important, as it will be useful. Particularly, the autobiographical books wrote by M.S. Gill and Bhure Lal are notable. All of them has served as an IAS officers and collected their experience on political and administrative behaviour. Their main focus is on corrupt practices by the Indian politicians. Bhure Lal in his book 'Corruption : Functional Anarchy in Governance' analyzed various factors responsible for corruption in Indian society. He pointed out various attributes for rising corruption such as unrestrained authority, monopoly, power, lack of accountability, absolute political power, perverse inclination of officials, personal loyalties over objective rules, instability in government and concentration of political and economic powers in a few hands.[66] Many thinkers and authors tried to define corruption as 'multi-faced' Social Phenomenon with innumerable manifestations. Corruption is pervaded in every walk and form of life. The canal man is required to pay fixed amount even for supplying water. The Patwari is to be paid for any work of making records, verifying land holdings, etc. which is his duty. According to Syed Alatas Husain, Corruption is a crucial problem. It requires the crucial changes that need to go further than just changes in personalities and parties in power. Corruption is as old as the history of human civilization. According to him,

> "... A corrupt administrator is no longer only a financial liability, but is also a moral sore that saps the vitality of his personality".[67]

'Indian Panorama: Triumphs and Tragedies', a book published on completing 50 years of independence focuses the role of CBI & CVC in India. It also throws light on scandals and incidents of maladministration.

> "No one can accurately measure the extent of corruption in India....",[68]

is the opinion expressed by Rajender Puri in his article, 'Free At Last, To Loot And Plunder'. He pinpointed that only during Prime Minister Lal Bahadur Shastri's tenure, any serious effort was made to fight against political corruption.[69] His successor either avoided to fight or remained its supporters.

Some articles are also significant in this regard. One of the issue of 'One India, One People' is devoted to the issue of corruption.

"Judiciary is the only institution in the country which has no public accountability...,"[70]

is the opinion made by Arvind Bobde, Former Advocate General of Maharashtra. All the fields, such as politics, judiciary and bureaucracy have lost their accountability and credibility. There are some devices to control corruption, such as CVC, CBI, Anti-Corruption Bureau. etc. CVC is effective one; but its basic weakness is that it doesn't have statutory base. It needs a strong participation of people to control corruption and maladministration. The people's participation may be described as taking part in the events taking place in a community or a large area.

These are few articles on corruption in India, which throw light on Indian situation.

Transparency International is an agency which declares yearly the Corruption Perception Index. According to the index, India is 69th in rank of non-corruption in the world and 7th in Asia.[71] Besides the websites, there are some government documents, reports and acts on this subject. They include-

Report by the Santhanam Committee in 1964, the Prevention of Corruption Act, 1947; The Prevention of Corruption Act, 1988, Anti-Corruption Laws, etc. (These are discussed in the second chapter in detail.)

1.7 RESEARCH DESIGN

A very purpose of this study is to understand the functioning and the impact of Lokayukta in Maharashtra. It is not sufficient for this purpose to read the Acts only. It is also necessary to study the impact of the Maharashtra Lokayukta and Upa-Lokayukta Act, 1971. As per act, the machinery is expected to reduce the volume of corruption so that citizens, in various walks of life, are able to avail of the services on reasonable basis without fear or favour. In order to ascertain impact, it is proposed to make use of empirical method in this study.

Survey method is well suited to grasp the real situation. Hence, it is proposed to adopt the same for this study.

(a) The Universe of the Study -

The citizens bring their complaints of corruption, maladministration, irregularities against officials to the Lokayukta. They come with their grievances, sufferings and harassment to the Lokayukta for his intervention with a purpose to ventilation of these grievances. Hence, the complainants and the officials by and large, constitutes the universe for this study. It is through the survey of those complainants, we can understand and analyze the functioning of Lokayukta in Maharashtra. The important question in this regard is how to select complainants for survey. It was proposed to undertake a random survey of the complainants for the study. However, due to the secrecy maintained by the Lokayukta office under section 10(2) of the Maharashtra

Lokayukta and Upa-Lokayukta Act, the sampling was not possible. That is the office of the Lokayukta did not provide up-to-date year wise lists of the complainants with details of who approached the Lokayukta for their grievances and complainants so that a viable and random sample could be worked out. However, the annual Consolidated Reports by the Lokayukta proved useful for obtaining the names and addresses of complaints. There was no systematic list in the reports also. As a result the idea to prepare random sample was given up and the complainants were chosen from the names as given in the reports. Accordingly, 104 questionnaires were sent by post to these complainants. Similarly, 117 concerned authorities were also provided the structured questionnaire out of which 5 were served personally by the researcher and remaining were sent by post. Thus, the complainants and the concerned authorities which comprise of the universe for this study.

(b) The Questionnaire –

For purpose of survey, two types of respondents were prepared; i.e. questionnaire for-

1. the complainants;
2. the concerned authorities.

The separate questionnaire was prepared for each of them.

1. Questionnaire for the complainants consists of questions pertaining to different aspects of Lokayukta institute.
2. Questionnaire for the concerned authorities has 2 sections. The first section consists of 23 questions, which can be answered by any of the successor of the concerned authorities. The questions relate to the working of Lokayukta. The second section is to be answered by that particular authority or the administrative officer concerning the complaint. The concerned authorities were requested to give details of investigation and the disposal of that particular

case. (please, see Appendix III and IV for questionnaire of complainants and authorities.)

(c) In Depth Interview-

In addition to the survey of the complainants and officers the interview of the functionaries were necessary. Hence, the method of in-depth interview was adopted. The objective of the in-depth interview was to find the facts responsible for the working of Lokayukta institute in Maharashtra.

The respondents of in-depth interview were-

(i) Lokayukta of Maharashtra,

(ii) Upa-Lokayukta of Maharashtra,

(iii) Ex-Lokayuktas of Maharashtra,

(iv) Ex- Upa-Lokayuktas of Maharashtra,

In all 6 persons were interviewed as they were only available. These interviews helped us in cross-checking the information about the Lokayukta of Maharashtra which is available in the reports, acts and other literature.

(d) Data Processing-

The answers given to the structured questionnaires and responses to the interview, questions were processed, tabulated and data gathered was computed. The following are the elements of data processing.

(a) For the chapter related to the Ombudsman, the secondary data is used.

(b) For Lokpal both some of the secondary and some primary data are referred.

(c) The analysis of Maharashtra Lokayuktas is mainly based on the primary data. It covers the data collected from the sources such as the Maharashtra Lokayukta and Upa-Lokayukta Act, 1971; the Annual Consolidated Reports of the Lokayukta and Upa-Lokayukta; as well as the survey of the complainants and the concerned authorities and the interviews of the present and former Lokayuktas and Upa-Lokayuktas. The entire data is processed for this study to go at conclusions.

1.8 CHAPTER SCHEME

The first chapter of the thesis is divided into 3 sections-

(a) Section one comprises of the research methodology. It consists of problem formulation, importance of study, objectives, hypothesis, research design and the outline of the thesis including the chapter scheme.

(b) Section two deals with the rationality of Ombudsman institute. The attempts have been made to define corruption and maladministration in this section. It also presents the Corruption Perception Index of the world and the Asian countries.

(c) Third section takes the genesis of Ombudsman plan from its inception in Sweden in 1809. In addition to this, models of Ombudsman in the first 5 less corrupt countries in the list of TI are also presented.

The second chapter titled 'Lokpal in India' is a historical sketch of the Lokpal which is not in existence. It is also divided into 3 sections –

(a) The first section reviews the various machineries that are available at present to fight corruption and maladministration.

(b) The second section highlights the Lokpal Bill 1969, 1977, 1985, 1996, 1998, 2000, 2001 presented to the Parliament. It focuses on the circumstances, reasons, excuses for continuous delay and ultimately non-passing phenomena of the bill till this date. It also emphasizes the urgency of Lokpal in India in an atmosphere of rising corruption prone situation.

(c) The third section throws light on Lokayukta system as it is existed in 15 Indian States.

The third chapter, which is the main chapter concerns with the study, is on Lokayukta in Maharashtra. The provisions and its implimentation of the Maharashtra Lokayukta and Upa-Lokayukta Act, 1971 are discussed in this chapter. Besides its limitations as well as difficulties in its effective functioning are also discussed.

The fourth chapter gives the profile of the fieldwork of the present research study. The explanation and analysis of the data collected through questionnaires and interviews is processed and tabulated.

The fifth and last chapter summarizes the entire material for analyses. The conclusions are drawn for entire study in this chapter. Finally, in order to strengthen the institution of Lokayukta in Maharashtra some suggestions are also made to overcome the limitations.

SECTION 2

1.9 RATIONALITY OF INSTITUTION OF OMBUDSMAN

Corruption is a multilateral and systematic deficiency in a society. In a common speech, corruption is the phenomenon involving the act of something that is debased, impute and anti-ethical. Hence, it undermines the foundation of society. Corruption is all pervading in the sense that not a single country in the world can be described as non-corrupt and not a single department in any government is free from corrupt practices. No doubt, there is a wide discussion on how to tackle corruption and maladministration. Emergance of Ombudsman can be considered as an outcome of such discussion. In order to understand how does Ombudsman deal with these evils, it is necessary at the outset to go through the meaning of the terms maladministration and corruption through the ages.

1.9.1 Maladministration

'Mal' is a Latin word used for 'evil' or 'wrong'. Sir Edmund Compton, the first Parliamentary Commissioner of the UK pointed out, "...Maladministration is a dirty word with unfortunate association, conjuring up actions such as taking bribe or bias, or extreme example of bias or perversity."[72]

It is obvious that maladministration is an outcome of wrong doings and bad influencing. Red-tapism, errors in work, granting funds without receipts, ignoring own responsibilities, showing laziness, cheating people by the politicians or bureaucrats are manifestations of maladministration. Mistakes, committing errors and high degree of oversights, wrong application of rules, failures in imparting vital information, giving misleading advice, wrong interpretation of departmental rules and regulations, unjustifiable delays, all these constitute maladministration. They certainly result into weaknesses and low profile of the administration as a whole.

'Cross-man catalogue' set up by Richard Cross-man, a British Parliamentarian, defined maladministration as,

> "...bias, neglect, inattention, delay, incompetence, inaptitude, perversity, arbitrariness, might count as maladministration."[73]

The various manifestations of maladministration include bad rules, bad laws, improper use of power, etc. Selfishness and personal gains are primarily at the roots of maladministration. Occasionally ignorance and clerical mentality also result into maladministration.

However, all the forms of maladministration give birth to corruption. In fact, maladministration is the mother of corruption.

1.9.2 Corruption in Ancient Days

Corruption is all-pervading phenomena. It is observed all over the world. The malady of corruption prevailed in all periods of history; i.e. ancient, medieval and modern. It can be said that history of corruption is as old as the history of human being.

Kautilya, in 'Arthashstra' [4 B.C.] gives exhaustive list of practices and acts that can be termed corrupt such as,

> "..causing loss of government, misuse of government property, misappropriation of revenue, falsification of documents, obstruction in lawful process, exploiting the

public, corrupting the officials, embezzlement, failure of supervision in work, false measurement, allocating expenditure under wrong Heads, cheating with weight, etc..."[74]

Today, all these acts and many more are very much existing in the society.

In 120 B.C., Hamurabi of Babylon talks about inquiries into corruption cases – which indicate the existence of corruption in the Western countries. The Byzantine Emperor Justinian in 535 A.D. noted that he who pays for a job must sell his services.[75] By fifth century B.C., corruption had become a common feature in the political life all over Greece.[76] With the opening of new opportunities for speculation in Greece, bribery and corruption were on increase. The governors of provinces were paid low salary and therefore, they used to exploit the people for their own private material benefit. The Catholic churches were also used to sell priesthood in medieval times.

Corruption was deeply rooted in the religious matters in the ancient and medieval times. In Aurangzeb's period, to corrupt a judge was rendered for the first time a crime- the fees paid in the Courts of justice was ascertained accurately.[78] The medieval Indians and Westerners were also not free from corruption. It has risen to the high heaven in the Kuomintang rule in China where to get rich quickly was the supreme goal and no refinement of corrupt practices was neglected.[79] In those days, corruption was a problem in the society and administration; but was not as hot as in the modern times. Eventhough, it existed in the society, it was not defined terminology.

1.9.3 Corruption in Modern Days

In ancient days, corruption existed and was discussed, but not as high and as frequent as in the modern days. In the modern days, corruption is an economic, social, political, administrative, cultural, religious phenomenon. There is hardly any corner in Indian life, which has not been defiled by corruption. There are a number of books, articles, and researches on the topic recently.

There was a feeling of fear in olden days among people involved in corruption. Therefore, corruption was looked upon as a criminal deed- which in modern society becomes a fashion. Political life in nineteenth century America was said to be more corrupt than in the preceding and following centuries in Britain. The high point of corruption coincided with the impact of the industrial revolution and the emergence of new classes in the eighteenth and early nineteenth centuries. The modernization and globalization in a way provided space for corruption. The scholars gave some of the definitions of corruption as following.

1.9.4 Concept of Corruption

The phenomenon of corruption is multi-dimensional. Newer dimensions are added to it in the course of time. The views, the approaches, the typology, the definition, the stages, the manifestation of corruption are the matters of concerned for academicians, theorists, politicians since long time. An attempt has been made in the following lines to know above all there aspect so that we can proceed to fighting Indian situation of corruption.

According to World Bank,

> "...a Corrupt practice is the offering, giving and receiving or soliciting of anything of value to influence the action of a public official in the procurement or in the extract execution."[80]

B.S. Bindra looked upon corruption like cancer in the blood[81] – it needs major operation and lengthy treatment. Justice R.P. Shetty of Supreme Court in India views it like plague,[82] which is infectional; whilst A.B. Vajpayee, Ex-Prime Minister of India called it 'malaria'[83] in which medicine can be given to those who have been affected. It can prevent the breeding of mosquitoes of corruption. N. Vittal, Ex-Commissioner, CVC, India, quoted that corruption is like AIDS[84]–a serious and dangerous disease in modern society. It spreads not only in the human physic but also in the psyche.

Prof. Syed Alatas Hussain called it 'tidal' corruption.[85] Like a tide this practice grows to immerse everything in its path.

The tidal corruption multiplies the number of perpetrators of the illegal practice more rapidly than other types of criminal behavior. A question is raised as to who are prone to corrupt practices? It can be answered that normally the less salaried and highly greedy officers and politicians are in the mainstream of corruption.

It can be safely stated from these descriptions that corruption is something very serious, manispol in the society. Because men are selfish, they indulge in different kinds of corruption is a lesson from history.

There are different approaches given by the scholars and experts to look at corruption.[86] The following are few of them as given in a webpage launched in Yahoo, a search engine on internet—

1. 'Public-Interest-Centered' approach of Rogow and Loswel, who said that corruption is highly injurious to public interest.
2. 'Public-Office-Centered' approach by Theo bald stresses on the misuse of incumbency of public office for private gains.
3. 'Market-Centered' approach by Tillman states the norms of governing public office have shifted from free market to a mandatory pricing model. Thereby, it changes the nature of corruption.
4. 'Legalistic' approach, by Scott stresses on legal criteria in governing public interest, behavior and authority.
5. Gould's 'Moralist' view says that corruption is immoral and unethical phenomenon that contains a set of moral aberrations from moral standards of society causing a lot of respect and confidence in duly constituted authority. It concentrates on the difference between good and bad in society.
6. Ceff's 'Functionalist's' view expresses that corruption flourishes as a substitute for the market system.
7. Lo's 'Social Centurist' view (1993) expresses that to understand corruption, one should take into

consideration the capacity of the state to produce particular form of social relations and their shifts.

8. Paverola's 'Social Constructionist' view (1996) is a theoretical emphasis on the interplay of law, ideology and political economy. It also stresses corruption as a problematic factor that involves the corrupters in the system as well as in the political, economic and social considerations within which they function.

Both the social centurist view and constructionist view look at corruption as an abuse of authority of social-cultural variable.

If we try to identify the class of corrupt people from the various approaches and views given above, we come to know that the class of public officials, politicians, bureaucrats, businessmen, suppliers, contractors are the contributors in regularizing and institutionalizing corruption. This is a brief account of different approaches to look at corruption.

There are many functionaries in the acts of corruption adopting various modes of corruption. Therefore, their are different types of corruption. As an experienced Ombudsman of Pakistan and a learned judge, Alatas Syed Husain has given comprehensive typology of the phenomenon of corruption[87] in his book entitled, "Corruption: Its Causes and Functions":

1. Autogenic corruption: is the leakage of information by a person that is self-generated.
2. Defensive corruption: is self-defense that compelled a person to pay bribe otherwise his interests would be suffered.
3. Extortive corruption: is a compensation in exchange of services.
4. Intensive corruption: is undertaking with a future reward in view.
5. Nepotistic corruption: means giving preferential treatment to friends or relatives.
6. Supportive corruption: is that which protects the existing corruption.

7. Transitive corruption: is where the two parties willingly participate in the corrupt practices.
8. Collusive corruption: is an instrument of inducement to allure the authorities to do wrong or illegal activity.
9. Coercive corruption: is to take undue advantage of the position by the authorities.
10. Non-conjunctive corruption: is to obtain benefits by the corrupt at the cost of someone where the victim does not come to know of his victimization.

As a matter of fact all these acts and types of corruption and maladministration given by him are not new and hence a matter of routine to a common man. The fact remains that corruption through all these types and limits economic growth, opportunity and investment and brings administrative illness.

From the definitions, approaches, types of corruption as given above, the following characteristics of corruption and maladministration are revealed:

1. Corruption is not single persons deal. It requires more than one person. It is a joint venture.
2. Corruption on the whole involves secrecy, in the sense that it is an act in darkness - except when it becomes rampant deep rooted and manifestation of money power and muscle power.
3. Usually corruption is a nexus between two or more parties having mutual obligation, understanding mutual benefit among the concerned parties.
4. Those who practice corruption usually attempt to camouflage their activities by resorting to some form of justification.
5. Those who are involved in corruption would like to influence decision making.
6. Generally, act of corruption involves deception, of some section of society and betrayal of trust.

There are certainly some causes at the root of corruption. Lot many efforts have been taken place to find out such causes by the scholars, academicians and theologians. The following are a few causes some of which have been pointed out by Alatas Syed Husien:

1. MORAL AND ETHICAL:

(a) Non-following of religious and ethical teaching,

(b) Degeneration and deterioration of values;

2. HISTORICAL:

(a) Colonialism leading to poverty due to extraction of resources by empirical powers,

3. SOCIAL:

(a) Illiteracy and poor standard of education,

(b) Absence of positive socio-economic environment conducive to corrupt-free society,

(c) Lack of urge to come out of mental make-up tolerating corrupt practices.

(d) Social structure and governmental system that is generating and supportive to corruption

3. LEGAL:

(a) Absence of severe punitive measures to curb corruption based upon inequality.

4. ECONOMIC:

(a) Poverty and un-employment,

(b) Over population,

(c) Low level per capita and national income,

5. ADMINISTRATIVE:

(a) delay, red-tapism, officialdom, rigidity, hierarchy, indifferent and non-sensible working of administrative system, lack of integrity, inefficiency among functionaries, etc.

6. POLITICAL:

(a) The absence or weakness of leadership in key positions capable of inspiring and influencing conduct mitigating corruption.

(b) nexus between politicians and bureaucrats.

There are many more causes of corruption. The list is exhaustive and unending. More and more new causes are added to it. The causes lead to new modes of corruption besides, number and severity of causes of corruption. Its magnitude and extent also matter much, which can be ascertained from their estimates based on comparative analysis of the ranking of corruption in various countries.

Maladministration is associated with corruption. Maladministration gives birth to corruption and corruption leads to a rise in maladministration in government or other. It is commonly discussed and required to be dealt with. Hence, a number of researches, projects, committees and commissions in various countries have been desperately studying how to face and curb the problem. Several books are dedicated to this issue. The media have offered a large space on the aspects related to the problem. All opine that it is inborn in the society and is unending; but needs to be controlled for a healthy welfare state.

1.9.4.1 Corruption Perception Index

Transparency International (TI) is the Berlin based International institute which finds out the ranking of corrupt countries in the world. According to it, India ranked 69th in the year 2000 which slipped up to 71st in 2001. The Corruption Perception index ranked 2.8 from 2.7. In the year of 2009, India has ranked 85 – which indicates that corruption is getting worst. The ranking is as given below:[88]

Table-1.1

List of Corruption Perception Index

Rank	*Country*
1	Denmark, New Zealand, Sweden
4	Singapore,
5	Finland, Switzerland
7	Iceland, Netherlands
9	Canada, Australia
11	Luxemburg
12	Austria, Hong Kong

14	Germany, Norway
16	United Kingdom
18	Japan, Belgium
21	United States
22	Barbados
23	Chile, France, Uruguay
26	Slovenia, Ireland
27	Estonia
28	Qatar, Spain
31	Cyprus
32	Portugal
33	Israel
35	United Arab Emirates
36	Botswana, Malta
39	Chiana Taiwan
40	South Korea
41	Mauritius,
43	Baharin
45	Czech Republic
47	Costa Rica, Malaysia, Jordan
52	Latvia, Slovak Republic
54	South Africa
55	Italy
57	Greece
58	Turkey, Poland
61	Namibia
62	Croatia Brazil
65	Cuba, Kuwait
67	Ghana, El Salvador
70	Romania
72	Bulgaria, Mexico, Peru
80	Thailand, Burkina Faso,
85	India,
86	Belarus, Malawi

The ranking shows that India, a large democratic and most populated country is more corrupt then many underdeveloped and even undeveloped countries also.

From the point of view of our study, it can be observed that as per the ranking, Scandinavian countries are almost non-corrupt where Ombudsman is playing an effective role; i.e. Finland, Fenmark, Ideland, Singapore, etc. It is remarkable to note that on prima-facie, there is co-relation between existence of Ombudsman and high degree of control on corruption.

Of course there are exceptions, as many of the countries with high degree of corruption do not have the institution of Ombudsman. However, it cannot be universally said about this co-relation between Ombudsman and corruption. The Nigerian Ombudsman is effective and yet its ranking is first from below. It means that other factors may be responsible for corruption.

South Asian countries are highly ranked as compared to other countries in the world. Because of deeply ingrained institutions and attitudes carried over from colonial and pre-colonial times, rampant corruption is obvious, to some extent natural also in the South Asian countries. Amongst the South Asian countries, India is at the 10th position. It is very shameful on the part of our country that the undeveloped countries like Taiwan, Thailand and Philippines are less corrupt than India. In the first Global Corruption Barometer Survey, 42.1% felt that corruption in India would increase over the period of three years, 20% expect that it would be substantial whereas 20% felt that it would decrease. It indicates that day by day an increase in corruption is the most critical problem in India. Hence, the following section deals with the problem of corruption and faulty administration in Indian scenario.

1.9.5 Maladministration and Corruption in India

Corruption in India is a dysfunctional outcome of the interaction between the public and the private. This action includes corruption, bribery, nepotism, etc. According to Odegard, corruption in India is a product of the way of life of an acquisitive society where 'money talks,' where what 'works' is justified, and where people are judged by what they have rather than what they are.[89] Corruption is un-ending and mind-boggling in India which is a multi-caste, multi-religious, multilinguistic state.[90] During pre-independence days, according to drain theory of Dadabhai Naoroji Britishers were responsible for exploitation of India.[91] After Independence, British were replaced by our own officials and politicians; however the condition of exploitation remained as it was; helpless and voiceless are governed by the arbitrary low and use of force injustice and unrighteousness. Administration is rounded by the malpractises and corruption. Both citizens and administrators are responsible for corruption.

1.9.6 Bureaucracy and Corruption in India

The phenomenon of corruption cannot be understood without reference to the bureaucracy. Bureaucrats are responsible for mismanagement, frauds and pilferages. Bureaucracy actually fails to perform its duty in an accountable manner. It was so in the past it is so at present.

The Committee on Prevention of corruption observed,

> "... in the primitive and medieval societies scope of public authority was small; man of the matters that were looked after by the community have now become a function of the state".[92]

This is how the Committee explains widening role of bureaucracy.

In his 'Indian Panorama: Triumphs and Tragedies', Mr. S.K. Ghosh indicates that bribery is common for import licenses, building permissions, government employment, agricultural aids, liquor permits, bank employment and loans, admission to educational institutions, etc. In rural areas land records can be manipulated by bribing Amine.[93]

Many other village officials accept bribe from villagers besides the Amin. The village Sarpanch as often bribed from landlords to decide the cases in their favour. Since most of the villagers are poor, the officials, especially the tribal people for advancing loans and marketing their agricultural products, often exploit them. During land settlements the concerned staff operating in villages is heavily bribed to manipulate records.

Corruption exists not only in villages but in urban areas also. Usually, the Income Tax Inspectors are responsible for departmental corruption as the lawyers, doctors, film stars, proprietors of coaching classes, businessmen evade taxes.

The police authorities take bribe for verification of character antecedents report, which is a must before issuing the passports and arms licenses before joining jobs permanently. In an interview to 'One India, One People' Francis Ribero, the then Police Commissioner of Mumbai pointed out how the ministers extract money from the police officials to be transferred. The concerned ministers sent a list of persons of their choice for appointments as well as promotions with the considerations of money. Private residences of several Director General and Inspector Generals of Police have been raided by the CBI in different parts of our country and unaccounted wealth was seized by them.[94]

Police administrators often has the relationship with criminals, gangsters, mafias, shooters. This class of crime is always protected by the arms of police and politicians whom has to prevent those. The provender's hands become protectors of them. The Indian railway is the largest department in India and is spreader far and wide and is also known for its corruption. A traveling ticket collector earns thousands of rupees per day in addition to his salary. Daily, thousands of youth and political leaders travel by trains without tickets. As a matter of fact, railway reservation means nothing if one can 'manage' the ticket collector. Thefts of items from railway coaches, goods in railway yards and brake-vans in connivance with railway staff and RPF run into crores of rupees.

In the government hospitals, medicines are regularly stolen and sold by hospital staff, nurses and ward-boys. Death reports/postmortem reports are provided with fake causes of death. The ward-boys, attendants and ayahs charge heavy amount for visit and just taking a look at the patients. Stealing and selling of eatables, clothing, medicines by prison staff is habitual. In prisons and hospitals, sub-standard material is supplied because of close links between the contractors and the authorities. Usually, the part of material is found in the houses of superintendents and the officials.

Nationalized banks are also involved in fraud amassing money by illegal means. Smuggling is a big business in India. In Mumbai, the annual profit earned form smuggling is estimated to Rs. 8,000 crores year.[95] Leaders always have a strong link with smugglers. A smuggler provides money and muscle power to leaders during elections and naturally expects protection from them.

'Pay the price and the job is yours' is an all-pervasive condition for appointment in government jobs. Every appointment, assignment and transfer carries a price tag. The merit hardly matters. The employment exchanges undertakes bribe for registration of names and of course, for recommendation of names to various departments. In State Public Service Commission, corruption and bribery is rampant. Corrupt and communal persons are appointed as the members of the Commission. In some states, members are used as agents to collect money from the candidates. Before some days nearly 398 posts recommended by MPSC involving chairman, senior officers of the commission along with police officers as well as officers from Mantralya were traped for involving in malpractices, bribe and irregularities in those selection.

One can customize a case of injustice with him/her self in the court of law. Unfortunately, our judicial system appears to be blind. To quote Mr. Arvind Bobde, late Advocate General of Maharashtra,

> "..judiciary is the only institution in the country which has no public accountability. Judges are paid poorly, their status, dignity and independence is not assured."[96]

The impeachment of justice V. Ram Swami, of the Supreme Court the first ever impeachment motion against a Supreme Court Judge, noted by Krishna Ayer,

> "..Corruption inside the institution is mounting, even judicial officers are slowly coming into the suspect class."[97]

Judiciary in India is not far from corrupt practices. It is being discussed in the second chapter in detail.

Bureaucracy is not free from corruption not only in India but in any other country. In Nicaragua, 40% of the importers have to pay 'incentives' over and above legal tariffs and fees. In Pakistan nearly all women had to pay for their delivery even though government hospitals and primary health care centers claimed to provide service free of charge. In Uganda, 50% of the people surveyed expressed their opinion that they had to pay bribes while dealing with the judicial services. In Bolivia, 78% of the people paid bribes when regularizing their government documents. In Thailand, there has been corruption in military and many officers are members of the board of private firms doing business with defense ministry.[98] Official corruption in China is the most serious problem.

No bureaucracy is free from corruption and maladministration.

1.9.7 Politicians and Corruption in India

There are two opinions about the fact that there is a nexus between the bureaucrats and politicians. Hence, it is necessary to approach and locate corruption on the part of functionaries along with politicians. As a matter of fact, the main source of corruption in India is politics in spite of the fact that politicians must support the process of eradicating corruption. Elections and electoral imperatives faced by political parties constitute the basis of political corruption.

In Indian context, noninterference in administration by politician termed as political neutrality, which is a British tradition of civil service has been almost non existent today. The pressures of party politics are very strong. The pure and dynamic civil servants are disgusted due to black shaded politics. Hippocratic politicians make bureaucracy insincere.

Political process breeds corruption. Political leaders divert development funds for personal benefits and use their authority amiss.

Parliament is expected to be a mirror of public will. It is a representation of general morality. It is bonded with good governance. The role of Parliament in fighting corruption is essential. However, it fails to perform this role, may be because of a wrong choice of the representatives. The modus operandy of corruption in the past was to corrupt those in power. However recently people with corrupt background directly enter into arena of politics. As a result, the black marketers have their influence on Indian politics. They join political parties, become office bearers and eventually control the party easily.

Pundit Jawaharlal Nehru, the first Prime Minister of India by ignoring the changes of corruption against Krishna Menon, the then Defense Minister, in jeep scandal and T.T. Krishnammachari, the then finance Minister, in LIC- Mundra scam sowed the seeds of corruption in Indian politics. In Sino-India conflict, government raided and seized all papers in the bank of China and discovered that Nehru had an undisclosed account of 'royalty' for his books in the Soviet Union.[99] That was shocking for Indians. It is well known that Indira Gandhi used to describe corruption as a worldwide phenomenon. She allowed her son Sanjay Gandhi to sell licenses in market place. Mr. Lal Bahadur Shastri, is the only Prime Minister who fought against corruption with his short arms very largely and his short tenure very highly. He tried to evolve a policy of weeding out political corruption, which Indira Gandhi supported more to spread it out in Indian politics. Morarji Desai's son was persuaded in his business. Jain's dairy boldly and unreluctantly prove how Mr. Rajeev Gandhi got 2 crores in bofors scandal. V.P. Singh's Ministers also were involved with hawala that he was in vain to prevent corruption.

During Chandrashechar's term, money was made from telephone equipment to State Trading Corporation purchases. Narsimha Rao's term is a black period of Indian administration. He is the only Prime Minister of India who was sued in the court for the charges of corruption. Greed, forgery were governing virtues in his period. His son Prabhakar was arrested in urea scam. Kuldeep Nair says,

> "...Indira Gandhi may have corrupted the institutions, but Narsimha Rao institutionalized corruption."[100]

It was criticised that A.B. Vajpayee was not free from corruption. It is surprising that why Chandraswami and hawala scandals are the blemishes of Indian politics.

In short, political corruption in India is not confined to grass-root level only but also pervaded severly at the top. Thus politics and corruption are inseparable.

Not only in India but also in the developed countries, ministers and politicians are involved in scams and scandals. Corruption reigns supreme even in advanced countries like Japan where every other Prime Minister has had to resign on this charge.[101] Potential of politics is lost that weakens the government. The allegations of corruption are playing a more central role in politics in Belgium, Britain, Japan, Italy, Spain and many other countries. In Philippines, a political office is a privileged position. It can be bought and sold. In Morocco, access to political power ensures access to economic privileges. In Africa, political leadership is the primary force behind corruption. In Jakarta, (1967) 17 people were arrested, some of them were from the Indonesian Armed Forces, who organized a syndicate to sell or rent out firearms to those who needed them for private often criminal purposes. The great Chinese reformer, Wang An Shih (AD 1021 - 86) in his attempt to eliminate corruption was impressed by the two ever-recurrent sources of corruption, bad laws and bad men. As he put it, "... but what I wish particularly now to emphasize is that history proves it to be impossible to secure proper government by merely relying on the power of the law to control officials when the latter are not the right men for their job. It is equally futile to expect efficient government in having the right men in their proper positions, you hedge them by a multitude of minute and harassing probations."[102]

His view is extremely instructive.

Political corruption is an intentional and deeply affects the government. The confidence of the people in the authorities has been shaken due to deep-rooted corruption. It becomes only way to get the things done in a huge democratic set up of government in India. In such a situation a common man who is at the receiving end is rendered helpless.

Considering the spreading cancer of corruption in our country, there is an urgent need for a trustworthy, independent and impartial machinery with adequate power to end corruption. Certainly, it needs persons of courage to occupy the position of Ombudsman, and of course, there is a political will to appoint such persons of courage. Thus, there is definitely a rationality behind the office of the Lokpal at national and Lokayukta at the state level.

SECTION 3

1.10 GENESIS OF INSTITUTION OF OMBUDSMAN

1.10.1 Birth of Ombudsman

The world has been experiencing the problem of maladministration and corruption. The common man is a victim of political and administrative corruption. The effects of corruption can be seen on the economic and social conditions of any country.

An urgent need for a watchdog over the government is as old as the government itself. Over 2,500 years ago, the ancient Romans established a Tribune to protect the rights of the people from those of ruling them. 'Censors' also reviewed programme of officials and took complaints from citizens. The Chinese Dynasty thousands of years ago had a person called the 'control Yuan' who handled complaints about maladministration in government. The French also had their 'Protector du Citoyen'.[103] Thus, either in monarchy or democracy, each and every system, need a controller for the government. The smallest country like Korea also had such machinery. In 1402, the king created the 'Shinmungo' or drum of justice outside the palace.[104] Anyone could report a case of injustice by beating the drum. In 1713, King Charls II, of Sweden was out of the country for 12 years for Russian war. He created a post of 'Chancellor of Justice' to supervise his servants in his absence. After the war, the king returned and the post was replaced by 'Justitie Kansler'.[105] Only the title was changed besides the appointment by the king, Justitie Kansler got appointing by the representative bodies. In 1809, Sweden adopted its own constitution and parliament boosted the Ombudsman institution by providing the need of control over public servants and governmental decisions. The important reason to establish the institution was to check the Royal officers disregard for law who were king's men (JK) in the Parliament.[106] Thus, the Justitie Ombudsman in Sweden is derivate in 1809 with an aim to defend citizen.

Until now, nearly 150 countries assumed such an institution. Before going the worldwide scheme of Ombudsman, it is necessary to know what does it mean.

1.10.2 What is Ombudsman?

'Ombudsman' is a household word in Sweden; but Indians are unknown to the concept. The word Ombudsman looks as if its constituent would be familiar, judging from the elements of man, Ombudsman is a Swedish word-ombud means 'commissioner, or agent'. It is derivate from old Norse 'Umbodh' was charge commission. In old Norse, 'Umbodhsmadhr' was a deputy who looked after the interests and legal affairs of a group of such a trade union or business. In 1809, the office of Riksdagens (Parliament) created Justitie Ombudsman to look after the interest of Justice in the affairs between the government and citizens. According to Encyclopedic Dictionary.

> "..Ombudsman is an officer appointed to provide an extra check on the rights of citizens against action."[107]

But, this is not a broad and all pervasive concept. According to 'Collier's Encyclopedia',

> "..Ombudsman is a public official appointed to investigate governmental abuses and who intervenes for the sake of ordinary citizen in his dealings with co-machinery of the government. Ombudsman is a person who helps the government and citizens as well."[108]

21st Century Universal Encyclopedia traces out that Ombudsman is a Scandinavian term for an official appointed to investigate complaints against the action of government departments. Technically, Ombudsman is a person of institutional ability and outstanding integrity with regard to the complaints from the public on decisions, actions or omissions by public administration. Ombudsman can protect the people against corruption and maladsministration as well as, abuse of powers and unfair decisions. It should be very clear that Ombudsman is neither an advocate nor a defender of government servant. The word 'ombud' refers to a person who acts as a spokesman or the representative of another person. It is an institution, which can deal properly with the government by a common man. According to Caiden,

> "... Ombudsman is institutionalized public conscience- the essence of what the government ought to do; that is to cultivate the well being of the citizens, the preservation of individual liberty and equitable treatment of all citizens by the public bureaucracy. " [109]

The meaning of Ombudsman is clearly a 'Citizens Charter.'

There are different names for Ombudsman in different countries as Defensor Del Pueblo (Spain. Argentina, Colombia); Parliamentary Commissioner For Administration (Sri Lanka, UK); Me Diateur De La Re Publique (France, Gabon, Mauritania, Senegal); Public Protector (South Africa) Protector Du Citoyen (Que Bec); Volksanwaltschaft (Austria) Public Complaints Commissioner (Nigeria); Provedor De Justica (Portugal); Difensor Civico (Italy); Investigator-General (Zambia); Citizen's Aid (Jowa); Wafaqi Mohtasib (Pakistan).

Though, the names are different the major purpose of adopting the machinery everywhere is to protect the citizens interests from corrupt bureaucracy. So far organizational level of the machinery is concerned, some countries have Ombudsman offices at the national level only; some have Ombusman at the regional, state and national level. Australia, Argentina, Spain have Ombudsman at national level; Canada, India, Italy have at the sub-national or state level; whereas European countries, North America, Latin America, Africa have a combination of Ombudsman functionaries at the regional level, city level and also at the public – private level. The International Ombudsman Institution on Nov. 15, 1999 resolved

created by enactment of the legislative or quasi legislative body which, is empowered to protect citizens against maladministration, violation of rights, unfairness, errors, abuse of power or any injustice caused and to investigate their complaints.[110] 'Ombudsman' is a word which the developed countries apply in the private sector also. In the present study, five models of Ombudsman are taken which are prevalent in less corrupt countries according to Transparency International.

1.10.3. Ombudsman in Sweden

Parenting from Sweden, Ombudsman has constitutional status. Article(6) of Swedish constitution states,

> "..Ombudsman is supervising under instruction determined by the Risksdag." [111]

Sweden has given birth to the concept. It is at the third position of Transparency International's Corruption Perception Index. Sweden has four Ombudsmen. (1) The Parliamentary Ombudsman whom Swedish call as 'Watchdog of Parliament,' who assumed his role long back in 1809. (2) Justitie Ombudsman (3) Milititie Ombudsman the post and work of both Ombudsmen has divided in 1915. (4) The office of Deputy Ombudsman was introduced in 1914.

SELECTION – Sweden being a true democratic country where Ombudsman is elected and removed by the Parliament. He has a term of 4 years. What is remarkable about the institute in Sweden is that though, it is elected by the Parliament, it is not responsible to the Cabinet. Thus, it is immune for the political pressure.

AREA OF WORK – The public servants/officials, Parliament members, military, personel, Judges are under Ombudsman's jurisdiction. This shows a wide scope and jurisdiction for him. Justitie Ombudsman introduced a change wherein a person should not be arrested unless the charges against him/her are based on evidence.[112] It is surprising that the concept of Military Ombudsman was opposed because there was a doubt that discipline would be harmed by offering a soldier the opportunity to complain against his superior. [113] But, nowadays,

to procedural rule designed to protect rights of the individuals. It fulfils the object of providing an independent and impartial military performance in Sweden.

The Swedish constitution keeps away Ministers from Ombudsman's jurisdiction to secure Ombudsman's political neutrality. Sweden was in an urgent need of a protector of citizens from abuse of power which was fulfilled.

Considering the volume of work the Deputy Ombudsman was established to share his work. Accordingly Chief Ombudsman handles the major cases and the minor cases are handled by the Deputy Ombudsman. Deputy Ombudsman is not at all answerable to the Chief Ombudsman, he is directly selected and answerable to the Parliament. Thus it is his subsidiary position. But it is surprising that he is not empowered to overturn every error and to produce correct answers to all the difficult questions which modern government confronts.

Swedish Ombudsman is a world classic institution which is independent, impartial and economically viable in terms of seeking help on corrupt practices.[114] Hence, it has inspired confidence in public that the protector of people's rights at their back. The unique feature of Ombudsman system is its decisions and documents are always open to the public which is a sign of public orientation of the institution. Ombudsman is reviewed by his results in every case. In 1969, the private Ombudsman for the press was established. In 1971, Consumer Ombudsman was appointed for the protection of the consumers.[115] The word 'Ombudsman' has been used in the private sectors also, his decisions and results are publicly open; but the documents are not.

1.10.4 Ombudsman in Denmark

After the birth of Ombudsman in Sweden, it remained unnoticed for hundred and more countries. According to 'Parliamentary Commissioner Act, 1954', The Ombudsmand (in Danish language) institution was introduced in Denmark. Stephen Hurwitz, the first Ombudsman of Denmark was

It is surprising that in Denmark also the civil servants and other organizations were in opposition of forming the institution. However, after some years of its formation, the Presidents of major organizations expressed their opinion in favor of Ombudsman,

> "..In the beginning, we were suspicious. As a matter of fact, we were scared. But we have found that we were mistaken." [117]

The Ombudsman's work actually proved like a tonic for the Danish public administration.

SELECTION – Parliamentary Commissioner/Ombudsman a non-Parliamentary authority is elected by the Folketing (Parliament) for a term of 4 years. He can obviously be dismissed by the Folketing only.

The salary and the position of Ombudsman is the same as that of the Supreme Court Judges.

AREA OF POWER – The state administration, civil, police, military and since 1962, the municipal authorities are also considered under Ombudsman's jurisdiction. He has been specifically given jurisdiction over discretionary areas of the administrative decisions; but he can't change the administrative structure and further the administration. Thus considerable thought was given on the jurisdiction of the Ombudsman. Every care has also been taken to limit his authority. As usual it is recommendatory and mandatory authority. It is not obligatory on the part of Government to follow the recommendations of the Ombudsman. However, according to article(3),

> "...he is obliged to keep himself informed as to whether any person subject to his jurisdiction pursues unlawful ends, takes arbitrary or unreasonable decisions or otherwise commits mistakes or acts, of negligence in the discharge of his/her duties." [118]

Danish Ombudsman can also supervise the Ministers, civil servants and all other persons acting in the services of the state.

objectionable in any case which suspects his impartiality, he may inform Parliamentary Directives about the case and Parliamentary Directives only take a decision on such cases.

There are no administrative tribunals in Denmark so that Danish Ombudsman directly can question to the Minister's action. He can discuss policy matters of the government and can suggest reforms in the defective provision of the law.[119]

Danish Ombudsman is a teacher of society and binds as a doctor upto cure the disease of corruption without disturbing its efficiency.

The office of Denmark Ombudsman proved it's utility not only in the country, but also in other countries. Stephen Hurwitz – a man with magic eye provided a good model to the willing incumbents.[120] He visited the European countries. By writing articles, delivering speeches and conversing the authorities, he pushed up to form the institution; and these efforts made several countries to establish Ombudsman system.

1.10.5 Ombudsman in Newzealand

After second world war, the institution of Ombudsman attracted the western Asian, European and non-Scandinavian countries. New Zealand is the fourth in the world and first Anglo-Saxon country which adopted the Swedish idea of Ombudsman. The New Zealand government agreed that the means available to the citizens for administrative injuries were inadequate. Stephen Hurwitz, the first Danish Ombudsman read a paper on 'The Scandinavian Ombudsman' in the United Nations seminar held at Cylone in 1959.[121] R.B. Cooke, a lawyer in New Zealand was influenced by Hurwitz's ideas of a redressal. He presented a paper at the New Zealand Legal Conference in 1960 stressing the need to create an institution. The lawyers, public servants and ministers opposed him. Yet the National Party in its election manifesto put up a promise to create Ombudsman institution. An Attorney General, H.R. Honan stressed on the importance of Ombudsman.[122] He moved a bill for the 'Parliamentary Commissioner (Ombudsman) Act, 1962'.

In 1962, New Zealand adopted Ombudsman by Law. The jurisdiction under this act was limited. The Ombudsman could investigate the complaints from citizens about the central government departments and organizations.

SELECTION – The New Zealand Ombudsman is appointed by the Parliament for 5 years. He may be re-appointed. Sir Guy Powel, the former Foreign Commissioner of India, was elected as the first Ombudsman of New Zealand.

AREA OF POWER – As per the Act of 1962, central government departments and organizations had been under Ombudsman's jurisdiction, which was extended in 1968 by including education and hospital boards.[123] The local government authorities were included according to Ombudsman Act, 1975. The ministers were out of his purview. The New Zealand government was not assured of its success of the Ombudsman due to 'Official Information Act, 1982'. Ombudsman conveyed the role of investigating and reviewing decisions on the requests of access to official information, held by the ministers of the Crown. After 20 years of its inception, Ombudsman could have the jurisdiction to consider the cases against ministers. In Jan. 2001, the 'Protector Disclosures Act, 2000' or 'Whistle blowing' legislation came into force.[124] The act added Ombudsman to provide advice to an employee who has made or is considering making a protected disclosure. Though, the powers of New Zealand Ombudsman are extended time-to-time, yet he cannot consider the cases from those who have acted as legal advisers to the crown. As well as he cannot investigate an administrative act. Ombudsman can investigate military affairs; but municipal administration is not under his jurisdiction. Those were lacunas and contradictions in the working of Ombudsman. The Ombudsman avoids such cases under his jurisdiction which are unduly delayed, or which are trivial frivolous in nature or lacking in faith. It is essential for an Ombudsman to be independent of the government so that the people of New Zealand can have confidence in the servants. As the government of New Zealand supports the Ombudsman, it finds decreasing number of cases. As a result New Zealand could attain third position in 'Transparency International's ranking. New Zealand Ombudsman is treated as a model Ombudsman by other countries.

1.10.6 Ombudsman in Norway

Ranking sixth in Transparency International's Index, this smallest Scandinavian country has successfully adopted the Ombudsman institute. In Norway, there was a head of the district in king's administration who was similar to Ombudsman. After the Second World War, Norway needed a machinery for administrative development. By the Storting's (Parliament in Norway) resolution the Ombudsman was created for objectors on Nov. 23, 1956.[125] The Storting's Ombudsman for public administration came into force according to the Act of June 1962 and Andreas Schie was crowned the first Storting Ombudsman. In the Bill, Mr. Jens Haugland, Minister of Justice stressed that the Ombudsman should protect the interests of the individual from administration.[126] For this purpose, Ombudsman is formed in Norway.

SELECTION – Like other countries, Norwegian Ombudsman is elected by Storting for a term of 4 years and can be discharged by a two thirds of majority.

AREA OF POWER – The Defense Ombudsman looks after the matters of defense. It is effective for military and civilian service. The Storting's Ombudsman for public administration tries to assess and call the attention to the defects in administration.[127] He does not have any executive power. The Ombudsman in Norway can deal with complaints against municipal, administration, judiciary and cases involving deprivation of personal liberty. Storting itself is out of his jurisdiction. He has freedom to choose his method of work. It is his own decision whether the documents should be put up publicly or not.

The Norwegian Ombudsman makes the Public

effective and sometimes, harmful to high handedness arrogance of the officials in their work.[128] The main drawback of Norwegian Omudsman is that his powers are limited to express his opinion on the cases. The Act says that the complaints must be signed and must be submitted within a year from the vented date. There is the 'Ombudsman Board' led by Ombudsman and members to deal with economical and social rights, educational and welfare work, canteen services, pensions, clothing, food, accommodation, NGOs, armed forces.[129] The board has the extensive powers. But the Norwegian Ombudsman basically has a limited power. According to observers, he is successful in tackling corruption and maladministration.

1.10.7 Ombudsman in Finland

Finland is the least corrupt country in the world. This small and thinly populated country gives a lesson for need of a bold and fair initiative of citizen's guardian. It makes the idea of Ombudsman popular in the democratic world.

Finland was separated from Sweden in 1809 and was attached to the Russian empire. To prevent public officials' interference in citizens rights, there was a need of super-administrative authority. Finland created such authority as 'Procurement' on the background of Sweden's 'Chancellor of Justice'.[130] Constitutionally, in 1919, Finland adopted the office of Ombudsman.

SELECTION – Ombudsman, chosen by the Parliament, can enjoy his term for 4 years. He is irremovable in his term and after completing his term, he may be rejected or may not be continued. His salary is equal to that of the President of Supreme Court, but his jurisdiction and status is quiet different.

AREA OF POWER – According to section 49 of Finnish constitution, the President of the republic, ministers, public authorities, civil servants are within the jurisdiction of Ombudsman.[131]

He cannot oversee the Parliament, the procurator, foreign authorities, corporations and non-profit associations. He can assist the business sessions of the Council of State, tribunals and public departments. He has some judicial authorities also under which he can request the court to reopen the cases.

In Finland, Ombudsman is an independent body that acts upon his/her own judgment. Ombudsman can investigate a matter of concern on his/her initiative. Finnish Ombudsman conducts site inspections of public officials and institutions focusing particularly on prisons, military units and institutions in the social welfare and health sector. The Ombudsman makes sure that the laws are upheld generally in the officials capacity. The procedure of inquiry is very flexible. The views of Ombudsman and results are often released and are open to public.

Procurator/Chancellor of Justice is the similar important post to Ombudsman in Finland. The single difference is that procurator can review the decisions of the Disciplinary Committee of the Finnish Bar Association which Ombudsman cannot.[132] Ombudsman is the highest guardian of the law. The Finnish legal experts stress that their influence has been beneficial. He is more powerful than his counterparts in the other Scandinavian countries. He himself is an example of usefulness and effectiveness.

Netherlands initiated with the Ombudsman on Jan 1, 1982.

1.10.8 Ombudsman Experience in Other Countries

In sixties, after adopting the Ombudsman institute by New Zealand many other non-Scandinavian countries also followed its experience. It is matter of surprise that the people, civil servants or ministers in these countries were not in favour initially. But, some components in the society felt the institute of Ombudsman useful after the very creation of the institution. Certainly, the main purpose of forming the institute is to [illegible] of maladministration in these countries.

and articles tried to convince the importance of the institution in the modern welfare state.[133] And the European countries sprang up with the office of Ombudsman in Public and Private sectors. United Kingdom was one of them which was inspired by Hurwitz's speeches on Ombudsman. As per 'The Parliamentary Commission Act, 1967' Sir Edmund Compton was appointed as the first Ombudsman of the UK. The Police and Criminal Evidence Act, 1984 established a Prison Ombudsman.[134]

Ombudsman in the UK proved quite useful even though its' major drawback was indirect approach to him by the citizens. His existence was defended by the Select Committee of the House of Commons. His powers in obtaining evidence are equivalent to the High Court. Ombudsman can deal with the cases of housing, planning, education, social services, consumer protection, drainage and council tax.[135]

There are 3 Local Government Ombudsmen who investigate the complaints of injustice.

Israel was the first developing country, which introduced the office of Ombudsman. Israeli Ombudsman influences public policy. In fact, it was powerless and failure attempt in the begining. Dr. Izak Nebenza, a former Ombudsman says,

> "..God gave man the task for moral advancement not only in his individual soul but also in his society. This is a meaningful role assigned by us (Ombudsman)..." [136]

If an Ombudsman is a quality man, he can make it strong. There are dozens of Ombudsmen in Israel in public and private sectors.

Nigerian people think that Ombudsman is not an instrument to fight corruption; but it is a useful redressal of citizens' grievances against the public and private bureaucracy.[137] Nigeria established Military Ombudsman in 1975 and executive and civil Ombudsman in 1979. It is surprising that besides impartial and independent practice of

is an external device to curb corruption. It can't change the entire corruption prone culture that may be prevailing in Nigeria.

Manitoba, a province in America, established Ombudsman institution by 'Ombudsman Act, 1970' by appointing Mr. George W. Maltby as the first Ombudsman of the state. Since 1997, the jurisdiction of the Ombudsman was expanded to municipalities and in June 1990, the Regional Ombudsmanship was established.[138] The purpose was to promote fairness, equity and administrative accountability. Detroit city in the US has a City Ombudsman who provides investigative and informational service to the citizens regarding the city government.[139] City Ombudsman has discretionary power that he can build up the confidence of citizens.

Like Manitoba and Detroit, in the US, Yukkon territorial government has an independent Ombudsman. Yukon Ombudsman can investigate the complaints against government departments, public schools, colleges, hospitals, local authorities, crown corporations and governing bodies.[140] A major task of Ombudsman is to review administrative actions in Yukon.

The office of Ombudsman was established on Jan. 20, 1995 in Bosnia-Herzegovina. The purpose is to protect rights and fundamental freedoms of each individual against governmental errors.[141]

Greek Ombudsman began to function on 1 Oct. 1998 and gained a widespread identification in 4 years. Greek Ombudsman aims at resolving individual problems and shaping administrative culture.[142] In Sept. 1999, the earthquake complied Athens by sending 12 staff members for processing citizen's applications to the Government Natural Disaster Financial Assistance progamme. Greek Ombudsman proved its' social awareness. Greek Ombudsman joined IOI, a promoter of worldwide Ombudsmanship in 1999. P. Nikiforos, the first Ombudsman in Greek submitted a proposal to the council of

offered to them in 2000. Greek Ombudsman in a very short period proved its' utility. It can deal with the matter of civil services, local government, judicial services, international services, legal council of state, secret services. It's powers of dealing are quite large, which made it very popular amongst Greek citizens.

Netherland's 'National Syndicate' during 1801 to 1805 was similar to Ombudsman. The office of 'Investigator Commissioner' appeared in 1976 and he replaced the office of Ombudsman in 1982.[144] It was constitutionalized on March 25, 1999 by article 78(a). The Ombudsman in Netherlands is one of the appreciated models which took 9th position in the 'Corruption Perception Index' launched by the Transparency International. Netherland's Public awareness for the institute made it popular within a meantime. It properly determines whether the administrative authorities are acting properly in the matters under investigation.

Article (276) of Pakistan's Interim constitution in 1972 provided Federal and Provincial Ombudsman. It was included in the 4th Schedule of constitution and the office of Ombudsman became effective in 1983.[145] Ombudsman (Wafaqi Mohtasib) works non-politically to diagnose, investigate, redress and rectify maladministration. Court, defense, army, navy, air force, foreign affairs are excluded from Ombudsman's jurisdiction. In reality, Pakistani Ombudsman cannot work effectively as expected for the simple reason that vital areas of corrupt society are as stated above far away from the jurisdiction of Ombudsman.[146] Again lack of political support will make the institution blunt. The provincial Government of Azad Jammu-Kashmir has established Provincial Ombudsman. Mohtasib not only deals with cases but also initiates studies and research regarding maladministration.

1.10.9 Ombudsman in Public and Private Sector

Besides politicians and bureaucrats those usually constitute

Ombudsman is required to check and control them. However, the Ombudsman mechanism has also penetrated different sectors of socio economic set up of different countries. They include banking, police, education, children, mining Legal, criminal, dental, pension, prison, electrical, etc.

Banking Ombudsman

Banking Ombudsman scheme was adopted for the first time by the UK on 2 Jan, 1986. The purpose was of course to resolve individual complaints about banking services.[147] All the major banks are under its jurisdiction. After the UK, many countries are adopting the Ombudsman in private and government banks. India is one of those countries. (detailed study is in Ch.II)

Banking Ombudsman can deal with the complaints from individuals, sole trader partnership and unincorporated bodies. In some countries, a complainant is required to approach the bank authorities but the concern authorities do not respond to the complaints then he or she could approach the Bank Ombudsman. Ombudsman directly cannot deal with bank's commercial judgement, yet it can interfere in maladministration or unfair treatment in the decision. It cannot make a rule for banking industry or cannot advise on any financial matter or debit problems. The Banking Ombudsman in private sector is proved to be an impartial, independent and very useful body.

Police Ombudsman

The smooth source in the UK to prevent the maladministration in police is Police Ombudsman, which presently is occupied by Mrs. Nuala O'Loan.[148] There are three departments in the UK police Ombudsman's office- The first is the 'Investigator Directorate' which deals with the complaints lodged by citizen. The Ombudsman has access to all the documents related to the case. The second is the 'Corporate Service Directorate' that collects the information and statistics. It also creates the method of processing and prepares policy of

to the check of police Ombudsman, the police conduct code is exercised as well as maladministration and misuses of the post by officers and constables are under control in the UK. Some other countries are also trying to go with Police Ombudsman to tackle administrative defects in the police Department.

Educational Ombudsman

Approximately, 200 colleges, schools, universities and educational institutes have Ombudsman ship in the US and the UK. According to American concept, University Ombudsman is urgent for justice within the complex institutional system of higher education. Universities at Kansas, Texas, Chicago, Colorado, Florida have established University Ombudsman. By posting Edward Levi as the first student Ombudsman in 1968, Chicago University introduced the concept of Education Ombudsman.[149] The office of Chicago Ombudsman is run by the students to investigate grievances by students as well as suggests a need for changes in the university rules, procedures, policies. In Kansas university, Ombudsman institution is created according to 'University Senate Rules And Regulations Act' which can communicate with students, staff, faculty, administrators and service offices impartially, independently and confidentially.[150] Colorado Ombudsman has authority to explain university policies and procedures which other universities do not allow.[151] Ombudsman in Florida can give advice, guidance, interpretation and investigation as needed by the students, the staff, and can discuss with them openly academic cases, employment problems, housing issues, testing procedures.[152] The powers vested with Ombudsman in the different universities are different. Chicago public schools have established Ombudsman to respond to individuals request. The office aims to offer a good service to students and parents. The state of Hawaii's Board Of Education Ombudsman is committed to assured that proper attention is given to individual complaints as concerns.[153] The Board has a good communication with the students through Ombudsman's results and the same

Education Ombudsman has created a healthy environment in the educational field in the US.

Children Ombudsman

Presently, UN is convinced of the problem of child labor, hunger, death due to starvation. The rights of children are in need of a safeguard. Sweden formed Children Ombudsman. It is an independent body. The institute is working at the national and local level. The problems of children under 18 are dealt with by the Children Ombudsman.[154] The Ombudsman also takes care of children's rights and laws. In Sweden, Children Ombudsman is a good remedy for their problems.

Mining Ombudsman

Mineral rich countries like Australia have several problems in mining industry. Oxfam Community Aid Board has been working for the last 40 years on problems of this industry. It formally established Mining Ombudsman in Feb. 2000. It has effected the industries in Asia, the Pacific, Africa and Latin America. Accordingly, the Mining Ombudsman can deal with the person who looses his land without proper compensation and sustainable livelihood; degradation of waterways and other natural resources upon which people depend.[155] The Mining Ombudsman assists communities in developing countries also.

Legal Ombudsman

In April 1991, Great Britain formed a Legal Service Ombudsman Institution which has the jurisdiction over the behavior of lawyers. In the US and the UK there is a Legislative Ombudsman whereas Kansas Government Department of Corrections has Departmental Ombudsman. Michigan Department of Corrections established Ombudsman in 1975- Both Kansas and Michigan Corrections Ombudsmen could deal with the prisons, legislators, correction's employee. It can review or recommend policy, mediate resolution and update the changes made by the department. The Scottish Legal Service Ombudsman Mrs. Linda Baker thinks that it is

The prisoners can complain against their practitioners in the past or at present.

Crime Victim's Ombudsman

Crime Victims Ombudsman at South Carolina is neither an advocate nor a defender of bureaucracy. It provides a crime victim equitable and fair treatment. It refers for them an appropriate agency and reviews and attempts to resolve complaints against victim assistance programme.[157] Texas Department of Criminal Justice established the programme to assist in the communication between the department and public. Ombudsman responds to the queries and makes appropriate referrals to agency staff.

Dental Ombudsman

The Dental Ombudsman service was launched in South Africa at first. The aim was to provide consumers an access to an independent, autonomous person. This person was expected to advice the patients, to deal with complaints concerning the standards of services and fees of the dentists.[158] The utility of Dental Ombudsman depend on the relationship between the practitioner and the patients.

Pension Ombudsman

The secretary of State, in the UK, appoints pension Ombudsman whereas his role and powers are decided by Parliament. The Ombudsman can deal with the cases of pension schemes. David Leverick, the pension Ombudsman expressed his views that he can decide the complaints and disputes about the ways the pensions scheme are run.[159] The Ombudsman can deal with the cases like delay in pension.

Prison Ombudsman

By the recommendations on the prisoners in England and Wales, the prison Ombudsman was appointed in Oct. 1994. The intention was to investigate the grievances made by prisoners about their poor treatment by prison staff. Sir Peter Wood, the

annual report (23 Oct. 1996) that he dealt with 2000 complaints during 14 months in which most of the recommendations were rejected by prison services.[160] He identified that some particular areas of prison services functioning of which give rise to complaints including disciplinary adjudication, security categorization, property and transfers. Now, after 10 years of aging of prison Ombudsman it is observed that maximum recommendations are accepted and implemented. Since Nov. 29, 2001 the Prison and Probation Ombudsman office had been launched. The Ex-prisoners, prisoners on remand and people on rehabilitation can go to the Ombudsman. The sufferers by National Probation Service can also write to this Ombudsman.

Electricity Ombudsman

Electricity Industry in South Africa grounded Ombudsman for Electricity by appointing Nick Hakof on Nov. 30, 2000. The office determines the prompt resolution and complaints and disputes between the consumers of electricity services and the members.[161] It also provides a free, accessible and informal service to the customers of electricity services accomplishing the Ombudsman scheme in private sector. Unfortunately it is found that the main role of Ombudsman is diverted in private sector.

As a matter of fact, there has been debate on public and Private Ombudsman machineries. There is no need of it for private sector. Accordingly, Ombudsman is essential defender against governmental actions. The role of private Ombudsman, if at all any, is something different. It may be that of mediator between public and private administration.

This is a brief account of Ombudsman system in different countries dealing with various sectors of the countries.

To some extent Government ombudsmen are successfully preventing malpractice in administration and corruption in government. It becomes citizen's listener, friend and however, the private Ombudsman has yet to establish its utility as compared to its counterpart in Government.

1.11 INTERNATIOAL OMBUDSMAN INSTITUTE

Though Swedish Ombudsman was un-noticed for hundred and more years after it's creation the idea and concept of Ombudsman has gripped strongly after the Second World War. Nearly 187 countries have Ombudsman office. Some ombudsmen thought to come together under one roof and to give and take some ideas with the purpose experiences related to the Ombudsman institute. On this background, the International Ombudsman Institute was established in 1978. The Ombudsmen in developed and developing countries have reached a stage to gather and to pass some ideas of Ombudsman ship mainly to control a worldwide disease of corruption and maladministration.

IOI promotes and encourages the concept of Ombudsman throughout the world. It is instrumental in the exchange of information and experience between ombudsmen, throughout the world.[162] To achieve this purpose, IOI supports the researches and studies of Ombudsman system. It accords scholarships, fellowships and grants to the researchers and encourages the idea of Ombudsman.

IOI has proceedings in English, Spanish and French languages. Till date, IOI has 126 members from 86 countries throughout the world. Updated Website developed by IOI indicates the number of its members is May 12, 2002.

Among the members of IOI from which the Board of Director is formed. Secretariat is a responsible body for IOI's policy. IOI has members, i.e. Institutional, Associate, Individual, Honorary, Life and Library Members. After every 4 years it organizes conferences. The first conference was held at Edmond, Canada in 1978; second at Jerusalem, Isreal in 1980; third at Vienna, Austria in 1992; Fourth in Buenos Aires, Argentina in 1996; Fifth at Durban, South Africa in 2000;. The sixth conference affirmed the essential characteristic of Ombudsman institute as independence and credibility.[163]

The conferences and occasional workshops always focus on the promotion of the Ombudsman institute. At present, IOI is trying its efficiency, decentralization and democratization of it's regional branches. IOI has a publication of yearly reports, journals, occasional paper series, news teller, etc. It maintains a library and resource of monographs, articles, legislation and other research material related to Ombudsman in any country. Increasingly, IOI helps to develop Ombudsman institution for the protection of human rights to strengthen its efficiency.

1.12 EUROPEAN OMBUDSMAN INSTITUTE

In addition to International Ombudsman Institute there are similar bodies in other part of the world. For example, in Oct. 1982, the 'Working Association' for the Insurance at University of Innsbruck organized a conference in Innsbruck, which was dedicated to more scientific interest and to the ideas of Ombudsman. The proponents were Prof. Hans Klecatoky, Prof. Dr. Fritz Riechert Facilides, Prof. Norbert Wirner who inspired to associate 'European Ombudsman Academy'. This was not a legal organization. In 1988, it was transformed legally by naming 'European Ombudsman Institute.[164] This view of Ombudsman system world over reminds us of what Bryce says eternal vigilance is the price of democracy. The western countries provide a model where in there is concern for corruption free society on the one hand and need for attention towards grievances of citizens on other. It also makes us very clear that malady of corruption and maladministration is not confined to government sector alone bút has perporated to almost all walks of life Again the results of Ombudsman machinery is it same at all Maces. There are variations. The Scandinavian countries are more successful than others. May be due to their small size and comparative less complicated systems and relations. Lastly the underdeveloped countries have lot of things to learn from the experience of the western this regard. The EOI is housed at Innsbruck, Tyrol. It is associated with the Australian law. The EOI adopted a scientific view to analyze human rights; to give civil protection to the institution of Ombudsman. EOI conducts the research projects in the Ombudsman ship area to promote and disseminate in non-Ombudsman countries. EOI mainly is active in supporting the Ombudsman idea and to give publicity.

Besides IOI and EOI there are several associations of Ombudsman which are affected in these particular areas such as Ombudsman Association, USA; British and Irish Ombudsman Association; Australia and Pacific Ombudsman Association; Canadian Ombudsman Association, etc.

1.13 WHY OMBUDSMAN IS POPULAR?

Swedish Ombudsman after 140 years, received a world-wide recognition. Maximum developed and developing countries are going with Ombudsman office. Concluding in all these countries the concept becomes popular. The reasons of popularity could be:

1. Ombudsman is an impartial and independent machinery.
2. Ombudsman is easier to approach.
3. Ombudsman can operate openly.
4. Ombudsman can handle the minor cases.
5. There is not any age limit to go to the Ombudsman.
6. Ombudsman provides service without charging heavy fees.
7. Ombudsman is non-profit, non-political institute.
8. Ombudsman's method of handling appeals against administrative decisions is direct, informal and more speedy than the courts.
9. Ombudsman is public-oriented more then government-orientation.
10. Ombudsman can inspire the confidence and trust within all parties.
11. Ombudsman can deal through enter premises, oral information or media news if not complained by anyone.

For all these reasons Ombudsman institution is popular. It helps to correct negligent, defective, irregular, abusive, injurious and insufficient behavior that constantly affects the personal and corrective rights of individuals.

1.14 DOES OMBUDSMAN EXCESSIVE?

Of course, to create an interest in public affairs, and to further and promote those principles, which are believed to be important to the public welfare, the Ombudsman system is necessary.

A people's movement should be initiated to end the 'misdeeds' of the government. A common man should feel that there is someone who lovingly attends to him in an impartial, supportive and active manner. Ombudsman is supposed to resolve problems informally expeditiously of each and every citizen. Ombudsman is the only machinery, which investigates the citizen's relation with government authority.

One of the Swedish Ombudsman says,

> "..150 years experience proves that there is always a need for an agency independent of the administration for safeguarding the rights of the citizens. The Ombudsman institution, which was formed 150 years ago, still appears to be a useful and necessary instrument for the protection of the citizen's lawful interests in the rapid development of society. New conditions naturally demand continuing adjustment." [167]

1.15 CONCLUSION

Modern government is going at the crossroad of good governance. It needs effective, efficient, transparent and accountable administration. It demands faith in administration on the side of people. The Ombudsman is a flexible friend of people, which is capable to fight with rising challenges of government. In this chapter, a wide discussion has been made on its usefulness, independence and accesses. Ombudsman shows its integrity and utility to citizens around the world. Ombudsman, a citizen's defender is successfully running in the public and private field in the western countries. But, some countries like India do not have such a device. International Ombudsman Institute and European Ombudsman Institute are hopefully trying to expand the idea of Ombudsman in those countries, which are not having it. They are in hope of developing the institution with the changing times as the greatest challenge of public administration.

REFERENCES

1. Gelhorn Walter- Ombudsman and Others - 83
2. Stacy Frank- The Ombudsman - 05
3. Donald Rowat-Ombudsman - 48
4. Donald Rowat- The Judicial Ombudsman - 32
5. Caiden Gerald- Ombudsmen in Developing Democracies International Review of Administrative Science Vol. 50, No. 3 1984 227-231
6. Adamlokan Ladipo - The Nigerian Ombudsman - The Indian Journal of Public Administration, Vol. 32(2) -233-235
7. IBID
8. Donald Rowat- Maladministration: Issue for the Ombudsman the Australian Journal of Public Administration - 22
9. Yardely David -Ombudsman in UK, Indian Journal of Public Administration – Vol XLJ(2), April/June-1995-191
10. http://www.eduskunta.fi/efakta/eoa/.
11. Gelhorn Walter- Ombudsmen and Others –Chapter-1 Sweden - 25
12. http://www.synigorus.gr/en-who-is-in.ca.
13. http://www.ombudsmen.govt.nz/layinga.htm.
14. http://www.colorado.edu.ombuds/index/html.
15. http://www.unichicago.edu/student/ombudsperson/html.
16. http://www. uchicago.edu.studentperson/html.
17. http://www.falcon.cc.ku.edu/~ombuds.index/html
18. http://www. colostate.edu.
19. http://www.cvo-gov.state/us/.
20. http://www.Ombudsman.ci.detroit.us
21. http://www.milegislativecouncilortg.ioc/contact.htm
22. http://www.LIC.Ombudsman.htm
23. http://www.nr.state.ky.us/nrecp/dep/smbizair/index/html/.
24. http://www.policeOmbudsman.org/main/htm.

25. http://www.homeoffice.gov/uk/ppoweb/index.missionhtm.html/
26. http://www.go.org.uik/html/
27. http://www.fos.dircon.co.uk/Ombudsman
28. http://www.theiob.org.uk/
29. http://www.oea.co.uk/htm
30. http://www.pensions-Ombudsman.org.uk/html.
31. http://www.cvo-gov.state/us.
32. http://www.cao.org.au/campaign/mining/Ombudsman/2001.index/html/
33. http://www.bo.se
34. http://www.Ombudsman.or.kr/hostory/on/htm/
35. http://www.corp.com/customer-rights.html/
36. http://www.tirol-hph.highway.telecom.
37. http://www.irlgov.ie./okOmbudsman/speeches.co
38. http://www.ombud.gov.bc.ca/publicactions/reports-
39. Jain M. P.- Lokpal In India
40. Saxena D. R.-Ombudsman: A Redress of Citizen's Grievances-126
41. Sharma Giridhar B.- Implementation of Ombudsman Plan In India
42. Jagadham and Makhija- Citizen Administration and Lokpal
43. Ponnoly Josseph-Lokpal-A Watchdog, The Southern Economist Vol. 41, No.11 - 5
44. Editorial-The Radical Humanist - Jan. 1997, Vol. 60, No. 10 – 3
45. Gopinath P.K.-Central Vigilance Commission- A Profile Indian Journal of Public Administration Vol. XXII, 3-425
46. Tiwana S. S. Machiney For Redress of Public Grievances In India- Administrative Change-Vol. XXII(2) Jan-Jun,1995-90
47. Singh Bishwanath-Lokpal:Indian Ombudsman Journal of National Academy of Administrative Science, Massourie Vol. XV, No. 2&3 .1970 -56
48. Singh S. S. –Parliament Bill in Political Corruption Indian Journal of Public Administration, April-June,1997, Vol. XLIII(2)

49. Agrawal U. C.- Need for a National Level Ombudsman (Lokadhikari) Indian Journal of Parliamentary Information, 1983 - 13
50. Sinha V. M.- Ombudsman in India, Political Science Review-Vol.III, No, 1, May-1964 - 135
51. Rai Haridwar & Singh S.P.-Indian Journal of Political Science,1987 - 87
52. Shail Shanthinoy-The Ombudsman for India. The Calcutta Journal of Political Science - 103
53. Editorial- Corruption In Ancient India, Journal of Parliamentary Information -305
54. http://www.bjp.org/html
55. http://www.alfa.nic.in.isdeb.is11/ses2/20130996.htm.
56. http://www.expressindia.com/news/weather.htm
57. http://www.apnapunjab.com/txplanning/taxplanningindex.htm
58. http://www.indiainfo.com
59. http://www.unitedbankofindia.com/open.htm
60. Parmar Mary- Lokayukta - 58
61. Singh S. S. & Shukla K. S.- Lokayukta - 01
62. The Times Of India, 27 February 2002
63. The Indian Express, 12 May 1999
64. The Times Of India, 24 July, 2002
65. The Hindu, 4 December 2002
66. Lal Bhure-Corruption: Functional Anarchy in Governance - 04
67. Hussian Alatas Sayed-Corruption: The Destiny in Asia - 145
68. Ghosh S.K.-Indian Panorama : Truimphs and Tragedies - 52
69. Puri Rajendra- Free At Last, To Loot and Plunder, 50 Years Of Independence - 55
70. N. Vittal- Zero Tolerance Corruption, One India, One People Vol. 3/7 - 8
71. http://www.transparency.org/documents/cpi/bps.html-
72. Gregory Roy and Hutcheson Peter-The Parliamentary Ombudsman-279-282

73. Williams David-Maladministration:Remedies For Justice - 38
74. William H. Mac Niel & Jean W. Sedlar, Reading in World History- Classical India Vol. IV
75. Dr.A.S. Altekar- State and Government in Ancient India - 88
75. Stacy Frank- The British Ombudsman - 54
76. Hallaya M. –Emergency: A War on Corruption - 13
77. Stacy Frank- The British Ombudsman - 55
78. Hussain Wahed-Administrative Justice during the Muslim Period in India-13
79. IBID
80. http://www.worldbank.org/
81. Hallaya M. –Emergency: A War on Corruption - 93
82. http://www.corruptindia.com/rewards.htm
83. Vajpayee Atal Bihari-Four Decades in Parliament -43
84. N. Vital- Zero Tolerance Corruption One India, One People Vol. 3/7, Feb., 2000 - 08
85. Syed Hussain Alatas-Corruption and its Destiny in Asia - 12
86. http://www. ioiacc.org/progrrame.html
87. Syed Hussain Alatas-Corruption: its Causes and Functions -33
88. http://www.transparency.org/documents/cpi/bps.html-
89. http://www.ioiacc.org/progrrame.html
90. Naoroji Dadabhai-Poverty and Un-British Rule in India - 218
91. Ghosh S. K.-Indian Panorama: Truimps and Tragedies- 227
92. Report-Committee on Prevention of Corruption, 1962 - 03
93. Ghosh S. K. –Indian Panorama:Triumps and Tragedies - 992
94. Ribero Francis- The Police Are Not Corrupt, They Are The Most Visible, One India, One People Vol. 3/7, Feb. 2, 2000
95. Puri Rajendra- Free Last, To Loot And Blunder, India: 50 Years Of Independence-II(1947-1987)- 662
96. N. Vittal- Zero Tolerance Corruption One India, One People Vol. 3/7 - 08
97. Ghosh S. K. –Indian Panorama : Triumph and Tragedies - 992

98. IBID
99. IBID
100. IBID
101. IBID
102. IBID
103. http://www.abc.net.au/concon.school/eduo/html.
104. http://www.Ombudsman.or.kr/history/ombudsmal/htm
105. Donald Rowat-Ombudsman-17-18
106. Stacy Frank –The Ombudsman - 52
107. S. K. Das-Encyclopedic Dictionary-2 - 243
108. William Halsey-Collier's Encyclopedia-18 - 98
109. L. Collingwood-21st Century Universal-21- 334
110. Lewis & Singh- India And The World Community - 02
111. http://www. Law. Ualberta.com
112. Agrawal U. C.- Case for a National Level Ombudsman - Indian Journal of Public Administration Vol-34(2), April/ June 1988-250
113. Donald Rowat- The Ombudsman, Ch. 1 The Ombudsman For Civil Affairs- 37
114. Gelhorn Walter- Ombudsmen and Others, Ch. 1 Sweden - 25
115. Donald Rowat- The Ombudsman, Ch. 1 The Ombudsman For Civil Affairs - 39
116. D. R, Saxena Mehra-Ombudsman (Lokpal) Redress of Citizen's Grievances In India - 44
117. Gelhorn Walter- Ombudsmen and Others, Ch. 4 Denmark
118. Donald Rowat- The Ombudsman -Ch.3 Denmark's Ombudsman -77
119. Gelhorn Walter- Ombudsmen and Others -Ch. 4 Denmark -245
120. IBID
121. Monterio John-Corruption -Ch. 13 Ombudsman in Action - 209
122. Donald Rowat- The Ombudsman, Ch. 6 Newzealnd's Parliamentary Commissioner -14
123. IBID

124. http://www.ombudsmen.govt.nz/Laying.htm
125. http://www.adobe.com/products/
126. http://www. ombudsmen.govt.nz/Laying.htm
127. http://www.odin.dep.no/odin
128. http://www.odin.dep.no/odin
129. Gelhorn Walter- Ombudsmen and Others Ch. 3 Norway-192
130. Donald Rowat- The Ombudsman Finland's Guardians of Law -54
131. Gelhorn Walter- Ombudsmen and Others Ch. 1 Finland-12
132. http://www.eduskunta/fi/efauta/eoal/.
133. Stacy Frank-The British Ombudsman -16
134. Lewis Norman and Singh S. S.-Ombudsmen - 81
135. http://www.Ombudsman.Org.Ukl/Htm
136. Gerald Caiden-Ombudsman in Developing Democracies International Review of Administrativr Science, Vol. 50, No. 3, 1984 -228
137. Adamolekun Lapido-The Nigerian Ombudsman, International Jouirnal of Public Administration-133
138. http://www.ombudsmen.Manitoba.MB.CA
139. http://www.ci.detroit.mi.us
140. http://www. Ombudsman.YK.ca/omb-mainwhite.html.
141. http://www.kentlaw.edu.com
142. http://www.synigoros.gr/en-who-is-html
143. IBID
144. http://www. Ombudsman..ni/index/html.
145. Syed Husian Altas- Corruption and Destiny in Asia- 32
146. IBID
147. http://www.obo.org.uk/1/html.
148. http://www.policeOmbudsman.org/main/mission.htm
149. http://www.uchicago.edu.studentperson/html.
150. http://www.falcon.cc.ku.edu/~ombuds.index/html
151. http://www.colostate.edu.
152. http://www.rene.pixelsight.com/ps/html

153. http://www.hlinote.k12.hi.us/STATE/BOE/Ombudsman.nsf.complaint
154. http://www.bo.se
155. http://www.cao.org.au/campaigns/mining/Ombudsman/2001.index.html
156. http://www.slso.org.uk
157. http://www.tdcj.state.tx.u/adminrvw/home/htm
158. http://www.Dental-omkbud/SA/html.
159. http://www.pensions.Ombudsman.org.uk/html.
160. http://www.prison-Ombudsman.uk/html.
161. http://www.elec/Ombudsman.org.
162. http://www.irlgov.ie/okmbudsman/speech.com
163. IBID
164. http://www.tirol.hph.highway.eoi/htm

2

Lokpal in India

2.1 INTRODUCTION

In this chapter, it is proposed to review the system to control corruption and maladministration in the Indian set up over a period of time. With the spreading of literature on Ombudsman institutions, mainly in the western countries, beginning in the Scandinavian nations, the idea of introducing such measures in India at the central as well as at the state level, has emerged. Especially, the rising incidents and magnitude of corruption in the country has given an impetus to this process resulting in the enactment of Lokayuktas in one after another states. Lokayukta in Maharashtra is the focus of this study. In order to understand and analyze the Lokayukta in Maharashtra, it is necessary to go into the details depicting the overall working of different institutional set up functioning prior to the introduction of Lokayukta in the state. It is also necessary to study the system of Lokayukta's working for 35 years in various states of Indian union.

Therefore, this chapter is divided into 3 sections.

The first section deals with the device and the machinery to curb corruption and to reduce maladministration.

The second section is on the Lokayukta and it's functioning in the States.

The third section describes the efforts taken to pass the Lokpal Bill in the Parliament. It also looks upon the progress made with setbacks and suggestions on planned 'Lokpal Bill' at the central level. This exercise will help us to understand Lokayukta in Maharashtra, which will be dealt with in chapter III.

SECTION 1

2.2 DEVICE TO CURB CORRUPTION AND MALADMINISTRATION

Ever since Independence, India is committed to secure the life, property and freedom of the citizens. Our constitution provides equality before law, various freedoms, right to life in the chapter on 'Fundamental Rights'. 'Directive Principles of the State Policy' is concerned with socio-economic rights leading to social justice. They are the directives towards the state to increase the standard of life, to reduce inequality and concentration of wealth, etc. It is necessary to make administrative apparatus effective, responsive and sensitive to fulfill these objectives given in the constitution. In order to achieve these objectives with a view to streamline administration in this direction, various efforts have been undertaken. There are number of such devices operating at various levels. They have been introduced at different times. All of them may not directly aim at controlling corruption. But, some of them are primarily concerned with administrative reforms and supplementing the existing Judiciary. They can be categorized into different types, such as:

1. Commissions and Committees—deliberately appointed either for general problem or for a particular incident of corruption such as Santhanam Committee, etc.;
2. Judiciary-a constitutional machinery;
3. Regulations –based on law, government resolution, a creation of Parliamentary Committee such as Corruption Prevention Act, etc.;
4. Special institutions-such as Central Vigilance Commission, Central Bureau of Investigation, etc.

5. The processes- the result of democratic functioning such as PIL
6. Democratic devices-individuals and NGOs
7. Other agencies

2.2.1 Commissions and Committees

Table 1 introduces some of the Committees or Commissions—

Table 2.1

Commissions and Committees on Maladministration and Corruption

No.	*Name of Committee / Commission*	*Headed by*	*Year*
1	Report on the Health of Public Administration	A.D. Gorwala	1951
2	Report on Survey of Public Administration in India, Cabinet Secretariat	Paul H. Appelby	1953
3	The Committee on Prevention of Corruption (Santhanam Committee)	K. Santhanam	1964
4	Administrative Reforms Commission	Morarji Desai/K. Hanumanthaiya	1966

2.2.1 Gorwala Report

Prof. A.D. Gorwala presented a 'Report on the Health of Public Administration' based upon his study on Indian Administration. This 70 pages report tried to make administrative functions more dynamic in India. The major suggestions of the Report include:

1. The minister should hold consultations with high civil officials on all official matters.
2. To maintain discipline and responsibility in the civil service, better pay scales and proper system of punishment be introduced.
3. Responsibility of inspection and direction be entrusted to senior officials and of more responsible work be assigned to the junior officials.
4. The working procedure of the Cabinet be improved.

These suggestions made by A.D. Gorwala were effective in removing the defects in the original administrative reforms in Indian administration.[1] Unfortunately, the government didn't show interest in implementation of these suggestions and hence a very important opportunity of administrative reform was lost.

2.2.2 Appelby Report

The Government of India invited a well- known American expert Paul H. Appleby to study and suggest administrative reforms in India. He visited various Indian states, studied government documents, papers and met the officials and Ministers and submitted his report on the basis of his observations on 15 Jan, 1953. There were 12 main recommendations in 3000 words report. Some of the important recommendations were:

1. There should be integrated system in Indian civil services.
2. For proper study of Public Administration, there should be an Institute of Public Administration at the national level.
3. The mismanagement in staff and line should be controlled.

Appleby revisited India in 1956 and made some more recommendations as follows:

1. The applied principle of delegation of powers should be adopted in administrative system.
2. The Executive Ministers should develop their ability to handle financial and budgetary matters.
3. The Parliament should discharge positive and constructive responsibility with regard to the progressive administration.

Besides these suggestions, he made comments on a control of crooked in administration. He said that it is necessary to impose prompt and sufficient penalties. He said the ungracious suggestions reported against the colleagues be welcomed and those making them be protected against harm being done to them. Better laws for securing honest administration would do a good deal in this Matter.[2] Appleby advocates homogeneity among civil servants working as an agency or as a task force. He suggested doing well by homogeneity.[3] Though, the government itself invited Appleby, it is surprising that the government didn't take any interest in implementing the recommendations.

Gorwala and Appleby's recommendations would have been useful in correcting the rising maladministration in India those days. But, no due attention was given to the recommendations made by both the experts. This negligence of their suggestions resulted in increasing maladministration, which only gives birth to the widespread corruption in Indian administrative system.

Thus, there was an urgent need to think of growing corruption in society led to committees and commissions.

2.2.3 Santhanam Committee

To investigate and combat corruption and to suggest administrative reforms, a Committee was appointed in 1962 chairing K. Santhanam. It submitted its report to the government in 1964. The most important suggestions made by the committee were as follows[4]:

1. To establish the Vigilance Commission with its autonomy.
2. To review the public services and practical steps to be taken to make anti-corruption measures more effective.
3. The committee referred to the steps to be taken to fix the responsibilities of each department for checking corruption.
4. It also aimed at the changes in law, which would ensure speedy trial of cases of bribery; corruption and criminal misconduct and make the law otherwise more effective.

The committee in order to liberalize the existing rules under section (5) of its recommendations suggested to form the central vigilance commissioner.[5] Accordingly, the commission was constituted in 1964. The jurisdiction, powers, status, and role of commission were also dealt with in the Act. (it is discussed in 2.5.2)

2.2.4 Administrative Reforms Commission-I

Administrative Reforms Commission was set up on Jan. 5, 1966 to examine the public administration and make necessary recommendations. Morarji Desai was the first Chairperson. But as he became the Deputy Prime Minister, the chairmanship was assigned to K. Hanumanthaiya, an expert and a well-known Civil Servant. Its final interim report was submitted on Oct. 28, 1966. The commission was advised to give its report on the problem of Redressal of Citizens Grievances. In May 1970, the commission submitted a comprehensive report containing 578 recommendations.[6] Some of the recommendations that are as follows:

1. There should be 2 agencies for removing the public grievances against public officials-

   (a) 'Lokpal' at the National level and

   (b) 'Lokayukta' at the State level.

2. The size of Union Council of Ministers should be limited and be determined in accordance with the requirement.

Though, the government did not accept all its recommendations, yet some of them were accepted and implemented. The government accepted the recommendation of appointing 'Lokpal' and 'Lokayukta'.

These 4 commissions and committees are important in the study of Indian administration, as well as for the present study. Gorwala and Appleby Reports tried to reorganize Indian administration to tackle maladministration, whereas, Santhanam and Hanumanthaiya committees attempted to offer a remedy to curb growing corruption and maladministration. All the recommendations made by these experts were not implemented. The result was supporting to the present illnesses in administration. However, wide discussion on the problem of corruption and maladministration took place on the reports of these commissions. An urgency of a redressal of citizens' grievance was felt right from 1969 due to the experts' reports. This can be treated as positive aspect of the commissions.

2.2.5 Administrative Reforms Commission-II

On August 31, 2005, II d Administrative Reforms Commission had established under the Chairmanship of Shri Virappa Moili.(x-Chief Minister, Karnataka and presently Law Minister) Smt. Vinita Rai, Shri V. Ramachandra, Dr. A.R. Mukarji, Dr. A. H. Calaro are the members of the commission. Till a date, it has submitted its 8 reports on Right To Information, Human Resource, Disaster Management, Administrative Morality, Law and Order, Local Government, Efficiency and Terrorism. The commission in its report particularly on RTI and others also strongly recommended for Lokpal. Its important recommendation is giving constitutional status to Lokpal. It also argue on inclusion of ministers, chief ministers, MLAs and inclusion of prime minister in Lokpal's perview. The commission stressed on establishement of Lokayukta in all the states as well as the local level.

Eventhough, the commission recommended for Lokpal and Lokayukta, government has not given proper attention.

2.3 JUDICIARY

Justice is a cold virtue. A common man is offered security and safety by judiciary. In the present circumstances when people's expectations and aspirations are being totally ignored by both the legislature and executive, it is the Court, which has to come to their rescue. The judiciary has done a remarkable job, which cannot be brushed aside.[7] It is significant that structurely the judiciary is independent of the Executive; but habitually, the executive interference into the judiciary is experienced. Judiciary has been playing an important role in protecting citizen's rights for a long time. Judiciary has been the basement of a Welfare State since the ancient days. The Laws were not made by the Committees or Commissions or experts; but were followed by the kings and the citizens in ancient India. Justice was administered according to Smritis.

It was king's responsibility to give protection to the people as well as proper and impartial administration of justice. Kautilya in 'Arthashastra' speaks about 2 types of courts: Dharmasthiya and Kantakshodhana[8]— the first was to dispose off the cases of violation, of traditional rules and regulations- and the second was for the police, public safety, criminal punishment and other serious offences. Asoka's judicial system was based upon Dandaniti. The justice was very quick and inexpensive in not only ancient days but also in Mughal period. Mughal justice was tempered by circumstances of the age and the fear of God, popular discontent and rebellion[9]. It was also impartial and prompt though it did not depend on any written laws. Modern judiciary is depended upon the Laws and Acts.

In order to understand the advantages and disadvantages of judiciary, it would be necessary to discuss the Rules and the Acts with which it exercises its powers.

2.3.1 Role of Judiciary in Controlling Corruption

"The judicial system had a great role to play in ensuring the smooth functioning of democracy", says P.R. Gokulkrishnan the former Chief Justice, High Court, Madras.[10] Judicial gods in India have appropriate power to take action against corruption.

To know the present position of judiciary in controlling corruption, we talked to some of the District Judges informally. The discussion concludes that 2 cases are admitted monthly in the courts and 7 cases are acquitted yearly due to lack of evidence and proof and non-co- operation of the sanctioning authority concerning corruption matters,[11] is an information given by the District Judge, Nasik. It makes clear how far judiciary plays an active role in controlling corruption. The judiciary, which has to control corruption, seems occasionally corrupt. In the ancient days, during the case hearing, judges were not allowed to discuss the matter or to have any personal talk with the accused.[12] The judgement was supposed to consider the nature of crime, the age and the motive of the criminal and with humanistic approach. The cost was Brahmin 100 cows, a Kshatriya 55 cows, a Vaishya 100 cows and a

Shuddra by wriggled an important factor in the judgment-the murderer of a Brahmin 10 cows.[13] Accordingly, the judgment in the corruption or bribery cases was based upon caste system. The judiciary was independent and impartial but it considered caste. The caste system was based upon profession-i.e. economic condition of an accused.

The ancient judiciary was all in all humanistic and timid. Today, judiciary is a hope to tackle corruption and maladministration-inappropriately; it is trapped in the corrupt practices.

2.3.2 Corruption and Other Limitations of Judiciary

Bhrigusamhita suggested the punishment for corrupt or perverse judgment by twice the amount of fine inflicted on the guilty party.[14] It makes clear that there was corruption in judiciary in ancient days. In modem times, it has become a common practice.

It was said that Indira Gandhi, the Ex-Prime Minister offered bribe to the Chief Justice of High Court, Allahbad, who boldly refused. It was only when various charges of corruption against Justice V. Ramaswami came in light that the long arms of justice began moving openly.[15] During emergency, Indira Gandhi transferred 14 judges and 40 were allowed to file a suit when she was ousted from power for the injustice done to them. The integrity and independence of judiciary thus became doubtful. E.S. Venkataramaiha, former Chief Justice, India says, "Nearly half of our mails are related to the charges of corruption and communal bias against High Court Judges."[16] The misbehaviour of judges is also not new. There was a popular saying in Mughal period, "to trust a Quazi* is to court misfortune."[17] The problem has worsened. The five of the forty-four judges serving in Bombay High Court had relatives practicing.[18] Favoritism is there in not only politics but also in judiciary. Another 167 lawyers in the same Association proposed the resolution for the Supreme Court Judges also in which A.H.Ahemedi himself was included.[19]

---

* Quazi is a highest judicial officer. It is the religious post invented in Mughal periods.

Nepotism and favoritism are hurdles in judiciary. Fighting corruption is an act of constitutional necessity. It can be done at the expense of truth. Judicial accountability is impossible without an effective and responsible exposure by the bar and the media.

This corrupt practice in judiciary is the major difficulty in controlling corruption in the society.

There are a few limitations of judiciary due to which the courts cannot deal with the problem of corruption and maladministration effectively:

1. Delay in justice
2. Lengthy process
3. Prolonged vacancies of judges
4. Indirect remedy
5. Costly

2.4 ACTS AND REGULATIONS

The Parliament as well as State Legislatures has enacted laws time to time to prevent corruption and maladministration. The major acts are 'The Prevention of Corruption Act, 1947 and 1988'.

2.4.1 Prevention of Corruption Act, 1947 and 1988

Prevention of Corruption Act, 1947 was meant for the public servants only. Other political or social elements were not subjected to the Act. According to the section 5(1) (d), of this Act, it is necessary to prove that the accused received bribe was gratification—prosecution must prove that money paid was not towards any unlawful collection.[20] Phenolphthalein powdered currency from an accused was one of the main sources to be presented to the wants. In 'Yashwant Nanibhai Pingle Vs. The State of Maharashtra', the Bombay High Court declared that the powdered currency is not quiet a sufficient proof to satisfy the sanctioning authority.[21]

But, at the time of this result, the Act was modified and became outdated due to the effect of 'Corruption Prevention

Act, 1988.' Before that, with the help of powdered currency, many accused were sentenced punishment.

The 1947 Act was amended in 1952 and 1964. The Act was not preventive in the sense that it has created new offences as penal offences and thereby sought their prevention.[22] On many backgrounds, it was not sufficient to curb corruption; hence, there was another Act passed in the Parliament on September 8, 1988, namely, 'Prevention of Corruption Act, 1988'. It is multi-faced piece of legislation. The relevant provisions, which were scattered, previously related to bribery, corruption and criminal misconduct are to be found at one place in this act.[23] Today, the Anti-Corruption Bureau implements the Act; but unfortunately, there are a few cases in the courts involving offences of corruption. So far, disposal of cases is concerned, hardly 2 cases monthly are subjected in the District Courts on the matter of corruption and not a single case is admitted for maladministration, nepotism, favoritism, etc. is the conclusion of informal discussion with the District Judge, Nashik. It seems that though there are provisions in the act, there is very little response from the citizens as well as public servants. The overall atmosphere is not conducive for citizens to come forward in large number.

2.4.2 Special Police Establishment

In 1941, during the World War-II, Government of India established the 'Special Police Establishment.' The aim was to investigate the cases of bribery and corruption in 'The War & Supply Department'. After the War, the Central Government needed an agency to investigate the bribery and corruption by the employees of central government. Therefore, the government decided to enact the 'Delhi Special Police Establishment Act'. It was formulated in 1946. The Act was for the Union Territories; but under Section 3(1) Of the Act, Central Government had power to extend it to the States also.[24] The present Central Bureau of Investigation was established under this Act. The Central Bureau of Investigation investigates the offences notified by the Central Government under the Delhi Special Police Establishment Act.[25] As per the decision of Supreme Court in 1997, the Central Vigilance Commission supervises Central Bureau of Investigation. (It is discussed in 2.5.1) Presently, neither the machinery nor the Act is an effective solution to curb corruption and maladministration.

2.4.3 Right to Information Act, 2005

Right To Information is one of the effective instrument for transparent administration. Sweden only has given birth to an idea in 1744 A. D. Like ombudsman, RTI was also neglected for a decade and more. It was accepted by other Scandinavian countries and then in other countries. Sweden, Germany has given constitutional status. USA, Canada, Australia, England has enacted it separately.

In India, due to official Secretes Act,1923 a common man becomes unknown what government and administration is doing. People could not ask a question on governmental policy making and implementation.

2.4.4 Ministry of Personnel, Public Grievances and Pension

In addition to the acts, there are executive agencies and departments established to deal with matters relating corruption and maladministration.

One of the major efforts made by PMO to revamp administration is the establishment of the 'Ministry Of Personnel, Public Grievances And Pension.' Rajeev Gandhi, the then Prime Minister was, instrumental for the organization of this department, which was constituted in 1985. The Ministry is the central agency responsible for policy and co-ordination of all activities in the sphere of public personnel management, including administrative vigilance, reservation for Scheduled Castes, Tribes and other categories in services, machinery for joint consultation and compulsory arbitration, staff, welfare, pensions, administrative reforms and public grievances.[26]

The work of ministry covers in all Ministries, Departments, Subordinate offices and Public Sector undertakings. As part of procedure, on every Wednesday in the morning from 10 a.m. to 1 p.m. all the Deputy secretary level officers are supposed to be available for attending the grievances.

2.4.5 Directorate of Public Grievance

This process strengthened the grievance redressal activity as a result, an independent authority in the form of the Directorate of Public Grievances has been functioning in the Cabinet Secretariat since April 1, 1988. The Directorate handles grievances related to the Department of Railway, Post, Telecommunication and also of to the Civil Aviation, Surface Transport and Urban Development Department from Oct. 1,1989. The quarterly meetings of various Departments/ Ministries are held. The powers of calling of papers and making recommendations on the basis of scrutiny of the relevant files are vested with this Directorate.

2.4.6 Administrative Tribunal

Justice is a multi-dimensional action. Judicial power controls administrative bodies within the limits of the law and the constitution. Delay and huge backlogs of cases are bad patches of the courts. An administrative body may sometimes exercise judicial functions—when it does so, it is called a quasi-judicial administrative body or tribunal.[27] For disputes and complaints related to recruitment and conditions of service of persons appointed to public services and of posts in connection with the affairs of the Union and State governments, the Administrative Tribunals Act, 1985 was passed by the Parliament. Under this Act, Central Administrative Tribunal (CAT) was set up on Nov. 1,1985 to provide speedy and inexpensive justice to the central government employees in respect of their service matters.[28] Tribunals are other than the courts. Tribunals are schemed under Article 323(A)* by 42nd

* Article 323 (A)—"Notwithstanding anything in this chapter, the Supreme Court may, in it's discretion grant special leave to appeal from any judgment, decree, determination, sentence or order in any case/matter passed/made by Court or Tribunals in the territory of India."

amendment. A tribunal is an ad-judicatory agency, which is not deemed to be a Court. Its function is due to the rapid growth of civilization. The rising problems faced by administration and the overburdened judiciary be given its rationale. Tribunals can be established at the central and at the state level, too. Tribunal takes the adjudication of disputes related to the recruitment and conditions of service of the persons appointment to public services or posts of the union and of the state, out of hands of the civil courts and high courts and puts them into those of the administrative tribunals for the union or for the States. Different tribunals include:

1. Labor Tribunal
2. Bank Debit Appellate Tribunal
3. Income Tax Appellate Tribunal
4. Claims Tribunal
5. Rent Tribunal
6. Compensation Tribunal
7. Motor Licensing Tribunal

By way of difference between Tribunals and courts it can be said that tribunals deal with the related and specific grievances. These are not hamstrung by adherence to rigid judicial procedures.[29] The judicial processes used by the Tribunals are flexible. Again, Tribunals are cheaper than the courts of law. The Tribunal system is well established and deeply rooted in France and U.S.A. compared to the Great Britain. These countries have had an ad-hoc tribunals.[30]

It is true that tribunal is easily accessible, free from technicality, expeditious and with expert knowledge of a particular subject; but as mentioned above the tribunals can deal with the specific subject with a limitation. Tribunals can deal with the cases related to the corruption and the maladministration in a particular field. Even though Tribunal is not machinery engaged in dealing corruption and maladministration, yet it can work as deterrent for government servants so that they will behave properly with the citizens.

2.4.7 Lok-adalat

As way of promoting the voluntary settlement of disputes inexpensively and expeditiously disposable, judges of the Supreme Court in 1986-87[31] proposed the Lok-Adalats and subsequently the Act was passed to promote the social justice with the provision of such Lokadalats.

They are forced at the state and district level. The State or District is authorized to organize the Lok-Adalat at convenient places. The Lok-Adalats have wide jurisdictions. If they will run more effectively, it will be a strong arm of judiciary as the tribunals. There are possibilities of cases pertaining to corruption and maladministration appears before these Lok-Adalat.

2.5 SPECIAL INSTITUTIONS

There are special devices to face the problem of corruption and maladministration besides these machineries.

2.5.1 Central Bureau of Investigation

The Central Bureau of Investigation was established on April 1, 1963 under the Special Police Establishment Act, 1946. It is basically investigating agency. The Central Bureau of Investigation is involved in collecting criminal intelligence pertaining to 3 main areas of operation; viz.: anti-corruption, economic crimes and special crimes. Central Bureau of Investigation broadly handles the cases of corruption, fraud or malpractices by public servants of central government departments, central public sector, agencies as well as state services sector. The Bureau of Investigation has handled high-level cases against Ministers, Chief Ministers, Secretaries, high-level Government Officers, Chief Managing Directors of Banks, Financial Institutions, etc. The Central Bureau of Investigation investigates the major crimes and cases of corruption in the country. On an average, it investigates about 1,200 cases every year of a serious nature out of which 80% of the cases are related to bribery, corruption, misappropriation, cheating etc. involving public servants.[32] For example, in initial stages, the Bureau had taken initiative in investigating the Bofors case, but after some time, it lost its enthusiasm. It is said simply because the Ex-Prime Minister of the country was one of the accuse.[33]

In its premier days, Central Bureau of Investigation was very efficient. An enquiry by Central Bureau of Investigation had status and reputation. But now a days its authenticity is viewed with a doubt and the reason is the inevitable political interference in investigation and the registration of cases, filing of charge-sheets, examination of witnesses as well as in the posting, transfer, promotion of Central Bureau of Investigation officers, etc. Formerly, the bureau was under the Ministry of Home Affairs but Indira Gandhi transferred it to PMO[34] which has paved the way for direct and high level interference in its investigation. In Hawala Scandal, Central Bureau of Investigation took over 2 years to start the investigation since the PMO wanted it to be delayed.[35] Deliberating, the machinery which is created to explore corruption—is itself going to be corrupt; i.e. Central Bureau of Investigation becoming weak and inefficient.

On December 18, 1997 a three-person bench of Supreme Court headed by V.S.Varma settled down new rules, which made the Central Bureau of Investigation free from politicians. Accordingly, the court emphasized that the ministers should not have any right to interfere in the investigation and prosecution of the Central Bureau of Investigation in any individual case and should not seek permission to investigate government officials and bank officials.[36] The result expected was that the Central Bureau of Investigation should be more free and efficient.

This discussion concludes that the Central Bureau of Investigation determines more proficiency and freedom. A special Act to retard corruption and maladministration signifies that maximum cases registered/charge sheeted by Central Bureau of Investigation largely belong to victimize the public servants or the private persons. However, the politicians remain unaffected from Central Bureau of Investigation's charges. In nutshell it can be agreed that the bureau proved to be effective deterrent against corrupt politicians. Hence, as absolute and liberal machinery needed besides all present machineries.

2.5.2 Central Vigilance Commission

With a view to have a machinery with teeth, the Central Vigilance Commission was set up in February 1964 on the recommendation of the Committee on Prevention of corruption. The significant thing to note about this Commission is that it is free from executive control. In 1998, in the case of 'Vinnet Narain Vs. Union of India', the Supreme Court had directed the Central Government to confer statutory status to the CVC.[37] Accordingly the CVC which was previously just an advisory body, is now as per this act is a statutory body. CVC is independent body and directly responsible to the Parliament. The CVC is not merely an investigating or enquiring agency. It is empowered to enquire or cause enquiries to be conducted into offences alleged to have been committed under the Prevention on Corruption Act, 1988. The commission covers the vigilance over the Ministries, Departments of Central Government, Nationalized Banks, Government Sectors, Public Undertakings, etc.[38] The commission can enquire about the executive body. But, whether it should enquire about the Prime Minister is not made clear anywhere. The commission may enquire about the executive body; but the judiciary and legislature are out of CVC's jurisdiction.[39] There is no proper reason given to keep them away from its jurisdiction. Since 1997, following the Supreme Court's order, CVC enjoys the supervisory power over CBI. But in the result, it was not mentioned whether it pertains to charge sheets also. To clear up some doubts, CVC decided to approach the apex court in the Hinduja brother and the judgment in Hawala case. However, the judgment is awaiting in this regard.[40]

The CVC always tries to solve the case through penalties or administrative actions. After all its efforts, if the case is not solved or facts are not caught then CVC hands it over to CBI. The rising number of cases of corruption shows that CBI could not succeed in controlling it, hence, the CVC needs to strengthen its functioning.

According to the 'Corruption Perception Index' published by 'Transparency International' in 1998, India has ranked 66 out of 85 countries. N. Vittal, the then Central Vigilance Commissioner assured that before leaving his charge on September 2, 2002, India's rank should be improved to 40 at least.[41] On other hand, in his lecture on late B. Dorieswamy Iyengar Memorial Lecture Series held at Shimoga on January 7, 2000, he was compelled to state that India listed 66th in 1998 out of 85 countries in 1999. He pessimistically added pointing out that India's rank has gone down from 66 to 73. Actually, the list is going from the less to the most corrupt countries. Going on to 73 from 66, India becomes more corrupt- besides, he explained that from the bottom, there were 19 countries in 1998 that were more corrupt than India and in 1998,there were 27 countries more corrupt than India. He concluded that the index is improving with India.

In India there is no Ombudsman i.e. Lokpal at national level. However, maximum states have Lokayukta and the State level Vigilance Commissions. The State Vigilance Commission plays an important role; e.g., the Commission in Punjab raided Chief of Punjab Public Service Commission, put charges against the Vice-Chancellor of the University and teachers running private coaching classes in Punjab. The State Vigilance Commission has its own investigating machinery but it has its limitations. Machinery is trying at its best.

The CVC is not very successful in reducing corruption and maladministration in India. Central Vigilance Commission could be an alternative in curbing corruption and maladministration to other commissions and committees. It is not an absolute solution. In the view of the suggestions for appointing Lokayukta, some of the states abolished or suspended the working of vigilance commissioner as if it was felt that the appointment of the new agency will render vigilance commissioner superfluous.[42] It is clear that the states running with Vigilance Commissions are demanding some alternative to the machinery which is more bold than the commission.

2.6 THE PROCCESS OF PIL

Besides all the committees, commissions, institutions, laws and acts there is a process of public interest litigation to fight against corruption.

2.6.1 Public Interest Litigation

Under Articles (226) and (32) of Indian constitution, the High Courts and the Supreme Court can issue writs against public authorities[43] for violation of fundamental rights. Recently the High Courts and Supreme Court are hearing the type of cases, which are described as Public Interest Litigation. The PIL is fundamentally different from private law litigation. Under PIL, people can demand action against exploitation of laborers by contractors, the use of children as bonded labor, illegal detention under trials, torture while in custody, etc. The PIL cases provided socio-economic justice to the people. The court has preventive and remedial power in PIL. PIL is the name given to efforts to provide legal representation to interests that historically have been un-represented and under-represented in the legal process. These includes not only the poor and disadvantaged, but ordinary citizens who because they cannot afford lawyers to represent them have lacked access to court rooms, administrative agencies and other legal basic policy decisions affecting their interests.[44]

PIL are blamed for delay, inefficiency, misuse and over burden. So far it is successful in curbing corruption and maladministration.

2.7 DEMOCRATIC DEVICES

So far the present research problem is concerned, these constitutional and the non-constitutional device are not quite effective in tackling corruption and maladministration. In any democratic society, a common man is expected to be important element. It is implied that people's participation is necessary in each governmental and non- governmental action. Swami Vivekananda quoted, "all the wealth of the world cannot help one little Indian village if the people are not taught to help themelves."[45]

This participation expects the mental and emotional involvement. The participation can be made through involvement of voluntary agencies and individuals, e.g. 'Jan-Andolan' by Anna Hazare is one of the major efforts in this regard. He compelled two corrupt ministers to resign on the charges of corruption. He fought against political corruption as well as administrative corruption. Shiv Khera also fights against central ministerial corruption through his agency namely, 'Country First'. Arun Bhatia is one more name in this context. It is because of his initiative that the inquiry of corruption in Dhulia Employment Guarantee Scheme involving non-officials and IAS officers was conducted.

It can be said that these are the islands giving a strong fight against the ocean in corruption. Unfortunately, they are not supported strongly by people. Obviously, it appears that all the efforts of the individuals will go in vain in fighting against corruption.

2.8 OTHER MACHINERIES

Besides all these central/national machineries, there is state level/ local machinery, which tries to curb corruption and to evolve clean the administration. In Andhra Pradesh, the Government launched a scheme called 'Projala Vaddaku Paalana'.* It remarkably tried to improve the services to the people of Andhra Pradesh, which treated it as a leading state in information Technology. In Aug.1997, with the help of NIC the government initiated 'Computer Aid Administration of Registration Department' (CARD). The computerized administration proved to be speedy, accurate, and transparent. In Assam, 'Lok Adalats' and 'Rajah Adalats' had been set up for speedy redressal of public grievances. Other states and the union territories are also trying for the same. For example, Bihar Government launched 'Janta Darbars' at the panchayat level under the Deputy Collector of the district to redress the public grievances relating to the Government departments in Bihar and Chandigarh. The Delhi state government has devised a public grievances officer in every department. Karnataka

---

* Administration at Door Step of the people.

Chief Minister undertakes ' Janta Darshans' and audiences for petitioners. Kerala Vigilance Department has been empowered to be pro-active and carry out investigations and made arrests in Prima-facie cases, rather than being reactive and proceed only after government's sanction as was the procedure earlier. This is remarkable improvement. Madhya Pradesh has Lokayukta at state as well as divisional level. Manipur has Public Grievances Redressal

Committee for hearing public grievances and redressing the grievances on the spot. In Manipur, some districts have adopted computerization of the public grievance. Orrissa has a separate Directorate for Prevention and detention of corruption by public servants. Pondichery has a citizen's charters in every department.

Punjab has started a programme to sort out the grievances on the spot; namely, 'Sangat Darshan'. Vigilance Bureau in Punjab is quite active.Grievance Committee at Rajas than tries to make a time frame within which the applications for distribution of public goods or grievances redressal would be disposed of at the block and district level. Tripura has introduced the system of holding administrative camps in the remote areas to listen grievances of the people. Uttar Pradesh also has a computerized Public Grievances Directorate to curb corruption in offices. This part from anti-corruption measures, there are a lot of efforts at the state and at national level. As against of these, there are some states where not any strong and effective machinery is available; e.g. Haryana, Sikkim, Lakshadvip, etc. (Maharashtra is discussed in third chapter)

Thus there are some constitutional, legal, institutional devices emerged and developed in the last 50 years. Besides, the Parliament has enacted laws. The government many times was forced to establish Commissions and Committees to enquire into the acts of corruption including the measures to improve the administration. The special establishments such as CBI, CVC constitute by this time, the routine machinery in this direction. Added to them is the welcome feature of PIL in recent time. The efforts of NGOs and the conscious people and the activists have definitely played a role in bringing out the incidences/affairs involving corruption. However, corruption-free society has remained a distant dream. It is not surprising as these are the institutional devices and legal framework to discover and reduce if not eliminate corruption. The real question is how far these institutional devices and legal structures are rigorously enforced by the concerned. Hence, the search for more and more of new devices goes on. The Lokpal at the central and Lokayukta at the state are the steps in this regard.

SECTION 2

LOKPAL IN INDIA

On this background, there have been several efforts made to pass the 'Lokpal Bill' in Parliament during last 39 years. Before discussing these efforts, it is necessary to see the background of the very idea of Lokpal.

2.9 GENESIS OF AN IDEA OF LOKPAL

C. D. Deshmukh, the then Finance Minister and Chairman University Grants Commission, made a formal proposal for an Ombudsman like institute. He forwarded the idea in July 1959 in his lecture in Madras. He asked for the establishment of a high level, impartial, standing judicial tribunal to investigate and report on the complaints or lying of information.[46] This was the first and formal element of the machinery of redressal of grievances expressed publicly. Just after some months K.M.Munshi, the renowned legal expert and member of Constituent Assembly, in a debate suggested for the institution in the form of permanent tribunal of enquiry in Feb, 1960 Another notable person who expressed his opinion on this issue was M.C. Setalvad, India's first Attorney General. In his inaugural speech in the third All-India Law Conference in August 1962, he referred to such an institution. In July 1963 L. M. Singhvi, MP and Legal expert raised the issue in Parliament. P. B. Gajendragadkar, the then Chief Justice of the Supreme Court of India spoke on the importance of the institution of Ombudsman. On April 22, 1964. Mr. Singhvi moved the resolution on Lokpal in the Loksabha.[47] He say in his resolution:

"An officer of parliament to be known as the people Prosecution, broadly analogous to the institution of Ombudsman in Sweden and other countries should be appointed under suitable legislation for the purpose of providing effective and impartial investigation machinery for public grievances."

Nehru was fascinated by the idea of Ombudsman type institute. There was a long discussion on this issue. Mr. H. C. Chatterji was in favor of such institution whereas Sinhasan Singh, S. N. Chatutrvedi, S. M. Banerjee and Yashpal Singh opposed it.[48] J. H. Hathi, the then Minister of State in the Ministry of Home Affairs stated that Government was thinking of evolving suitable machinery for redressal of public grievances;[49] hence, Mr. Singhvi withdrew his resolution. Meanwhile, there was an appointment of the Committee on Prevention of Corruption in 1964. The Central Vigilance Commission was established on the recommendations made by the Committee.

Again, in November 1967, the ARC strongly recommended the appointment of Lokpal and Lokayukta with the following features:

1. They should be demonstrably independent and impartial.
2. The investigations and proceedings of these functionaries should be conducted in private and should be informal.
3. The appointment should be non-political.
4. The status should be equivalent to that of the highest judicial functionaries.
5. They should have discretionary field to decide cases.
6. The proceedings should be free from interference of the judiciary.
7. They should not look forward to any benefit or pecuniary advantage from the executive government.

The Government accepted the recommendations made by Administrative Reforms Commission for the machinery of redressal of citizen's grievances. In December 1967, P.K. Deo moved a private Bill on the basis of ARC draft bill in the Parliament. Finally, 'The Lokpal and Lokayukta Bill, 1968' was introduced and was referred to the Joint Select Committee of both houses of Parliament in May 1968. After that for several times, the bill was introduced in Loksabha or Rajyasabha. Several times, it was discussed at length but has not passed yet.

Here are chronological aspects of the deliberation on Lokpal Bill.

THE LOKPAL AND LOKAYUKTA BILL, 1968

According to the bill, there should be a 'Lokpal' for central Government with 'Lokayukta' as its second member. The bill was introduced on May 9, 1968 and was sent to the Joint Select Committee of parliament.[50] The bill made amply clear that the public servants working outside India would also be amendable to the jurisdiction of Lokpal and Lokayuktas. One more important thing was that the complainant was not required to pay any fee along with complaint. The bill was referred to the JSC. It gave its report on March 21, 1969. The witnessing gist of the report given by Mr. Bagwan Sarup Bhatnagar, Mr. N. N. Wanchoo, was,

"Lokpal should be the most powerful limb of the Parliament."[51]

There were some changes made by the committee in the original bill. The Prime Minister was included but later was excluded by the JSC. The bill was forwarded in Loksabha in 1969.

LOKPAL AND LOKAYUKTA BILL, 1969

The revised version of the Bill by the JSC was moved by Vidya Charan Shukla on August 20, 1969.[52] The Bill previously included the PM. But when the bill was discussed in JSC, majority excluded the PM. The argument was made that if the PM was required to vacate his post the whole government automatically ceases. While discussing the Bill in Loksabha,

V. P. Mandal, MP, Savepura proposed that the jurisdiction of Lokpal should include the cases of caste violence, atrocities which were not accepted.[53] On the same day the bill was passed in Loksabha but was not discussed in Rajyasabha. President of India in December1970 dissolved the Loksabha for midterm poll. The attempt to pass the bill proved unsuccessful.

LOKPAL BILL, 1971

In August 1971, the bill was again introduced in Loksabha with minor changes. At that time the Prime Minister was included in the jurisdiction of Lokpal bill. However, a major drawback of the bill was that the State Govewrnment Servants were out of the sphere of Lokpal.[54] The Bill again was approved after discussion. But meanwhile Maharashtra, Rajasthan and other States established the State Lokayukta. The country was passing through a critical political situation in this period. Therefore, no serious and urgent attention was given to pass the bill. Even though, the Lokpal at the center could not be introduced at this juncture , Maharashtra and Rajasthan established Lokayukta in their states by enacting the laws by respective State Legislature. Besides, in Assam, the law was almost ready.

LOKPAL BILL, 1977

Once again, on July 28, 1977 the bill was proposed and moved. It included the cases of corruption, nepotism and abuse of position, but did not cover the grievances of maladministration. One more lacuna was the camera inquiry, which was not incorporated in the bill. Similarly, the procedure regarding the transfer of complaints to competent authority to review the system was such that Lokpal could directly deal with the 'middle man' without aggrieved.[55] At this time, the Bill firstly included the provision of Lokpal for speedy disposal of cases. It contained a provision of a fee of Rs 1,000 to be

---

* Public Functionary Under The Act Means A Person Who-

(a) Holds The Office Of Prime Minister, Minister Of State/Deputy Minister Of Union.

(b) Is,Or Has Been A Member Of Either Those Of Parliament.

deposited by the complainant along with the complaint. Basically, the bill remained a permanent commission of inquiry against political officers; because the government servants were excluded from its jurisdiction. The bill was sent to the Joint Select Committee of the House which excluded the CMs of the states from the jurisdiction of the Lokpal. But, the Home Minister recommended the Chief Ministers be brought in the purview of Lokpal. Because It was a period of emergency the bill became invalid in the House.

LOKPAL BILL, 1985

The then Union Minister Mr. A K Sen on August 26, 1985 again introduced the Lokpal Bill. The object was the same as it was in the past. Again it was referred to the JSC for the 4th time. The PM & CM were excluded from the jurisdiction of Lokpal. Lokpal had the jurisdiction to punish any insult or the causes while discharging of his duties. The Bill also did not cover public servants. However, it maintained the fee clause.[56] The bill was withdrawn without giving any strong reason.

LOKPAL BILL, 1989

The Lokpal Bill was reintroduced on December 29, 1989 during the 9th Loksabha. The bill was similar to one 1985 Bill; except inclusion of Deputy PM in the jurisdiction of Lokpal.[57] Due to the defeat of the government on the floor of the Loksabha, the bill once again became invalid.

THE LOKPAL BILL, 1996

Once again an effort was made for the formation of Lokpal on 13 September 1996 by introducing the bill in Loksabha.

The sailent features of the Bill are:

1. Structure: There shall be multi- member body of Lokpal. A chairperson shall be a Chief Justice of India or a Judge of Supreme Court. Other two members should be persons of knowledge and experience of judiciary and administration.
2. Appointment procedure: The Lokpals shall be appointed by the President in consultation with the

Chief Justice of India, the leader of the opposition in Loksabha and the Speaker of the Loksabha.

3. Age and tenure: The Lokpals shall hold the office for 5 years. They shall not be removed except by an order made by the President on basis of the recommendation made by the Chief Justice or any other authority.
4. Under the scheme of the bill, Lokpal shall inquire into complaints and allegations against public functionary as defined in the bill for an offence punishable under the Prevention of Corruption Act, 1988.[58]

At this time also the bill was not passed.

LOKPAL BILL, 1998

On 23rd July 1998, M. R. Janardhanan kept the statement of the Bill. According to the article 11(2) of the Bill,[59] Lokpal shall not inquire into any matter concerning any person if the chair person or any other member has any bias in respect of such matter or person and if any dispute arises in this behalf; the President shall on an application made by the party aggrieved, obtain in such manner as may be prescribed in the opinion of the Chief Justice of India and decide the dispute in conformity with such opinion. The bill again was dropped.

LOKPAL BILL, 2001

The repeated acts of presenting the Lokpal bill does not end here. It was again introduced on July 9,2001. Vasundhara Raje, the then Minister put up the Lokpal Bill, 2001. A major change in the bill this time was the requirement of tenure of Lokpal. It required that there should be a chairperson with two members for a fixed tenure.[60] It added with a view to ensure independence of the Lokpal and to discharge its functions without fear or favor and shall not remove except by an order of the President. To enable the Lokpal to function effectively and in a quasi-judicial manner the power of the civil court in respect of summoning and enforcing the attendance of any person and examining him on the data requiring the discovery and production, any document and receiving evidence etc. have been confirmed.[61]

The PM was included the bill whereas Judges of Supreme Court and Election Commissioners were kept out of his purview. The Bill sought to make special provision for discouraging, frivolous, vexatious and false complaints.

14 AUG., 2001

On 9th July, the Bill was again presented on the table. On 14th Aug, 2001, it was discussed in detail. In this Bill article 10(1) provides that the Lokpal shall not enquire into the matter involved in or arising from or connected with any such allegation against the PM in so far as it relates to national security and maintenance of public order.[62]

The Constitution Review Committee also considered this bill. At this time, it was referred to the Parliamentary Standing Committee. On June 28, 2003 it was again kept for discussion. The cabinet agreed to keep the PMO in its purview. Sushma Swaraj, the then Parliamentary Affairs Minister told that it would be a simple measure and not a constitutional amendment.[63] The cabinet also agreed that the bill would be passed in monsoon session of the Parliament. However, could not stick to its words. Once again efforts to establish the Lokpal had gone vain.

The forgoing discussion about the introduction of the bill several times in the Parliament is presented in following table:

Table 2.2

Positions of Lokpal Bill from 1968 to 2003

No.	*Date and Year*	*Feature of the Bill*	*Position about inclusion of Prime Minister*	*Fate of the Bill*
1.	May 9, 1968	(a) Public Servants were includedb) (b) Complaints without any fees	Yes	Referred to the Joint Select Committee
2.	August 20, 1969	Cases of castism should be included (suggestion was not accepted)	Yes	Passed in Lok Sabha — but not passed in Rajyasaba due to dissolution of Loksabha for midterm poll

No.	*Date and Year*	*Feature of the Bill*	*Position about inclusion of Prime Minister*	*Fate of the Bill*
3.	August, 1971	(a) Central Government Servants were included) (b) State Government Servants were not included	Yes	Left without discussion
4.	July 28, 1977	(a) Complainant was required to pay Rs. 1000/- as fees (b) Excluded cases of maladministration	Yes (Excluded the Chief Ministers of States)	Referred to the Joint Select Committee
5.	August 26, 1985	(a) Complainant was required to pay Rs. 1000/- as feesb) (b) Excluded Central Government Public Servants	No	Referred to the Joint Select Committee
6.	December 29, 1989	Deputy Prime Minister was included	No	The bill was lapsed
7.	September 29, 1996	(a) Inclusion of public functionaries	No	Lapsed due to dissolution of Loksabha
8.	July 23, 1998	(a) Inclusion of public functionaries	No	Lapsed due to dissolution of Lok sabha
9.	July 9, 2001	(a) Judges of Supreme Court and Election Commissioner were excluded	No	Presented but was not discussed
10.	August 14, 2001	(a) Judges of Supreme Court and Election Commissioner were excluded	No	Referred to the Constitution Review Committee
11.	June 28, 2003	(a) To be formed as a public grievance redresal	Yes	Cabinet approved and agreed to move the bill—but was not passed

(Table—Self compiled and edited by the Researcher)

2.12 PRESENT SITUATION OF THE BILL

Historically, the Bill remained without passing with delay, uncertainty and callous neglect on the part of the Cabinet and the Indian Parliament for a long period of 35 years. There was lack of consensus among lawmakers about the exact functions of the Lokpal and whether to include the office of the prime minister in the definition of public servant. I. K. Gujral, the Ex-Prime Minister and Subhash Kashyap, a Parliamentary Secretary were not in favor of inclusion of the Prime Minister.[64] Vajepayee himself was in favor of including Prime Minister, under its purview. In October, former Prime Minister Narasimha Rao and his ex-cabinet colleague Buta Singh were sentenced to three years in jail by a special court in a vote-buying case. The case involved allegations that in 1993 Rao tried to influence a parliamentary vote of no confidence by bribing four lawmakers of a regional group.[65] In a country where ex-Prime Minister—a supreme authority is charged as a corrupt is difficult to speak about a clean government. A recent survey by a private agency showed 2/3rd or more than 2,500 people who were questioned thought that there is corruption in Indian government high offices that took a country back by 25 years. Nearly half of those interviewee said they or someone close to them had given a bribe to obtain a government service.[66] While the introduction of the Bill in the Parliament is a step forward, there are many more hurdles to be crossed before the Lokpal Bill is finally passed by the Parliament, receives assent of the President and is notified officially. There are already rumblings and murmurs among the Members of Parliament that the Bill should not be made applicable to them.

2.11 SALIENT FEATURES OF PROPOSED LOKPAL BILL

Even though the process of enactment of Lokpal Bill is incomplete, considering the provisions of the Lokpal Bill, 2003 salient features are as given below:

(1) Establishment: Lokpal shall be appointed by the President in consultation with the Chief Justice, Supreme Court as well the leader of the opposition party. He shall hold the office for the term of 5 years. There should be 2 members to assist him. There is no mention of age limit of the person. The status or the position of the Chairman i.e. Lokpal shall be the same as that of the Chief Justice of

India. Others shall be the same as judges of Supreme Court.

(2) Tenure: Every member in Lokpal shall hold office for 5 years[67] and shall not be removed except by an order of the President on the ground of the proved misbehavior or in capacity after an inquiry to be made by the Chief Justice of India or by other judge of the Supreme Court of India.[68] For that, misbehavior or incapability of the chairperson/member shall be proved in the Legislature.

(3) Jurisdiction:

(a) According to Clause 9 (1) the Lokpal may inquire into any matter involved in or arising from or any complaint alleging the public functionary has committed any offence punishable under the Prevention of Corruption Act, 1988.

(b) Lokpal may inquire into any act or conduct of any person other than a public functionary in so far the purpose of its enquiry into any allegation.

(c) Referring to Clause 7(1), the President can ask the Lokpal to inquire into any allegation specified in the order in respect of public functions and not withstanding anything contained in the Act. The Lokpal shall comply with such order.

(4) Matters out of Jurisdiction: The clause (10) of the bill requires that the Lokpal shall not inquire into any matter in respect of any person or matter, or into any matter that has been referred for inquiry under the commission of Inquiry Act, 1952 on its recommendation or with its prior concurrence.

(5) Miscellaneous

(a) The Lokpal has been provided with the power to search and seizure any document, which in its opinion will be useful for, or relevant to any inquiry.

(b) The Lokpal is authorized to punish any person with simple imprisonment for a term that may extend to 6 months or with a fine or with both in case of intentional insult or interruption to or bringing into disrepute the institution of Lokpal.

(c) The Lokpals have to report the President annually.

(d) The Lokpal can award or reward the compensation.

(e) The Lokpal can sentence imprisonment for a term of 1-3 years or fine up to Rs. 50,000 to a false complainant.

(f) The Lokpal can hold the inquiry as expeditiously as possible and complete it within 6 months from the date of complaint is received.

(g) The Lokpal shall discharge his functions to the subordinates. Under clause 8(1) of the Act, he can appoint a secretary in consultation with the president. He can secure the services of any officer who shall be subject to the exclusive administrative control and the direction of the Lokpal.

These provisions carry no meaning as long as they are not statutory.

2.12 WHY LOKPAL IS DELAYED?

The following reasons can be by way of consolidated positions for constant delay incurred to pass the Bill:

1. Ambiguity in the draft of the bill.
2. Controversial nature of the bill.
3. Ignorance and non-seriousness of the ruling as well as opposition parties.
4. Fear among the politicians about the Lokpal institution.
5. Lack of political will towards passing of the bill.
6. Lack of strong public support.
7. Lack of adequate interest shown by NGOs, media, experts and the people in general.

This long and callous delay to the enactment of Lokpal Bill clearly indicates the absence of desire and initiative on the part of society and the government. It needs an organized effort.

2.13 SHORTCOMINGS OF THE BILL

There are certain shortcomings that can be pointed out in the proposed Bill.

(a) The Bill is restricted to merely offences punishable under the Prevention of Corruption Act, 1988.

(b) A complainant is required to pay the fees Rs. 1000/-.

(c) The Bill excluded the Civil Servants from its jurisdiction for political corruption that can be dealt with the political functionaries.

(d) The political corruption, which occupies larger area in corruption, is excluded from the jurisdiction of proposed Lokpal. The Civil Servants are supposed to report cases of administrative corruption. This is probably the inference from this provision.

(e) One of the defects in this bill is that the power of the Lokpal is confined to the offences punishable under the Prevention of Corruption Act, 1988. The act covers the cases of illegal gratification and possession to the lawful sources of income. That is why, the cases of corruption arising from nepotism or other motivating factors would not fall within the ambit of the Lokpal.

The institution of Lokpal should be thought of as an alternative and absolute solution to the present machinery on corruption and maladministration. But, with the present defects and drawbacks in the bill, there is possibility that the institution will be rendered inefficient and week. Hence, there is need to give over it and adequate changes be incorporated in it.

2.14 SUGGESTIONS

Let us hope there shall be a Lokpal in future. Some of the suggestions for this future office shall be:

1. Lokpal should have sue-motto power of investigation to protect community right.

2. The public servant constitutes the major factor in the cases of corruption and maladministration. Hence, he should be included in the purview of Lokpal at different levels-national, state or local. For example, in Denmark, civil administration is under the Ombudsman's purview that is exclusive of the courts. But, it is controlled due to consideration of the Ombudsman.
3. In Sweden, Ombudsman is the constitutional body and has a status in the governmental system. Lokpal in India should be given a constitutional status so that it can get a high position in the governmental process.
4. Lokpal should create confidence in people and should build up image like Swedish Ombudsman.
5. Lokpal should not only investigate the complaints made by the citizens against the administration; but also seeks to create a better image of administration like one in Sweden.
6. Foremost important thing is that Lokpal should be explicitly free from the Government, mainly from the Executive.
7. Lokpal should have the power to publicize the cases involving serious offences of maladministration. The recommendations of Lokpal also should be publicized. It would be in tune with right to information.
8. Lokpal should have its own investigation agency on the line of Scandinavian and European countries.
9. Like Ombudsman in Sweden, Lokpal should exercise great restrain on unnecessary fact finding and panelizing officials.
10. In a poor country like India, it is advisable not to charge any fee for the complaints to the Lokpal or there should be a nominal charge of fees like the Scandinavian countries such as Finland and Denmark.

The constitution has created a few independent machineries. But it has been observed in the studies that many a times adequate funds and other facilities are not made available to them. Considering this it should be made obligatory on the part of the Government to provide funds and facilities from time to time to Lokpal. This will also help to activate the Lokpal. This will help also in building confidence among the functionaries as well as the people about the mission to create corruption-free society.

SECTION 3

LOKAYUKTA IN INDIAN STATES

There are quite good number of efforts for the 'Lokpal' at the Center. The Lokpal Bill is yet to be enacted. But fortunately, more than half of the states in India have adopted the Lokayukta in their states. They are -Orrisa, Maharashtra, Rajasthan, Bihar, Uttar Pradesh, Andra Pradesh, Gujarat, Himachal Pradesh, Aassam, Madhya Pradesh, Karnataka, Kerala, Goa, Punjab. We have the beginning of this safeguard system against corruption in the country through the Lokayukta system. It has been well settled in those states by this time. Following is the brief account of emergence of Lokayukta in the states—

ORISSA: Orissa is the first State, which has passed, the Lokayukta Bill. The 'Lokpal and Lokayukta Act, 1970 was passed on 28th October 1970 and started its implementation in 1983. In 1983, the Act with a view to include the Chief Minister in Lokayukta's purview was amended.[69] In Orissa, as per the act, 'Lokpal' is the head of the institute to curb corruption, maladministration and nepotism—'Lokayukta' is the second one after 'Lokpal'. Thus, there are two persons in the office of the Lokayukta.

Maharashtra is the second state that passed the act and first that implemented the Lokayukta institution at state level.

RAJASTHAN: The Administrative Reforms Committee, Rajasthan recommended in September 1963 for the appointment of an independent and high-powered body in the nature of an Ombudsman.[70] Rajasthan Administrative Reforms Commission was the first to speak on Ombudsman in India.[71]

The Rajasthan Lokayukta and Upa-Lokayukta Act, 1973' was presented in the Assembly on August 28, 1973 and was passed. Mr. Inder Dev Gupta took over as the first Lokayukta in Rajasthan.

BIHAR: Bihar constituted 'Lokayukta' on May 28, 1973 by appointing Dr. S. V. Sohani as the first Lokayukta as per 'The Bihar Lokayukta Act, 1973'. The Chief Minister was excluded from the act earlier; but by the amendment made on April 1983 he was included.[72] Bihar Lokayukta has to submit his Annual Report to the Chief Minister and Governor. Both of them send their comments on its reports, which are confidential. Then the report is submitted to the House.

UTTAR PRADESH: The 'Uttar Pradesh Lokayukta and Upa-Lokayukta Act, 1974' was passed in 1975 and B.Dayal the former Chief Justice of Madhya Pradesh High Court was appointed as the first Lokayukta of Uttar Pradesh.[73] The Uttar Pradesh Lokayukta can operate for the Ministers, Public servants, all Government officials at the District and at the local level, however, the Chief Minister is excluded from its jurisdiction.

ANDHRA PRADESH: The report of the Administrative Reforms Committee, Andhra Pradesh recommended for appointment of a receptionist of the rank of U.D.C. in each Collectorate with the purpose of streaming administration.[74] With the passing of 'Andhra Pradesh Lokayukta and Upa-Lokayukta Act, 1981', the state Government in Andhra Pradesh adopted Lokayukta on September 4, 1982. Mr. Avula Samba Siva Rao was sworned in as the first Lokayukta in 1983. For a long period, the common man in Andhra Pradesh was unknown about the existence of the office of Lokayukta. In July 2002, R. Ramanujam took over the post and made lots of efforts to popularize the office.[75] This is the first effort in Andra Pradesh in that direction. N. Chandrababu Naidu, the then Chief Minister, Andhra Pradesh also expressed his opinion to strengthen the office to check corruption in administration. A complainant in Andra Pradesh is required to pay Rs. 150/- as a fee by draft or money order along with the complaint. A remarkable point is that Lokayukta has its own investigating team led by an officer of the rank of IGP. So far the jurisdiction of Lokayukta is concerned, it cannot deal with the all India public servants. The Chief Minister is excluded from its purview.

GUJARAT: The 'Gujarat Lokayukta and Upa-Lokayukta Bill, 1974' was introduced in the Gujrat Legislative Assembly and could not be passed. But in 1983, the Chief Minister Madhav Singh Solanki announced the decision of the government to appoint the Lokayukta.[76] According to the ' Gujarat Lokayukta Act, 1986' the state has appointed the Lokayukta to curb corruption and maladministration.

HIMACHAL PRADESH: In Himachal Pradesh the 'Himachal Pradesh Lokayukta and Upa-Lokayukta Bill' was introduced in 1975, but it was lapsed. Again in April 1980 and March 1982. It was discussed and finally passed in August 1983. J.V.R. Tatachari, Jusitce, Himachal Pradesh High Court took over the charge of the first Lokayukta of Himachal Pradesh.[77] Himachal Pradesh Lokayukta office tried to take the institution nearer to the people. In other states, Lokayukta deals with complaints of citizens against civil servants but in Himachal Pradesh, the civil servants also can complaint under the Act.[78] Every citizen has easy access to the Lokayukta.

However, the limitations of the Lokayukta in Himachal Pradesh are-

1. He does not have the power of suo-moto.
2. There is no independent investigating machinery.
3. No prompt action on the reports of the Lokayukta is taken.

An active co-operation by the executive and government is necessary in the successful working of the Lokayukta in Himachal pradesh.

ASSAM: Assam state Government enacted 'Assam Lokayukta and Upa-Lokayukta Act 1985'.The Assam Government was achieving for a clean administration through the Lokayukta office as it has been stated in the act. [79]

MADHYA PRADESH: 'Lokayukta and Upa-Lokayukta Bill, 1974' was passed by Madhya Pradesh Assembly in April 1975 and was forwarded to the President. There after the Assembly was dissolved and obviously the Bill was lapsed.[80] The Bill was again introduced in September 1980 and came into force on September 16,1981 namely 'The Madhya Pradesh Lokayukta and Upa-Lokayukta Abhiyan, 1981'. According to this act, the Chief Minister is not included in his jurisdiction. However, there is a provision that if there is any complaint against the Chief Minister, it is to be submitted to the Governor directly. It is obligatory for the Governor to accept the complaint and to ask the Lokayukta to enquire the same.

KARNATAKA: As per the promise made in the Election Manifesto, Ramkrishna Hegde, the former Chief Minister introduced the 'Lokayukta and Upa-Lokayukta Bill' in the Assembly on March 28, 1983. It was passed in both the houses and enacted on Jan. 16, 1986. It is said that the Karnataka Lokayukta is more independent than other states.[81] It is because he has its own investigating machinery. The Chief Minister and the public servants are accountable to Lokayukta; but MLAs are not included in his jurisdiction. It is to be noted that, S M Krishna, the then Chief Minister of Karnataka expressed his opinion in the Legislative Assembly that MLA, should be under the purview of Lokayukta.[82] In 2001, a case against V.S. Koujali, Agriculture Minister came to the Lokayukta. As the MLA is out of its purview the same could not be investigated. The case was dismissed. Later on, MLAs were brought under Lokayukta's purview. In Karnataka, the office of Lokayukta is a positive intervention in establishing popular faith in democratic governance.[83] Karnataka is the only state that uses the two-tier system of Lokayukta. Government of Karnataka has transferred some of its powers and functions to the elected body; i.e. The Zillah Parishad. The Zillah Parishad Officer, who is enjoyed the powers, can act as a Mini-Lokayukta at the district level. Thus, it is a moderate beginning of controlling at local level through Lokayukta. It is yet to be proved whether implementing office like CEO can impartially and objectively conduct the functions of Lokayukta.

KERALA: The Administrative Reforms Committee, Kerala longback in its report (1965-67) says,

"Indiscipline among Government servants has been sweeping the State." The report emphasizes the importance of integrity and efficiency at all levels as basic to good administration.[84] Kerala has passed 'The public Men (prevention of Corruption) Act, 1983. Besides State level Lokayukta, as per with this intension, Kerala Panchayat Act, 2000 Ombudsman for local Government was constituted in Kerala. It consist of 5 members including,

(a) The High Court Judge as the head;
(b) Two District Judges;
(c) Two Public Men;

Ombudsman has its own staff. It can utilize the service of any officer in the Government for enquiries. The officers are required to provide the information if necessary for investigation. The Ombudsman can deal with the public servants including the President, Chairpersons, all the members, secretaries, and other staff of the local Government including the local officials transferred to them.[85] Kerala Ombudsman for local government is expected to put a check and maintain a balance to make it efficient, autonomous and dedicated.

Kerala is an example of two-tier Ombudsman ship.

All the Lokayukta Acts are similar. The main difference is the jurisdiction, mainly whether the Chief Minister is included or not. The acts of Orrisa, Kerala, Karnataka and Gujarat cover up the Chief Minister within the jurisdiction of Lokayukta while others do not. Most of them include public men and public servants, corporations, Universities, all the Government sections and Undertakings.

Kerala Lokayukta has a major limitation that it doesn't have any infrastructure.[86]

GOA: Goa titled the act as the 'Goa Public Men's Corruption (Investigation and Equiries) Act. The Act includes Chief Minister, ministers, leaders and officers. It is criticized that the title of Act disrespects the public servants- 'Public Men's' refers to the public servants-i.e. it is to control the public servants only. Hence, it is required to be changed.[87] The Act includes the complaints of corruption. But it does not include the grievances and allegations of maladministration. Another drawback is that it deals with the public men and not with the government servants; i.e. the secretaries, joint secretaries, under secretaries, officers in panchayats, municipalities, etc. This act is not quite successful in cleaning the Goa administration.

PUNJAB: In 1992, during the tenure of Beant Sing, 'The Lokpal Bill' was passed in Punjab. Justice S.S. Sodhi was appointed as the first Lokpal. In 1999, the Lokpal indicated three ministers of the congress government with 'major corruption changes' in his report submitted by Lokpal Justice H.S. Rai to the Governor.[88]

The Lokpal office on this issue has sent a number of reminders to the Punjab Raj Bhawan. The ministers were congressmen and a report was a godsend on the eve of the election. The Governor was also a congressman at that time. Therefore, he kept mum. The report remained without any discussion. Besides, justifying and changing the concerned ministers on the charge of corruption, the Punjab Lokpal was caught in the crossfire between political parties. Justice Rai was entrusted with reviewing all the complaints lodged with the disbanded Lokpal office. But in this said complaint against Ministers, Governor was not co-operative. This explains the fact that how far the executive is helpful to the Lokayukta in Punjab. It is also clear that Lokayukta cannot argue in the ministerial cases effectively if the Government is with him.

Tamilnadu has its 'The Tamil Nadu Public Men (Criminal Misconduct) Act, 1974.

Above table makes it clear that there is uniformity in the Acts. There are number of factors where there is no unanimity and the mode of investigation also differs.

Though, Lokayukta is successful on the state level yet, there is a need for impartial, independent and public oriented

Table 2.3

Table of the Position of Lokayukta in Indian States

Name of the state	*Rank in Corruption*	*The description of the Act*	*Provision of the Upalo-kayuktas*	*Tenure of the Upalo-kayuktas*	*Inclusion of Chief Minister*
Orrisa	12	The Orrisa Lokpal & Lokayukta Act, 1970	Yes	5 yrs.	Yes
Rajas Than	10	The Rajasthan Lokayukta & Upa-Lokayuktas Act, 1973	Yes	3 yrs.	No
Bihar	1	The Bihar Lokayukta Act, 1973	No	5 yrs.	No
Uttar Pradesh	2	The Uttar-Pradesh Lokayuktas upa-Lokayuktas, 1985	Yes	6 yrs.	No
Andra Pradesh	5	The Andra Pradesh Lokayukta & Upa-Lokayukta, 1983	Yes	5 yrs.	No
Gujarat	9	The Gujarat Lokayukta Act, 1986	No	5 yrs.	Yes
Himachal Pradesh	NA	The Himachal Pradesh Lokayukta Act, 1983	No	5 yrs.	Yes
Assam	4	The Assam Lokayukta & Upa-Lokayukta Act, 1985	Yes	5 yrs.	No

Name of the state	*Rank in Corruption*	*The description of the Act*	*Provision of the Upalo-kayuktas*	*Tenure of the Upalo-kayuktas*	*Inclusion of Chief Minister*
Madhya Pradesh	6	The Madhya Pradesh Lokayukta Evam Upa-Lokayukta Adhiniyam, 1981	Yes	5 yrs.	No
Karnataka	11	The Karnataka Lokayukta Act, 1984	Yes	5 yrs.	Yes
Goa	NA	Goa Public Men's Corruption (Investigation And Enquiries Act)	NA	NA	NA
Punjab	NA	The Punjab Lokpal Act,1992	No	5 yrs.	No
Tamilnadu		The Tamilnadu Public Men (Criminal Misconduct Act), 1974	—	—	—

Source—INDIA TODAY November 24, 1997.

machinery. After going through the articles in the newspapers; i.e. The Times of India, Indian Express, The Hindu, etc. on Lokayukta in the states, it seems that it is working successfully. But, all the institutions have teething troubles. All the defeciencis and shortcomings were sorted out at the First All India Lokayuktas' and Upa-Lokayuktas' Conference held at Shimla in 1986. Again in 1991, the Third All India Lokayuktas and Upa-Lokayuktas Conference was held at Hyderabad. Under the Chairmanship of Justice A. Sitharam Reddy, the then Lokayukta, Andhra Pradesh. An Implementation Committee was constituted for this conference. The Committee designed the draft of Model Lokayukta Bill. [89] Following are the points of resolution passed by the Committee:

1. There should be the institution of Lokayukta in every State.
2. Lokayukta should be given the Constitutional status.
3. There should be uniformity in the provisions of the various enactments.

The efforts are going on to implement these by the Lokayuktas of various States.

Some suggestions by the way of observation based on the news and articles in the newspapers and periodicals are made in this study on the administration of the State Lokayuktas:

1. The Lokayuktas need administrative reforms in its personnel management.
2. The Lokayuktas need a separate investigation team.
3. The offices of Lokayuktas need autonomy and independence while dealing with the ministerial cases.
4. An active role of the press and media needs to popularize the institute.
5. A large number of people's active participation is needed.
6. Efforts should be made to frame the model Lokayukta bill followed by all the states.

Summarizing the Lokayuktas in Indian states, it can be said that it can be effective to redress injustice of the citizens. It can also make a balanced and sound relationship between administration and citizens. It can also be said that by and large the states are coming forward to have this machinery on regular basis and support to the Lokayukta acts. Therefore, the large number of states has come forward to institute Lokpal. However, the range of the appointing Lokayukta from 1970 to 2002 is an indication of a very slow process of adopting the machinery in the states.

The moot problem is how to make a corruption-free country from the national to the local level. To that extent there is an absence of a tool proof machinery. Hence, there is a need of national level machinery i.e. 'Lokpal'. How far Lokayukta in Maharashtra is successful is discussed in third chapter. It's limitations and difficulties are discussed in the fourth chapter.

2.15 BANKING OMBUDSMAN

Besides Lokayuktas at state level to curb corruption in Government Departments, the banks have also instituted Ombudsman. There is machinery in the banking sectors to control irregularities and corruption. The goal is to accumulate money in the affluent and mobile society. The matters related to finance are going complicated. To solve these complications to the customer's satisfaction RBI has brought up the Banking Ombudsman in 1995. Corruption has spreaded enormously among bank officers and employees, posing a serious threat to the banking industry. It is not always the small try in banking sector who are involved; but it is the high shots who seldom get wedged are responsible for massive frauds as well as the services rendered by the banks.[90] Banking Ombudsman is there mainly to check the frauds in the banks. The scheme was brought under the section 35(A) of the Banking Regulation Act, 1945 by the power conferring on it.[91] In its initial stage office of the banking ombudsmen was established in Bhopal, Bang lore, Chandigarh, Mumbai, New Delhi and Hyderabad. Now, 15 states in India has Banking Ombudsmen. All

Scheduled Banks, Scheduled Commercial Banks, Regional Rural Banks, Co-Operative Banks are covered under the scheme.[92] The Banking Ombudsman is an expeditious, efficient and prompt in the resolution to customer complaints through expensive. It covers the Indian customers as well as NRI'S in respect of remittances and deposits.[93] Banking industry today requires more socio-economic satisfaction to the customers. The offices need to be more accountable and responsible[94] in respect of various activities relating to customer services. Citizen's Charter; i.e. Banking Ombudsman is a customer friendly scheme run by RBI. Banking Ombudsman is continuing to serve the customers to their entirely satisfaction.

2.16 INSURANCE OMBUDSMAN

The institution of Insurance Ombudsman was created by the Government of India Notification dated 11 Nov., 1998. It aims at quick disposal of the grievances of the insured customers and to mitigate their problems involved in redressal of those grievances. Insurance Ombudsman are drawn from Insurance Industry, Civil Services and Judicial Services for the term of three years. The Governing body of Insurance Council has appointed twelve Ombudsman across the country. Their offices are located at-

Bhopal, Bhubneshwar, Cochin, Guwahati, Chandigarh, New Delhi, Chennai, Kolkata, Ahmedabad, Lucknow, Mumbai, Hyderabad. All the Ombudsmen have a secretarial staff. They perform two types of function-(1) Conciliation (2) Award making. Their powers are restricted to insurance contracts of value not exceeding Rs. 20 lacks. Since 1998, there is a steady increase in the lodging and disposal of the complaints[95]. The institution has helped to generate and sustain the faith and confidence amongst the consumers.

2.17 CONCLUSION

There are lot many efforts to curb corruption. Many more devices try to control maladministration. But, very little could be achieved through all these efforts. In the Western countries, Ombudsman deals with the problem successfully. In India, the attempts are made to establish such machinery. One of the failures is a strong opposition to the Lokpal Bill. It shows non-integration in Indian administration. Due to lack of public and political will, Lokpal Bill is opposed since last 39 years. But, hopefully 15 Indian states have Lokayukta at the state level. While stressing for Lokpal at the central level, it was necessary to see whether the Lokayukta at state level is successful. Besides, some drawbacks, Lokayukta in the States is doing well. Those are discussed in the present chapter in general and Lokayukta in Maharashtra is discussed in particular in the next chapter.

REFERENCES

1. Dr. S.C. Sharma- Public Administration-338
2. Appleby Paul – Public Administration in India : Report of a survey -48
3. *Ibid.,* 50
4. Gazetteer of India-123
5. Commission and Committee—5 –1962/63-2
6. Commission and Committee—5 –1965/66—10
7. Ravi Prakash— Constitution, Fundamental Rights and Judicial Activism— 281
8. *Ibid.,* 33
9. Agrawal B.R.— Our Judiciary—14
10. The Hindu—02 Dec.2002
11. Interview—District Judge—Nasik—05-06-02
12. State and Government In Ancient India— Dr. A. Saltekar— 260
13. *Ibid.,* 208
14. Bhrigusamhita—54
15. Indian Panorama: Truimps annd tragedies — 925
16. *Ibid.,* 932
17. Indian Panorama- 925
18. Mahajan V.D.— India Since 1526—251
19. *Ibid.*

20. Section—2 Prevention of Corruption Act, 1947
21. Crime Legislative Journal—Bombay High Court—1996—1270
22. Mansukhani H. L.-Corruption and Public Servants—Vikas Publishing House Ltd, New Delhi—1979—15
23. Bhure Lal— Corruption: Functional Anarchy in Governance—8
24. http://www.cbi-spe.nin.in/.
25. http://www.cbi.nic.in/.
26. Annual Report— Ministry of Personnel, Public Grievances and Pension, 1988-989
27. Prasad Vishnu - Administrative Tribunals in Action
28. The Gazetteer of India — 404
29. Singhvi Nita—Administration and Citizen— 50
30. *Ibid.*
31. Agarrwal— Our Judiciary—165
32. Joseph Ponnoly Dealing with Corruption 22-27 CBIE CBI Publication Vol. IV No. 1 Jan. 1996
33. http://www.fas.org/irp/world/india/cbi.htm
34. S.K. Ghosh - Indian Panorama:Truimphs and tragedies— 754
35. http://www.cbi.nic.in/.
36. *Ibid.*
37. http://www.cvc.nic.in/vscvc/rajne/ws.htm
38. IJPA—July-September, 1997-Vol. XLIII No. 3 —427-427
39. The Times of India, June 5, 2001
40. The Times of India June 21, 2002
41. One India One People Feb. 2000 Zero Tolerance Corruption—N. Vittal 6
42. Singhvi Nita Administration and Citizen —163
43. Tiwana S.S- Machinery for Redressal of Public Grievances India Administrative Changevol. XXII(22) Jan. July— 166
44. PIL- In Quest of Justice Dr. Sonia Hurra Mishra & Com., Nov. 1993 - 56
45. *Ibid.*
46. Dhawan R.K- Public Grievances and Lokpal (A Study of the Administrative Machinery for Redress of Public Grievances) - 207

47. *Ibid.*
48. Loksabha Debate
49. *Ibid.*
50. Loksabha Debate, 1968
51. Report- Joint Select Committee on The Lokpal and Lokayukta Bill,1968 Secretariet Loksabha, New Delhi March 1969
52. Information Bulletin—Lokpal For India – Loksabha Secretariet, New Delhi 1969
53. Loksabha Debate, 1969
54. Loksabha Debate, 1971
55. Loksabha Debate, 1977
56. Dr. D.R. Saxena/K.P. - Mehra Ombudsman - 425
57. *Ibid.,* 1
58. The Lokpal Bill, 1996
59. Loksabha Debate, 1998
60. Loksabha Debate, 2001
61. The Hindu-July, 2001
62. The Hindu- August, 2001
63. Times of India-30 June, 2003
64. Times of India-20 August, 2002
65. Times of India-30 June, 2003
66. The Lokpal Bill, 1968
67. *Ibid.,* Clause 3(1)
68. *Ibid.,* Clause 3 (7)
69. Dr. Saxena D R— Ombudsman (Lokpal : Redress of Citizen's Grievance in India) - 377
70. http://www.persmin.nic.in/arpg.
71. Sharma Giridhar— Implementation of Ombudsman Plan in India— 25
72. Dr. Saxena D R— Ombudsman (Lokpal : Redress of Citizen's Grievance In India) - 375
73. *Ibid.,* 373
74. http://www.persmin.nic.in/arpg.

75. The Hindu—Dec. 4, 2002
76. *Ibid.*
77. Indian Journal of Public Administration— Jan-Mar, 1989-Vol. XXXV No.1-177-179
78. Mary Parmar—Lokayukta—76
79. Dr. Saxena D R—Ombudsman (Lokpal : Redress of Citizen's Grievance In India- 375
80. Indian Journal of Public Administration—Jan-Mar, 1989-Vol. XXXV No.1-177-179
81. The Times of India— 24 July, 2002
82. *Ibid.*
83. The Hindu— 8 August, 2002
84. K. Rajasekharan— Ombudsman For Local Government In Kerala 24-28 Kurukshetra—April, 2001
85. K. Rajasekharan - Ombudsman For Local Government in Kerala - Kurukshetra (April, 2001) - 24-28
86. Times of India— Feb.27, 2002
87. http://www.persmin.nic.in/arpg.
88. The Indian Express—12 May 1999
89. Annual Consolidated Report of the Lokayukta and Upa-Lokayukta, Maharashtra— Jan. 1 to Dec. 31, 1995—2
90. S.K. Ghosh -Indian Panorama: Truimphs and Tragedies— 675
91. The Banking Ombudsman Scheme- Reserve Bank of India—11
92. http://www.Denabank.Ombudsmen.Com
93. http://www.Unitedbankofindia.Com/Open.Htm
94. http://www.Obcindia.Com/Iindex.Htm.27 Dec. 2001

3

Lokayukta as it has been Functioning in Maharashtra

3.1 INTRODUCTION

The institution of Ombudsman is being recognized as an important device to control corruption and maladministration. It is an important tool with the citizens to ensure smooth and corruption-free administration. Even though there is no Ombudsman at national level, the Lokayukta has been functioning at the state level in number of states. They include, Maharashtra, Uttar Pradesh, Madhya Pradesh, Andhra Pradesh; Kerala, Karnataka, Punjab, Goa, Gujarat, Rajashtan, Orissa, Bihar, Tamil Nadu, Assam and Himachal Prasesh.

In this chapter, Lokayukta in Maharashtra is being discussed. To begin with how the Lokayukta Bill was passed in both Houses of the State is described. Later on, the Lokayukta and Upa-Lokayukta Act is discussed in detail. The process of appointing the Lokayukta, its tenure, salary, functions, powers, authorities, etc. are reviewed. Its actual functioning, problems, difficulties, limitations faced during operation are also considered.

3.2 LOKAYUKTA BILL IN LEGISLATIVE ASSEMBLY

The Indian Constitution makes a resolve to ensure equality before law, social justice and egalitarian society. In order to realize these objectives, the work and the responsibility of administration has been increasing day by day. The vital presence of the institution of Ombudsman and its attention into the public administration would definitely serve same purpose in this regard. It will help to achieve many objectives of the ideal and philanthropic administration. It can take some steps to reduce the inaccessibility of bureaucracy to the common people. Under its influence the irresponsiveness and insensitivity, (which is becoming a general trend in the Indian administration nowadays) of the bureaucratic class can be reduced. It can instill a new spirit in public life. And the most important achievement would be that it will educate the public to fight corruption and other unwanted trends present in the administration. The concept of the Institution of Lokayukta is based on the Institution of Ombudsman in Scandinavian countries. Maharashtra is the first Indian State implemanting the Lokayukta Institution.

On Oct. 9, 1971 'The Lokayukta and Upa-Lokayukta Bill, 1971' was moved by Mr. S.K.Wankhede, the then Finance Minister. The Bill was discussed in detail. Specially, the matter such as whether the Chief Minister and the Co-operative sectors should be included in the jurisdiction of Lokayukta or not was discussed in the house. V.G. Deshpande, MLA, Vidarbha Graduate Constituency, referring to Ramshastri Prabhune, an ideal of impartial justice, stressed that the Chief Minister should be included within the jurisdiction of the Lokayukta.[1] He also added that the Ex-Chief Minister of Punjab, Mr. Pratap Sing Kairon was proved guilty in the corruption cases. So he argued as to why the Chief Minister should not be included under the purview of the Lokayukta. The question was of special concern. Advocating the stand of Mr. Wankhede, N.D. Patil put forth a novel way of handing over the powers to the Governor about the corruption charges against the Chief Minister.[2] One of the MLAs, Mr. A.R. Jadhav expressed the fear of instability in the governance if the Chief Minister is subjected to the purview of the Lokayukta. The view was supported by some of the members in Assembly. But the majority of the members were on the side of the inclusion of the post of Chief Minister under the purview.

As far as the Co-operative Sector was concerned, V.G.Deshpande and some other members of the house opined to include the sector in the jurisdiction of the law but the move could not gain the mandate. Thus, excluding the post of Chief Minister and the Co-operative sector from its jurisdiction, the bill 'Lokayukta & Upa-Lokayukta, 1971' was passed. It has been enacted on Dec. 10, 1971

SECTION 1

LOKAYUKTA IN THE ACT

3.3.1 Appointment and Qualifications

The process and system of appointing the Lokayukta is prescribed in the third and fourth section in the 'Maharashtra Lokayukta and Upa-Lokayukta Act, 1971'.

According to it, a person holding the office of Lokayukta is similar to that of High Court judge. The Lokayukta generally is selected from the retired High Court judges. The person to be appointed as Lokayukta should necessarily fulfill the following conditions:

1. The person should not be a member of Parliament or of the Legislature of any state.
2. The person should not hold any office of trust or profit.
3. He should not be directly or indirectly connected with any political party.
4. He should not be allowed to keep his relationship with any private management of any concern or be involved in any business thereof.
5. He should leave his profession if any before holding the post.

A person who fulfills the above conditions could be appointed as the Lokayukta. Obviously, the Governor makes the appointment. Before the appointment the Governor has to consult the Chief Justice of the High Court and the Leader of the opposition party in the Legislative Assembly. The consultation of the leader of the opposition party is necessary to make an impartial appointment. There should be political neutrality in the selection. Democratic aspect is taken in to consideration in the process of selecting the Lokayukta. Till date, the appointment process appears to be sound. There was not any other irregularity in the selection.[3] Another welcoming thing is that only the retired Judges are appointed as the Lokayukta. Probably, the judges are indisputable. Fortunately impartial and bold persons only adorned the crown of Maharashtra Lokayukta. So far following judges have been appointed as Lokayukta:

Table 3.1

Presiding Period of Lokayukta and Upa-lokayukta from 25th October 1972 to this Date

Lokayuktas—

Sr.	*Name*	*Period*
1.	**Justice** S. P. Kotwal	25 October 1972- 24 October 1977
2.	**Justice** A. R. Shimpi	2 January 1978- 25 January 1979
3.	**Justice** N. D. Kamat	6 September 1979- 5 September 1984
4.	**Justice** V. S. Deshpande	27 September 1979- 26 September 1989
5.	**Justice** P. S. Shah	26 October 1989- 25 October 1994
6.	Justice H. H. Kanthatria	27 October 1994-30 November 1998
7.	Justice V. P. Tipnis	1 January 1999-31 December 2003
8.	**Justice** G. D. Patil	27 January 2004-26 January 2009
9.	**Justice** Purushottam Gaikwad	2 July 2009- till a date
Upa-Lokayuktas—		
1.	**Shri** L. M. Nadkarni	1 October 1973-30 September 1978
2.	**Shri** S. V. Bhave	16 November 1978 15 November 1983
3.	**Shri** S. P. Mohani	16 November 1983- 15 November 1988
4.	**Shri** K. Sivarakrishnan	4 February 1989- 3 February 1994
5.	**Shri** N. Jayraman	28 February 1994-27 February 1999
6.	**Shri** R. C. Iyyer	8 March 1999-7 March 2004
7.	**Mr.** Suresh Kumar	14 June 2004–13 June 2009
8.	**Mr.** John Joseph	1 December 2009 to till a date

(Reference: The Annual Consolidated Reports)

3.3.2 Oath

After the appointment and before assuming the charge of the post, the person must take an oath. Consequently, the Oath for Lokayukta is entitled in the first schedule. He is bonded by the faithfulness, allegiance to the post and for the best judgment to the common man. The Governor gives the oath or some person appointed in behalf by him.

3.3.3 Tenure and Removal

As per Section 5 (1) of the Act, Lokayukta can hold office for five years.[4] On the charges of misbehavior or incapacity of the person, he can be removed from the office before completing his tenure. The Governor has to address each of the Houses of the State Legislature on that matter. In case of removal, the resolution will have to be supported by a majority of not less than one third members of the House. After getting sanction of both the Houses, Lokayukta is removed from the post. There is no simple way to remove Lokayukta. Lokayukta is given adequate security of his tenure so that he can ably discharge his duties without any disturbances or any fear of removal.

3.3.3 Leave

The Lokayukta shall be entitled to a leave for one month in a year with the allowances. Besides, he can avail a vacation of 15 days in summer and 7 days in winter.[5] At the time of retirement he may encash his pending leave if any. There is an adequate leave facility to the Lokayukta so that he could responsibly do his work.

3.3.4 Salary and Allowances

The second schedule of the Act prescribes a basic of pay Rs. 4000/- to Lokayukta, which after the revision is Rs. 14300/-. He gets dearness allowance Rs. 30,000/- and above per annum. Lokayukta is entitled to get free hospitalization, medical attendance and treatment in the Government hospitals including the dependent family members. In addition to it, he gets Rs. 3,000/- per month as city compensatory allowance from August 1, 1997.[6] In 2009, the salary structure has been revised and Lokayukta gets the salary same as it is to chief Justice High Court, i.e. 90,000/-.

If a person holding the post is drawing any pension or gratuity for the previous service, that amount is deducted from the current amount of salary. Throughout his term Lokayukta is entitled to rent free accommodation. In case he occupies any other accommodation he is entitled to Rs. 9000 per month as has home allowance.[7] The residence of the Lokayukta can consume 3,600 kiloliters of water and 10,000 units of electricity uncharged. He is provided with a motorcar with the allowance of its maintenance, oil and a chauffer.[8] He is given traveling allowance and daily allowance for his on duty journeys.

Lokayukta is entitled travel concessions for himself and dependent members of the family residing with him for visiting any place in India or his permanent residence during his leave, twice a year with the option of traveling by air or air conditioned first class by railway. The provisions of salary and allowances of the Lokayukta are such that he should not get attracted towards bribe or any gift or any irregular practice.

According to the Contributory Provident Fund Rules; the Lokayukta is a subscriber to the contributory provident fund. He is given a pension for the same post. But, after 1990, the government stopped pension of a person who is getting pension for his previous post.[9] As the Lokayuktas are Ex-Judges and Upa-Lokayuktas are ex-public servants, they get pension from those posts. Hence, the pension from the post of Lokayukta is stopped. But, it doesn't affect Lokayukta's functioning within his service period.

3.5 JURISDICTION

3.5.1 Power and Function

According to the requirement made in the Act,

> "An Act to make provision for the appointment and functions of certain authorities for the investigation of administrative action taken by or on behalf of the Government of Maharashtra or certain public authorities in the state of Maharashtra, in certain cases and for matters connected therewith."[10]

---

* Minister of Council; I.E. State and Deputy Minister and Officer in Connection with the Affairs of the State of Maharashtra.

The purpose of establishing the machinery is clear. To investigate the matters of grievances and allegation of corruption and maladministration is Lokayukta's main function. Hence, Lokayukta is given adequate powers and jurisdictions.

Jurisdiction of Lokayukta largely means the type of cases, complaints Lokayukta can deal with. It also means the range of investigation he undertakes. As per Section (2) of the Act, Lokayukta can investigate any matter of allegation or grievance covering corruption or maladministration within the jurisdiction.[11] According to section (2) of the Lokayukta Act, 'allegation' means any action taken by the public servant:

(a) Which is in his own or any others cause undue harm or hardship to any other person.

(b) Which serves his personal interest or improper or corrupt motives

(c) Which is guilty of corruption or lack of integrity.

Whereas grievance means a claim by a person that he sustained injustice or hardship in consequence of maladministration.

The distinction between the two is if the complainant says that he has sustained injustice or hardship in consequence of maladministration, what he alleges is a grievance because he has himself sustained some injury or hardship. But, in the case of 'allegation' the complainant need not personally have sustained any injury himself. It is clear that any one can make an allegation but only the person aggrieved can make a grievance.

Under section (7) Lokayukta may investigate into any action of 'grievance' or 'allegation' of following offices and institutions:

(a) Public servants

(b) Local authorities under-

(i) The Municipal Corporations;

(ii) Every president and vice-president of a Municipal Council and chairman of the standing or subjects committee;

(iii) Every president and vice- president of a Zila Parishad, chairman and Deputy chairman of Panchayat Samiti;

(iv) Any Special Secretary, Additional Secretary or Joint Secretary to the State;

(v) Any person in the service of any Government Company;

vi) Any society registered under the Society Registration Act, 1860.

Lokayukta has to render his advice in the matter of grievance and allegation made against the public servants if asked by the governor. If the office bears one or more Upa-Lokayukta, the Lokayukta may assign them the matter to be investigated to Upa-Lokayukta..

3.5.2 Matter Out of Jurisdiction

Whether the jurisdiction of Lokayukta is broad or narrow depends on the blocking the sphere of his activities. Again the lack of jurisdiction makers much if the post of institution is kept away from the jurisdiction of Lokayukta.

The existing Lokayukta Act does not give Lokayukta access to the Chief Minister of the Sate. The Chief Minister is out of Lokayukta's jurisdiction. Under the third schedule, actions related to-

(a) crime investigating action;

(b) and action on protection of the security of the state;

(c) action taken in the exercise of power in relation to determining whether a matter shall go to the court or not.

(d) action taken in respect of appointment, removals, superannuation or other matter relating to the condition of service of public servants.

(e) grant of honours and rewards are out of Lokayukta's jurisdiction.

These matters are out of Lokayukta's jurisdiction. Further, according to Section 8(5), the Lokayukta cannot investigate-

(a) Any complaint involving a grievance, made after the expiry of 12 months from the date on which the action complained against becomes known to the complainant;

(b) Any complaint involving an allegation, after the expiry of 3 years from the date on which the action complained against is alleged to have taken place; but, if the complainant provides any reason satisfactorily, the Lokayukta can discretionarily consider the complaint.

Thus, there is time limitation for the complaint to be made. Referring to the 18th section of the act, if the state government recommends so, in a special case, Lokayukta keeps the matter out of investigation. Similarly, if he thinks that dealing any case is harmful in the public interest, he can dismiss it and restrict his own jurisdiction.

He is not authorized to investigate any action which is taken by or with the approval of-

(a) Any judge as defined in section 19 of the IPC,

(b) Any officer/ servant of any Court of India,

(c) The Accountant General, Maharashtra,

(d) The Chief Election Commissioner, the Election Commissioner, Article 324 of the Constitution and the Chief Electoral officer Maharashtra State,

(e) The Chairman/member of MPSC,

(f) The Speaker, Maharashtra Legislative Assembly or the Chairman, Maharashtra Legislative Council,

(g) Any member of the Secretarial staff of either House of Legislature.

(h) Universities,

(i) Ex-public servants, Ex-Secretaries and Ex-Ministers

He has to work in addition if Governor notifies or indicates—

(A) By specific notification anything about the grievance and eradication of corruption.

(B) To supervise the agencies, authorities or officers constituted for the redressal of grievances and eradication of corruption.

Lokayukta within his jurisdiction can contact any government office or summon him for witness or can ask for any paper or document or any file from any government office or authority for the purpose of investigation. The offices are obliged to provide information required by the Lokayukta. If they do not, the Lokayukta might punish them.

Thus, the above mentioned provisions definitely reduce the sphere of activity of Lokayukta. In short, he has to function with many ifs and buts. How far is it justifiable especially from point of view of safeguarding interests of common man in the face of wide range of irregularities around him is a matter of serious concern. Lokayukta requires more powers and extensive jurisdiction for its efficiency, effectiveness and success. Owing to the exclusion of above-mentioned authorities, Lokayukta's jurisdiction becomes limited. However, in spite of the limitations, Lokayukta is effective in Maharashtra than any other state.[12] Lokayukta investigates the matters of allegation and grievances.

Under section (19), Lokayukta can assign his power of investigation to the Divisional Commissioner or Collector for the geographical reasons. Any officer in the Lokayukta office or any offices of the state or central government or any person or any agency can exercise the powers handed over by the Lokayukta. He can also delegate a complete case to the Registrar or Additional Registrar in his office.

For the past 30 years, the Lokayuktas and Upa-Lokayuktas have delegated powers partly to the government officers. It is for the first time that Mr. Tipnis and Mr. Iyer, Ex-Lokayukta and Upa- Lokayukta delegated powers to the Registrar and Additional Registrar as a whole.

Delegation is a principle of organization that can extend its efficiency and effectiveness. It is observed that the disposal of cases has increased and got speeded up due to delegation.[13] Delegation has proved to be useful to the Lokayukta office.

3.5 REPORTS OF LOKAYUKTA

Lokayuka has to give report of his findings in any case to the concerned authority and the Governor. Lokayuka reports whenever—

(a) he finds that the action has resulted undue hardship to the complainant, he reports to the concerned for the redressal within a specific time.

(b) The competent authority has to intimate and report to the Lokayuka that such an action has been taken. If not, considering that the redressal is not solved, the Lokayukta can investigate more and substantiate the report in writing including his findings and recommendations along with the relevant documents, materials and other evidence.

(c) The Lokayukta annually presents the Consolidated Report to the Governor. If his recommendations or findings in any case do not result in action, he can report it to the Governor. The Lokayukta can also report any special matter or subject to the Governor.

The Governor shall cause a copy thereof together with an explanatory memorandum to be laid before each House of the State Legislature.

Till date the Lokayukta and Upa-Lokayukta have submitted 32 annual reports from 1972 to 2004 besides some special reports to the Governor. The annual reports from 2005 t 2009 are on the way of preparation.

3.6.1 Procedure of Inquiry

The Lokayukta Act has laid down specific procedure for the conduct of the enquiry and investigation in Section (10). Accordingly, the complainant has to file the complaint in the prescribed form and affidavit. An affidavit drawn in the first person shall be sworn in before the Registrar or the Assistant Registrar. A complainant can attach any attested document along with the form of complaint. If a registering officer finds that the form is not according to its official rules, he postpones the registration and informs the complainant to change it within a specified time.

The Registrar or his authorities firstly scrutinizes a filed complaint. If he finds any defect or any required information not furnished, the complainant is informed and is asked to change it within a stipulated time. This constitutes the pre investigation process.

3.6.3 Investigating the Case

After receiving the complaint the office of Lokayukta forwards a statement to the competent authority or public servant. It informs them about the complaint made against him. The concerned can send any person to attend or can present related document. He can also produce requisite record or a copy from any court or any office. This is the legal way of Lokayukta to investigate the case.

In a particular case, Lokayukta can appoint a commission for the examination. If anyone refuses to provide any document the Lokayukta can order to produce whatever he thinks fit in that case.

Normally, no Advocate, Mukhtyar or other legal representative is allowed to appear before the Lokayukta; but in a specific case, the party is allowed to appear through any such person.

Lokayukta sends a notice to the complainant and the concerned to appear before him witnessing with any other person if necessary through the police station in that area.

During hearing, both the parties have a right to examine their witnesses and to cross-examine the second party, with the permission of the Lokayukta. If necessary, he can appoint an interpreter for solving the problem of language.

3.6.4 Refusal of Case

Lokayukta can refuse to investigate any grievance or any allegation if he does not think it proper or sufficient reason of complaining. If the complaint is made after expiry of 12 months from the date on which the action complained against becomes known to the complainant or after the expiry of 3 years from the date on which the action has taken place. He has to record the proper reasons of refusal of complaint and also has to inform the complainant and the concerned.

Lokayukta can close down the case if there is legal difficulty or if the Government orders it. After closing, if he gets any sufficient cause, he may revive the complaint or re-open the case and re-hear it on merits.

3.7 HEARINGS AT DIVISIONAL AND DISTRICT HEADQUARTERS

Lokayukta and Upa-Lokayukta have their sittings at Divisional and District Headquarters. The complaints compeiled to visit the Mumbai office also. Mr. V. S. Deshpande started the practice of arranging the hearing at the Divisional and District levels to save the time and money expenses of the complainants so far procedure is concerned.

The press note is given about divisional sittings of Lokayukta in the local newspapers. By meeting the complainant or the officials directly, the Lokayukta decides whether the complaint could be entertained for formal recommendations and for the redressal.

The experience of Lokayukta shows that many persons take benefit of this arrangement and come forward with their complaints during such sittings.

3.8 UPA-LOKAYUKTA

The Governor can appoint an additional Upa-Lokayukta in consultation with the Lokayukta. The terms, conditions, oath and jurisdiction of the both Lokayukta and Upa-Lokayukta are same. Under section 3(3) Upa-Lokayukta is responsible for the administrative control of the office of Lokayukta for the purpose of convenient conduct of investigations and disposal of cases under the Act.The Upa-Lokayukta is provided a residence and if he is residing elsewhere, he gets House Allowance Rs. 7,800 per month with 3,600 kilometers of water and 10,000 units of electricity per annum. He is provided with a motorcar and leave facility similar to the Lokayukta. If Lokayukta office becomes vacant or due to any reason if he is unable to perform his duty then by an order of the Governor, the Upa-Lokayukta enjoy his powers. If the office of Upa-Lokayukta becomes vacant, the Lokayukta directs it. Under section 7(1) & 7(2), a clear-cut division of powers is laid down as regards the work to be done by the Lokayukta and Upa-Lokayukta. By a notification issued on July 18,1973, the Upa-Lokayukta can proceed against the Municipal Corporations of Bombay, Poona, Nagpur, Sholapur and Kolhapur. The provisional rules and regulations of the Lokayukta are given in the above table:

Table 3.2

Lokayukta and Upa-Lokayukta in Maharashtra

No.		*Lokayukta*	*Upa-Lokayukta*
1.	Notification enforced on	October 25, 1972	October 1, 1973
2.	Term	5 years	5 years
3.	Oath	Given by Governor	Given by Governor
4.	Appointment (by the Governor)	After consulting with the Chief Justice of High Court, opposition leader in legislature assembly	After consulting with Lokayukta
5.	Salary	Rs. 90,000/-.	Rs. 80,000/-
6.	Accommodation	By State Government	By State Government
7.	Consolidated House Allowance in lieu of house	Rs. 9,000/-	Rs. 7,800/-
8.	Dearness Allowance	As per rule	As per rule
9.	Samptury Allowance	Rs. 3,000/-	Rs. 2,000/-
10.	Pension	At the rate of Rs. 2,700 per month	At the rate of Rs. 2, 025 per month
11.	Matters to investigate	Minister, Secretary, any Public servant, etc.	Public servant not being a Minister, Secretary or Public Servant of any class or sub-class

3.9 STAFF OF THE LOKAYUKTA OFFICE

The constant increase in the workload of the Lokayukta shows a need for more officials. Initially, in 1972, the staff numbered 10.[14] In 1973, due to increase in the work, it augmented to 49; it grew up to 73 and to 84 in 1997; whereas the office needs 42 more officials to attend the increased work load. The present position of staff of Lokayukta office is shown in Chart 3.1

Owing to inadequacy of the staff, Lokayukta has a large pendency of the cases. The former Lokayuktas explain that due to inadequate staff and lack of its own investigating machinery, Lokayukta finds it difficult to work efficiently and effectively.

3.10 ROLE OF LOKAYUKTA

A glance on Lokayukta's functioning makes it clear how far Lokayukta is successful in Maharashtra, whether it could reduce corruption and curb maladministration. The empirical findings relating to this has been discussed in the next chapter. However, his role as per act is high lighted here—

(a) He helps the citizen in solving their grievances.

(b) He helps the process of the government and governmental organizations. It controls governmental bodies also by handling the ugly part of governmental working; i.e. irregularities, corruption, etc.

The influence of the Lokayukta is persuasive. Lokayukta has tremendous moral force acting on the state to undo the wrong done to the individual or group of individuals. It is a unique institution, which flexibly provides an inexpensive and comparatively quick justice to the citizens. Maharashtra being the first state implementing the Lokayukta, other 12 or 13 states inspired by the concept and established Lokayukta. In Maharashtra, the institution has progressed in its ability to fulfill its mandate of redressing the grievances of the citizens.

CHART 3.1

Organisational Chart of the Office of the Lokayukta and UPA-Lokyukta

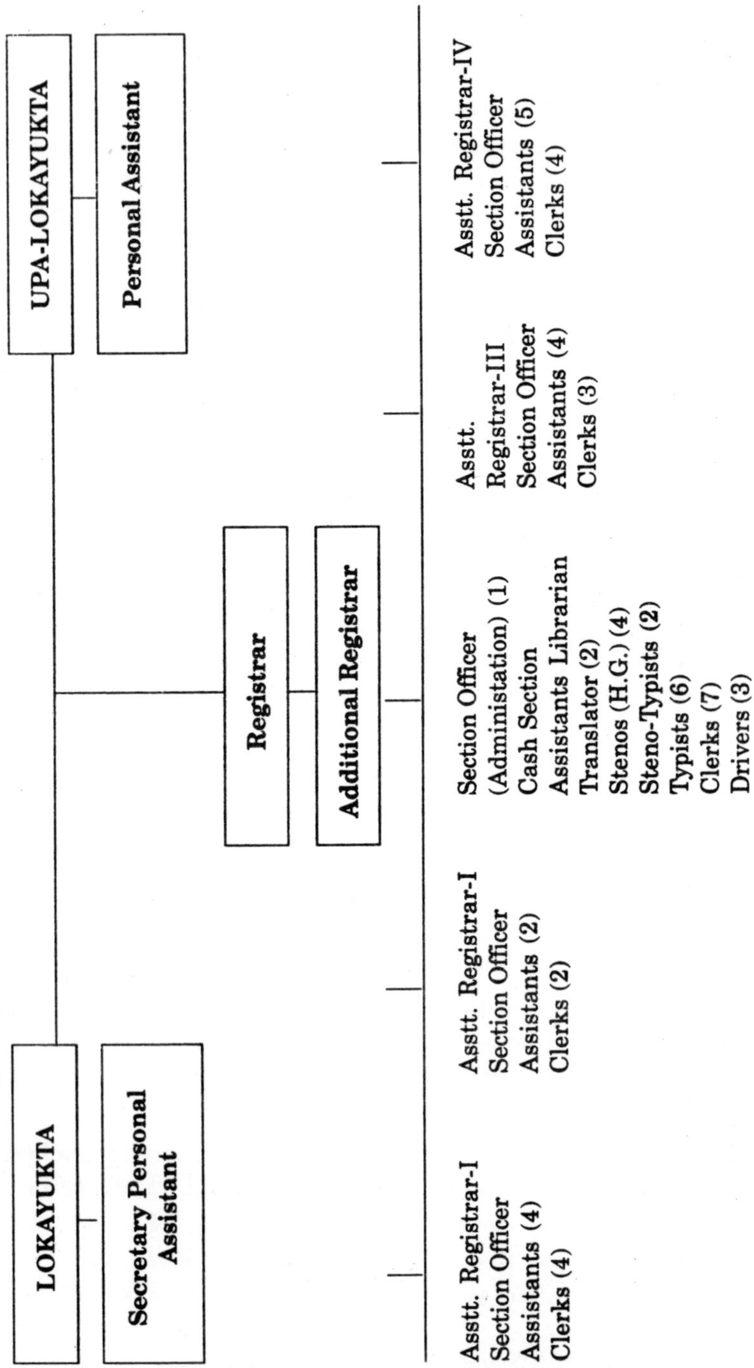

Lokayukta is a friend, guide, and philosopher of the citizens. Its role is that of an administrator. It is a watchdog of the citizen in a democratic state.

3.11 PROBLEMS FACED BY THE LOKAYUKTA

The institution like Lokayukta aimed at finding fault with others, is bound to face number of difficulties. His is not a smooth path. He has to experience displeasure of many powerful sections of society.

Successive incumbents occupying the post of Lokayukta come across many problems. They have undertaken their task with many odds. Following are some of the problems faced by the Lokayukta:

1. Inadequate Staff: Lokayukta office is deficient in staff. A large number of complaints require a matching staff.[15] The pendency of cases might decrease with an adequate staff. The government is not always keen and serious in this regard.

2. Investigating Machinery: Non-provision of independent and well-trained investigating machinery has remained a major lacuna in the Lokayukta Act, 1971. The government does not approve it. The institute takes the help of the governmental investigating machinery such as Police Department or CBI. It means, the institute has to depend on outside force for its work.

It makes the institute helpless due to lack of public confidence in the investigation by these Governmental machineries. Karnataka Lokayukta has it's own investigating machinery. Lokayukta depends upon CBI, Anti-Corruption Bureau for investigation, but as per narration given by the Lokayukta, experience is not satisfactory.[16] Many a times it takes months or years to get the reports of investigation. It results in huge pendency of cases. Hence, Lokayukta urges for its own investigating machinery. Independence of the institution is inconceivable without such machinery.

3. Inadequate Accomodation: The provided accommodation to Lokayukta office is in Administrative building of a State Government at Mumbai. The functionaries in the office told that it is not adequate.[17] It requires more space to cope up the increasing work.

4. Ignorance of the People: The effective role of the Lokayukta largely depends upon the use of his services by the people. The first thing necessary is that people must know Lokayukta and its functioning. We observed in our visit that the people know very little about the institute of Lokayukta and Upa-Lokayukta. Probably, publicity of the institution and the Act is not adequate.

5. Inordinate Delays: We have observed that there is an inordinate delay in the execution of the decisions and recommendations made by Lokayukta to the concerned administrators. Further, the concerned authorities take long time to respond to the queries made by Lokayukta. Reports by Lokayukta have to be kept in Legislative Assembly in the first month of the following year. But usually, the reports are kept late due to other bussiness of the House. Thus, it takes a lot of time to pass it in the assembly.

In its 20th report, Lokayukta has pointed out that the government discloses some documents and avoided giving it to Lokayukta. It is due to keep it away from governmental actions. In fact, according to the act, it is compulsory to give Lokayukta any required document.

6. Inadequate Budget: While providing money to the office of the Lokayukta, the total administrative expenses of the institute are not taken into account. Hence, The Lokayukta is required to cut the expenditure. In year of 1999-2000, the Lokayukta's expenditure was about Rs. 1,43,38,000/-:[18]

Salary	Rs. 1,32,48,000
Traveling allowances	Rs. 2,31,000
Officials	Rs. 6,94,000

Petrol, oil, other	Rs. 1,54,000
Visitors	Rs. 11,000
Total	Rs. 1,43,38,000

The officials as well as the Ex-Lokayuktas and Upa-Lokayuktas stated in our visit that budget provided is not adequate to run the office. The programmes such as annual divisional sittings, attending the international ombudsman conferences, national conferences, etc.[19] could not be undertaken due to paucity of funds. It shows that inadequate budgetary provision is the major difficulty faced by the Lokayukta.

3.12 PROPOSALS FOR AMENDMENTS TO THE LOKAYUKTA AND UPA-LOKAYUKTA ACT

Right from inception, the Lokayukta office has been consistently asking for amendment in 'The Maharashtra Lokayukta and Upa-Lokayukta Act, 1971' for its effectiveness. It is just natural that the Lokayukta and Upa-Lokayukta Act, 1971 needs modification over a period of long time in the light of difficulties and problems it faced. According to the officials and the ex and present Lokayuktas and Upa-Lokayuktas, following amendments are required to be made as early as possible:

1. Section 10(2) of the act does not permit the Lokayukta to disclose the public or the press the identity of the complainant and of the public servant affected by the investigation. But, if the name is disclosed in some cases, it would put some check on others and could act as deterrent. Further the recent trend of right to information is also in favour of such disclosure. Therefore, the amendment to disclose the identity of public servant be undertaken.
2. A serious limitation which has been encountered by the Lokayukta and Upa-Lokayukta in the performance of their functions is found in the provisions of section 8(1) (a) & (b). The section 8(1) says except as hereinafter provided, the Lokayukta and Upa-

Lokayukta shall not conduct any investigation under this act in the case of a complaint involving a grievance in respect of any action,—

(a) If such action relates to any matter specified in the Third schedule,

(b) If the complainant has or had any remedy by way of proceedings before any tribunal or court of law.

Clause (a) specified the IIIrd schedule as follow:

(a) Action taken for the purpose of investigating crime—

(b) Action taken in the exercise of powers in relation to determining whether a matter shall go to a court or not.

(c) Action taken in matters which arise out of the terms of a contract governing purely commercial relations of the administration with customers or suppliers, except where the complainant alleges harassment or gross delay in meeting contractual obligations.

(d) Action taken in respect of appointments, removals, pay, discipline, supperannuation or other matters relating to the conditions of service of public servants but not including action relating to claims for pension, gratuity, Provident Fund or to any claims which arise on retirement, removal or termination of service.

If the grievances fall within any of this clause of the III rd schedule then the Lokayukta/Upa-Lokayukta will have no jurisdiction. Section 8(1) (b) says that the Lokayukta shall not conduct any investigation

"...if the complainant has or had any remedy by way of proceedings before any tribunal or court of law".[20]

Thus, when the section uses the words "has or had no remedy", it contemplates a case where in theory a remedy is available. For example, in the matter of corruption, Anti-Corruption Bureau is a remedy to the complainant. So long as the remedy is available on paper the Lokayukta and Upa-

Lokayukta have no jurisdiction. It is rather difficult to see, therefore, in which case in the matter of corruption the Lokayukta or Upa-Lokayukta have jurisdiction at all. The provision to section (1) (b), no doubt, creates an exception. It gives the Lokayukta the power to hold an investigation if he

"...is satisfied that such person could not or cannot, for sufficient cause, have recourse to such remedy".[21]

This would ordinarily mean that exception again is full. Under section 8(1) (b) the citizen has in theory another remedy open. Thus, it means, in the matter of corruption, the jurisdiction so hedged in by limitations becomes practically ineffective.

It is necessary to rethink on the restrictions imposed on approaching the Lokayukta through these clauses so that more and more acts and posts be brought top the purview of Lokayukta by way of amendment.

(3) According to section 2(h) & 2(l)—

2(h)—'Minister' means a member (other than the Chief Minister) of the Council of Ministers, by whatever name called, for the State of Maharashtra that is to say, a Minister, Minister of State and Deputy 'Minister'.

2(l)— 'Secretary' means a Secretary to the Government of Maharashtra and includes a special Secretary, an Additional Secretary and a Joint Secretary.

Lokayukta thinks that it is necessary to include 'ex-minister' and 'ex-secretary' within this section

4] In its IInd report, Lokayukta suggested to amend section 10(5). The words—

> "...in case where the Lokayukta or an Upa-Lokayukta decides not to entertain a complaint or to discontinue any investigation in respect of a complaint, he shall record his reasons and communicate the same to the complainant and the public servant concerned."[22]

The section directs that the Lokayukta or Upa-Lokayukta shall only in two cases mentioned, record his reasons and communicate the same to the complainant and the public servant concerned. The two cases in which he has to do this are (1) where he decides not to entertain a complaint; or (2) where he decides to discontinue any investigation in respect of a complaint. What is to happen after the Lokayukta entertains a complaint, continues the investigation and comes to a final conclusion is nowhere mentioned in act. There is no provision for communicating the reasons and findings to the complainant or the public servant concerned in cases where the Lokayukta gives finding after recording evidence and fully hearing both sides. Lokayukta suggested in its IInd report that in section 10(5) after the words—

> "in respect of a complaint" the following words should be inserted: "or gives a finding on merits after hearing both sides".[23]

These are the amendments required for more effectiveness of the Act.

SECTION 2

These are some of the provisions of the Lokayukta Act. The preceding section highlighted the organization and structure of the Lokayukta institution. But, the real problem is how do these structural arrangements and facilities given in the act come to the rescue of citizens who have been deprived of the due claims. It is necessary to understand the real functioning of the Lokayukta office.

LOKAYUKTA AS IT IS FUNCTIONING IN MAHARASHTRA

In 1997, Maharashtra Lokayukta completed its 25 years. Within this period, the Lokayukta office dealt with nearly one lakhs and more complaints. The question arises, whether the complainants or common citizens are satisfied with this machinery. Whether the incidences of maladministration and corruption have mitigated after due working of the Lokayukta. For this purpose, a light is thrown on Lokayukta's functioning on the basis of Lokayukta Reports.

3.13 CASES RECEIVED AND DISPOSED BY LOKAYUKTA

To begin with the frequency of approaching the Lokayukta by the complainants a comprehensive table is given in the report of the Lokayukta:

Table-3.3 shows the number of complaints received and disposed off from 25th October 1972 to 31st December 1998—

Table 3.3

Table Showing Number of Complaints Received and Disposed from 1972 To 2003

Year	*Opening Balance*	*Institutions Complaints Received*	*Total*	*Disposal*	*Closing Balance*
1972-73	—	903	903	594	309
1974	309	764	1073	744	329
1975	329	982	1311	776	535
1976	535	1259	1804	1087	717
1977	717	1433	2150	915	1235
1978	1235	1314	2549	1132	1417
1979	1417	1552	2969	1302	1667
1980	1667	2079	3746	2827	919
1981	919	1669	2588	1916	672
1982	672	1868	2540	1691	849
1983	849	3153	4002	2506	1496
1984	1496	4430	5926	3966	1960
1985	1960	5421	7381	3775	3606
1986	3606	6713	10319	7530	2789
1987	2789	6102	8891	6652	2239
1988	2239	6281	8520	6460	2060
1989	2060	6967	9027	656	2465
1990	2465	7053	9518	6263	3255
1991	3255	8760	12015	8436	3579
1992	3579	8709	12288	8142	4146

Year	*Opening Balance*	*Institutions Complaints Received*	*Total*	*Disposal*	*Closing Balance*
1993	4146	9038	13184	8942	4242
1994	4242	9613	13855	9267	4588
1995	4588	10029	14617	9486	5131
1996	5131	12757	17888	11041	6847
1997	6847	14351	21198	16534	4664
1998	4664	13000	17664	12299	4665
1999	4664	10493	15608	11531	4077
2000	4077	10800	14877	11135	3742
2001	3742	12279	16021	11323	4698
2002	4698	11047	15745	11631	4114
2003	4114	9620	13734	10179	3555
2004	3474	10004	13478	10247	3231
2005	3231	10402	13633	9517	4116
2006	4116	8200	12316	7346	4970
2007	4970	7579	12559	6267	6293
2008	6293	7610	13903	—	—

Source: The Annual Consolidated Reports, The Lokayukta and Upa-Lokayukta.

It can be safely said that large number of people have approached the Lokayukta in Maharashtra. This is an indication of rising difficulties and grievances of the people due to irregularities done in multifarious functionaries of government departments.

On this background it is necessary to consider as to what extent the Lokayukta could dispose of these complaints. In spite of the fact that the reports make yearwise statistics about the disposal of the cases as per the act, the act is silent on definition and meaning of 'disposal'. It seems from reports that there are various categories of complaints when they are treated as 'disposed'.

They are:

1. Complaints in the form of grievances;
2. Complaints in which complainants are at fault;
3. vague complaints;
4. anonymous or pseudonymous complaints;
5. not having jurisdiction as per sections 8(1) (a), 8(1) (b), 8(3), 9(1) (a), 9(1) (b);
6. recommendations made under section 12(1), 12(3) and special report made under section 12(5)

The Lokayukta considers the complaints on corruption and grievances as per the jurisdiction provided to him in Section (2) of the Act. He rejects the complaints on the grounds mentioned above besides the vague, faulty, anonymous, psuedonemous cases which have no mention in the Act.

As far as the cases undertaken for disposal under the above said sections are concerned, the inquiry and the pre-investigation process will not be possible. Therefore, some of the cases carried forward for the next year will be rendered as pending cases with their percentage in the same year.

Table 3.4

Table Showing Percentage of Desposal of Cases from 1972 to 2003

Year	*Total No. of Cases*	*Total No. of Disposed Cases*	*% of Disposing the Cases by Lokayukta*
1972-73	903	594	65.78
1974	1073	744	69.33
1975	1311	776	59.19
1976	1804	1087	60.25
1977	2150	915	42.55
1978	2549	1132	44.4
1979	2969	1302	43.85
1980	3746	2827	75.46
1981	2588	1916	74.05

Year	Total No. of Cases	Total No. of Disposed Cases	% of Disposing the Cases by Lokayukta
1982	2540	1691	66.57
1983	4002	2506	62.61
1984	5926	3966	66.92
1985	7381	3775	51.14
1986	10319	7530	72.97
1987	8891	6652	74.81
1988	8520	6460	75.82
1989	9027	6562	72.69
1990	9518	6263	65.08
1991	12015	8436	70.21
1992	12288	8142	66.25
1993	13184	8942	67.82
1994	13855	9267	66.88
1995	14617	9486	64.89
1996	17888	11041	61.72
1997	21198	16534	77.99
1998	17664	12299	69.62
1999	19608	11531	58.81
2000	14877	11135	74.85
2001	16021	11323	70.68
2002	15745	11631	73.87
2003	13734	10179	74.12
2004	13478	10224	75.85
2005	13633	9517	69.80
2006	12316	7346	59.64
2007	12559	6267	49.90
2008	13903	—	—
Total	321229	218705	66.08

Source: The Annual Consolidated Reports, The Lokayukta and Upa-Lokayukta.

GRAPH 3.1

Disposal of Cases from 1972 to 2003

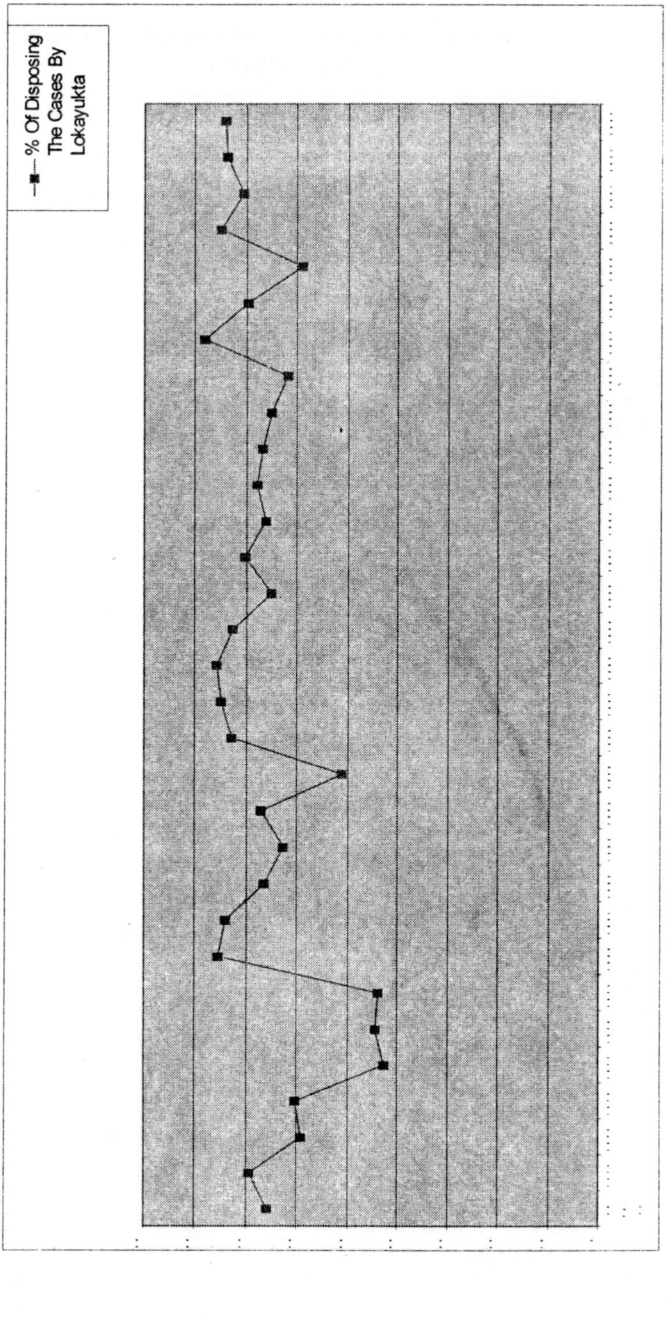

Table 3.5

Table showing Percentage of Pending Cases from 1972 to 2003

Year	Total Cases + Closing Balance of Last Year	Closing Balance for Present Year	% of Balanced Cases
1972-73	903	309	34.12
1974	1073	329	30.66
1975	1311	535	40.80
1976	1804	717	39,74
1977	2150	1235	57.44
1978	2549	1417	55.59
1979	2969	1667	56.14
1980	3746	919	24.53
1981	2588	672	25.96
1982	2540	849	33.42
1983	4002	1496	37.38
1984	5926	1960	33.07
1985	7381	3606	48.85
1986	10319	2789	27.02
1987	8891	2239	25.18
1988	8520	2060	24.17
1989	9027	2465	27.30
1990	9518	3255	34.19
1991	12015	3579	29.78
1992	12288	4146	33.74
1993	13184	4242	32.17
1994	13855	4588	33.14
1995	14617	5131	35.10
1996	17888	6847	38.27
1997	21198	4664	22
1998	17664	4665	26.40

Year	*Total Cases + Closing Balance of Last Year*	*Closing Balance for Present Year*	*% of Balanced Cases*
1999	15608	4077	26.12
2000	14877	3742	25.15
2001	16021	4698	29.32
2002	15745	4114	26.13
2003	13734	3555	25.88
Total	283911	86567	30.49

Source: The Annual Consolidated Reports, The Lokayukta and Upa-Lokayukta

According to Table 3.4, for the period from 1974 to 1979 the number of disposed cases are in decreasing order and obviously, the balance is in the increasing order. Thus, the disposal process is slow. Probably, this was a formative period of the institution. The office was not yet prepared for a speedy disposal. However, after 1980s, especially up to 1984 the disposal has increased. In 1980, 75.46% cases were disposed and only 25.96% were carried forward as pending cases. From 1981, onwards, it was again in the descending order. In 1985, the number has descended by 11%, i.e. 66.92% in 1984 and 51.14% in 1985. But, again from 1986 onwards, it was good. May be because the office was well equipped.

After 1990, Lokayukta disposed off more than 65% cases. It means, the Lokayukta dealt with more than 65% of the cases per year filed to it. As the office received more and more response from the concerned authorities.

The main reasons for the pending cases are inadequacy of personnel in the office and lack of proper follow up on the part of the concerned authorities and departments to complaints referred. It can be said from the Table 3.5 that at the beginning, the pendency was around 40% however after 1998 it came down than 30%. Again after 2005 it can be observed that the percentage of pendency is upraised.

Graph-3.2

Pending Cases during the Period from 1972 to 2003

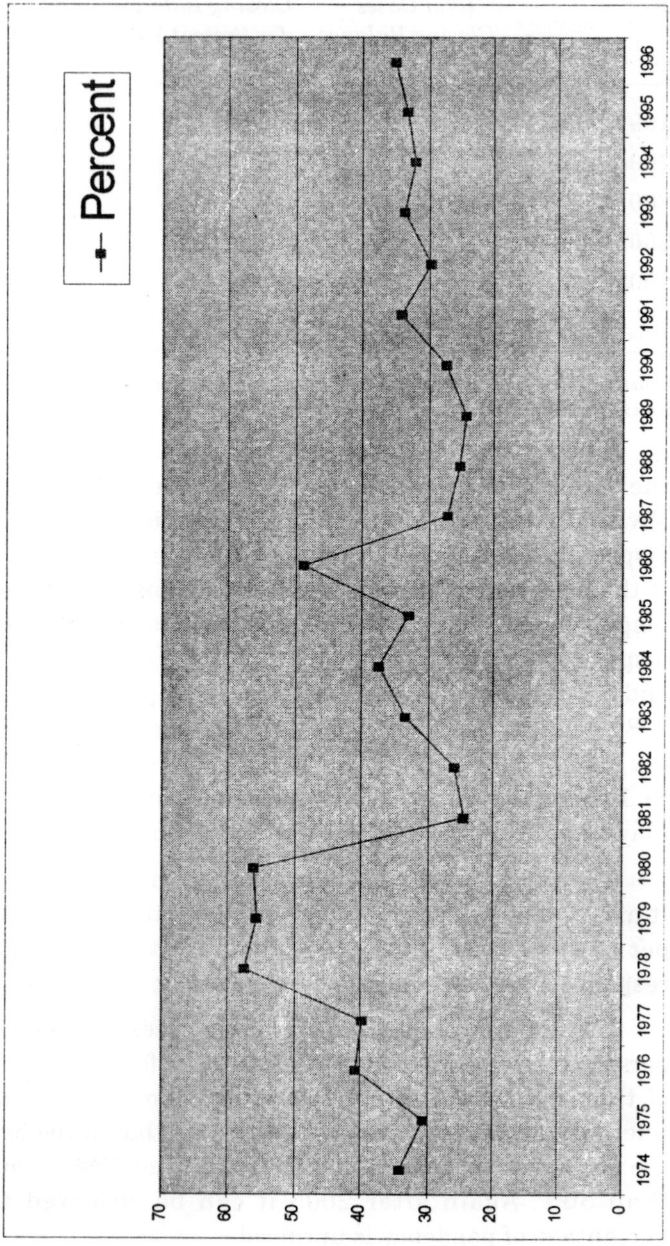

But it is difficult to estimate the volume of pending cases by the office of Lokayukta from the period referred above. It is because the pending cases of the current year are included in previous year's cases.

It is difficult to know the current year's absolute pending cases and of course, disposed cases. Hence, it is also difficult to judge how far the Lokayukta is prompt, efficient to decide the cases and aware about the agony of the people.

In general, from the above tables it can be roughly said that:

(a) There has been by and large a constant increase in the number of registered complaints.

(b) Disposal of complaints has reasonably improved after first five years

(c) Yet as a matter of fact there has been overall decline in the pending cases. However as it has been observed that there are as many 9 years out of 29 when the numbers of pending cases are in the increasing order. Thus, the phenomena of pending cases are mixed one.

(d) As stated above the disposal of the complaints include several titles.

Therefore, it is difficult to work out the disposal cases.

The Lokayukta office receives thousands of cases every year. The quantum of work of Lokayukta office due to rising complaints has increased over a period of time. These cases cover manifold varieties. Obviously, the Lokayukta has to classify them in the lights of nature of complaints, their seriousness and urgency. Again he has also keep aside meaningless complaints which are vague, anonymous and not properly presented. Further he has also to take into account very meticulously, whether these cases fit into his jurisdiction according various provisions of Act. There is wide scope for use of discretion and discrimination on the part of Lokayukta to interact the sections of the Act in this regard. Thus, the cases received by Lokayukta are both considered and therefore, not disposed. As per section (8) of the Lokayukta Act, 1971 he is required to give proper reasons for non-disposal or non-consideration of the cases he receives.[24] In order to understand the situation in this respect, we tried to make use of the data available in the reports of the Lokayukta. These yearly reports give the number of complaints registered in the office of Lokayukta and manner in which they have been dealt with. Even though there are some missing links in the tables on complaints available in the reports, we would like to present meaningful part of it so that we can come to know the actual yearly cases Lokayukta considered and disposed, the cases he had not considered.

We would like to categorize and to project these non-disposed cases in two parts e.g.

(a) those which were reported as out of the jurisdiction of Lokayukta under various sections.

(b) Those cases which were according to Lokayukta faulty, vague and anonymous.

Such break up of cases would help us to work out percentage of cases out of total cases reported and disposed. This, according to us, constitutes the core of the performance of the Lokayukta and the functionaries in his office.

Further, this presentation will throw light on the tendency of killing the cases in the name of jurisdiction not available. We can safely say larger is the proportion of cases covering lack of jurisdiction of the Lokayukta the watchdog of citizens so far their grievances and their suffering due to corrupt practices and irregularities on the part of Government officials are concerned. Before proceeding towards the presentation of the reports as stated above, let us try to familiar with the sections of the Act, 1971 pertaining to jurisdiction of Lokayukta.

The cases are refused for investigation under various sections in the act. But, the break up of these numbers are given section wise from 1974 to 1988. After 1989, the figures are given in the report but not given section wise separately. The sections under which the cases are disposed as 'No

Jurisdiction' are as follows;

(1) Section 8(1) (a)—if such action relates to any matter specified in the Third Schedule.

Third schedule[25] is as per following:

(a) Crime investigating action;

(b) Action protecting the security of the state;

(c) Action taken in the exercise of power in relation to determining whether a matter shall go to the court or not.

(d) Action taken in respect of appointment, removals, superannuating or other matter relating to the condition of service of public servants.

(e) Grant of honors and rewards are out of Lokayukta's jurisdiction.

It means Lokayukta cannot investigate the cases those are criminal related to the security of the state, matters of the court, rewards and honors given by the Government and related to some of the conditions of the public servants.

(2) Section 8(1) (b)—if the complainant has or had any remedy by way of proceedings before any tribunal or court of law and is satisfied that such person could not or cannot have recourse to such remedy for sufficient reason.[26]

It means if in any case, if it was lodged to the court and court had been justified, Lokayukta could not consider that case. Even though the complainant is not satisfied on the court's decision, Lokayukta refuses the case by giving reason that court had proceeded on that.

(3) Section 8 (3)— public servant who is[27]—

(a) Any local authority in the State of Maharashtra;

(b) Any corporation authority;

(c) Any Government Company held by State Government;

is not in Lokayukta's jurisdiction.

It means, some of the local and corporation authorities and public sectors are not under Lokaytukta's purview.

(4) Section 8 (5)—if a grievance is made after the expiry of 12 months and allegation is made after expiry of 3 years from date on which the action have taken place.[28]

It means, there is the limitation of time when should the case be submitted.

(5) Section 9 (1) (a) and 9(1) (b)— if the complaint is made by any person other than a complainant or public servant where the aggrieved is dead or unable to act himself. In this case if Lokayukta thinks it is not proper to deal with and can refuse to investigate.[29]

It means that this is Lokayukta's discretion that if the case of a dead person or disable person to act should be considered or not.

In all these situations, Lokayukta doesn't have jurisdiction to investigate. Table 3.6 and Table 3.7 shows a large number of cases disposed by refusing under these sections.

The table shows that maximum cases are disposed non-jurisdiction under section 8 1(a). The number of cases has been increasing from 1972 to 1988. The percentage of disposal, as non-jurisdiction is cratic. During 1972 to 1988, totally 43,873 cases are disposed of which 10,766 cases are not considered due to non-jurisdiction of Lokayukta. This is considerable number. It indicates a loss of efforts made by the complainants to approach the Lokayukta besides the institutional loss. Of the 5 types of complaints given under 8(1) (a), one deals with service matters i.e. appointment, removal, superannuation, etc. It mean the Lokayukta is not supposed to listen the grievances of employees in this regard. Considering the lapses, irregularities, delays incurred about these issues, the non-availability of jurisdiction to Lokayukta had to injustice on the part of employees. There are a few cases of complaints of pensioners in our survey. But, they are limited to delay in release of pension and sums of retirement benefits.

Eventhough section 8(1)(b) is clear about not to approach the Lokayukta when alternative remedies are available. This table shows that there are large number of rejected cases

Table 3.6

Table Showing Percentage of Disposal of Cases under Sections 'No Jurisdiction' of Lokayukta

Year	*Disposed Cases*	*Sec 8(1)(A)*	*Sec 8(1)(B)*	*Sec 8 (3)*	*Sec 8 (5)*	*Sec 8 (6)*	*Sec 9(1)(A)*	*Sec 9(1)(B)*	*Other Reasons*	*Total*	*%*
1972-73	594	266	45	–	–	–	NIL	NIL	NIL	311	52.36
1974	744	40	28	21	2	4	NIL	NIL	106	201	27.02
1975	776	67	25	3	5	NIL	NIL	NIL	116	216	27.84
1976	1087	123	49	5	NIL	NIL	NIL	NIL	174	351	32.29
1977	915	0	0	0	NIL	NIL	NIL	NIL	NIL	0	0.00
1978	1132	149	43	1	7	4	NIL	NIL	198	402	35.51
1979	1302	158	71	15	9	NIL	NIL	NIL	266	519	39.86
1980	2827	264	100	6	42	NIIL	23	7	NIL	419	14.82
1981	1916	179	42	7	18	48	19	12	185	491	25.63
1982	1691	215	45	2	20	NIL	11	6	NIL	288	17.03
1983	2506	326	97	2	26	44	15	16	306	817	32.60
1984	3966	474	134	10	18	47	09	13	NIL	696	17.55
1985	3775	407	158	11	19	58	25	9	429	1091	28.90
1986	7530	681	309	12	64	84	14	12	NIL	1176	15.62
1987	6652	1499	153	12	38	31	9	5	18	1765	26.53
1988	6460	1506	181	10	71	40	11	6	198	2023	31.32
	43873	6354								10766	24.54

Source: The Annual Consolidated Reports, The Lokayukta and Upa-Lokayukta.

(10766) because the alternative remedy was available. This shows that the complainants are not educated and therefore, awareness of the proper jurisdiction of Lokayukta. As a matter of fact, there is anomaly in the very provision in the sense that it is because alternative remedy is not effective. The complainant is required to go to the office of the Lokayukta. This is not considered here. It can be safely argued by way of conclusion that the tendency of restricting the area of functioning under some protects observed in many places is repeated.

All in all the percentage of disposal is nearly 25 per year as per non-jurisdiction. It makes clear that amongst the disposed cases, 25% complainants are not satisfied but are justified in the eyes of the Lokayukta only. This is very crucial point under which a complaint can be set-aside conveniently without giving much thought to it. Technically and legally it is justified.

One gets an impression that by and large it is the discretion of the Lokayukta to decide the cases. But, he has to give a satisfactory explanation for the refusal of cases. It is necessary to understand what Lokayukta means by default, vague, non-proper and anonymous cases that it disposes by refusal.[30]

1. Default Cases: If there is any default of the complainant, the registering authority postpones the registration. He informs the complainant to rectify the error or omission within a specific time. If the complainant does not, the case is considered as disposed off. This disposal is only on the side of Lokayukta office and not of a complainant.

2. Vegue Cases: If there is no clear mention of the nature of allegation or if there is absence of the name, address or office of the concerned authority or if the grievance is vague the case is considered as disposed.

3. Anonymous/Psuedonymous/Cases: If there is absence of the name of the complainant or concerned public servant or is made by some other name the compliant is considered as disposed off. The receipt of anonymous and pseudonymous complaints indicates the fact that people do not have the courage to face the powerful and the influential persons like politicians and administrators.

4. **Non-proper Cases**: If the information in the application is not sufficient the case is considered as disposed off.

After going through the reasons of refusal of the cases under various reasons, it is necessary to analyze the statistical working of the Lokayukta. Following table presents percentage of the cases refused showing several causes:

Table 3.7

Table showing the Percentage of Cases Disposed as Refused under Various Reasons

Year	*Diposed Comp-laints*	*Default of Comp-laints*	*Vague Comp-laints*	*Anony-mous Pseudon-ymous Complaints*	*No Proper Complaints*	*Total*	*Per cent*
1972-73	594	43	78	134	—	255	42.93
1974	744	119	125	121	4	369	49.60
1975	776	—	243	143	4	390	50.26
1976	1087	—	354	145	55	554	50.97
1977	915	87	195	109	_	391	42.73
1978	1132	133	275	81	_	489	43.20
1979	1302	120	188	138	28	474	36.41
1980	2827				_	0	0.00
1981	1916	83	32	108	343	566	29.54
1982	1691	77	18	117	214	426	25.19
1983	2506	156	28	179	313	676	26.98
1984	3966	156	43	563	472	1234	31.11
1985	3775	162	36	220	628	1046	27.71
1986	7530	455	45	124	479	1103	14.65
1987	6652	470	3	27	62	562	8.45
1988	6460	—	28	46	93	167	2.59
Total	43873					8702	19.83

Source: The Annual Consolidated Reports, The Lokayukta & Upa-Lokayukta.

This table shows that Lokayukta refused nearly 45 to 50% cases within 7 years of its inception, in 1972, it disposed 42.93% cases refusing under all above mentioned reasons. During 1981 to 1984, the percentage of disposal is between 25 to 30%. It means, the ratio of refusal was decreased in this period. From 1986, it decreased a lot- in 1985, 27.71% cases were refused whereas in 1986, 14.65% cases were refused. In 1987, it was only 2.59%-in this year, maximum cases were disposed and not were refused. After 1989, the Lokayukta office had not given the break-up of refused cases under various reasons. Hence, it was not possible to study and criticize those years. The picture presented in the reports of disposal during 1972 to 1988 makes clear that Lokayukta disposes the cases, which actually is refusal under several reasons. Though there are a lot of limitations to Lokayukta's jurisdiction, he tries to dispose off the cases in favor of a common man.

The purpose of this study is to know the absolute utility of the Lokayukta office. It is necessary to see the number of grievances redressed and satisfied the common people. In order to arrive at the actual redressal of the grievances, the total number of cases rejected either due to non-jurisdiction or other reasons has been deducted from the total number of complaints received by the office of the Lokayukta. The yearwise solved cases and their percentage has been shown in the table given below:

Table 3.8

Table Showing the Percentage of Grievances Redressed

Year	*Disposed Cases*	*Grievance Redressed*	*Percentage of Redressal*
1972-73	594	18	3.03
1974	744	89	11.96
1975	776	107	13.78
1976	1087	138	12.14
1977	915	60	5.46
1978	1132	191	16.43

Year	*Disposed Cases*	*Grievance Redressed*	*Percentage of Redressal*
1979	1302	194	14.20
1980	2827	419	14.82
1981	1916	421	21.97
1982	1691	385	22.76
1983	2506	424	16.91
1984	3966	724	18.25
1985	3775	774	20.50
1986	7530	1389	18.44
1987	6652	132	1.98
1988	6460	918	14.21
1989	6562	1002	15.27
1990	6263	1057	16.87
1991	8436	1526	18.08
1992	8142	1250	15.35
1993	8942	1726	19.30
1994	9267	1942	20.95
1995	9486	2115	22.29
1996	11041	2019	18.28
1997	16534	4104	24.82
1998	12299	3442	27.98
1999	11531	2670	23.15
2000	11135	1929	17.03
2001	11323	1870	16.52

Source: The Annual Consolidated Reports, The Lokayukta and Upa-Lokayukta.

The table shows that the highest percentage of grievances comes to 28 (27.98)%. It means through out this period, Lokayukta could not come to the rescue of even 1/3 complainants for at least 4 years. The number of cases decided is less than 10%. From 1979 onwards up to 1986, the

Lokayukta kept its utility from 14% to 24%. In 1987, it was only 1.98%. This number is very remarkable during the last 30 years of the Lokayukta institution. The number of redressal never decreased as it was in 1987. After that again the percentage is in increasing order. After completing its 25 years in 1997, it grew up to 25%. This raises very important question about the utility and very existence of office of the Lokayukta. Again, this also leads to the question as to who should be blame – the sorry state to affairs Is it law ? (The Lokayukta and Upa-Lokayukta Act, 1971) The complainants? (their lack of education and awareness), or the incumbents? (Lokayukta, Upa-Lokayukta and functionaries). The only hopeful thing that can be observed is there has been increasing number of cases disposed after the format period (5 to 7 years) of the office of Lokayukta.

Besides, due to its limited jurisdiction, Lokayukta cannot work and investigate the cases lodged with it. The second reason is that the legislature and executives do not show interest in Lokayukta's functioning.

One more aspect of disposal of the cases is to recommend under section 12 of the act. This section is for submitting the special reports. Lokayukta under this section can report to the concerned authority.

These sections are as below:

(1) Section 12 (1)— If, after investigation of any action in respect of which a complaint involving a grievance has been made, the Lokayukta think it has resulted in injustice or undue hardship to the complainant or any other person, by writing to the public servant and concerned competent authority he shall report them.[31]

Under this section, if Lokayukta think that the concerned authority insult or injustify the complainant, Lokayukta by reporting to the concerned and public servant can warn them.

(2) Section 12 (3)— If, after investigation of any action in respect of which a complaint involving an allegation has been made, the Lokayukta is satisfied with that such an allegation can be substantiated either wholly or partly, he shall by report

in writing communicate his findings and recommendations along with the relevant documents, materials and other evidence to the competent authority.[32]

(3) Section 12 (5)—if, the Lokayukta is satisfied with the action taken or proposed to be taken on his recommendations or findings referred to in sub-section (1) and (3), he shall close the case under information to the complainant, the public servant and the competent authority concerned, but where he is not so satisfied and if he considers that the case so deserves it so, he may make a special report upon the case to the Governor and also inform the complainant concerned.[33]

Lokayukta can make a special report to the competent authority and if he does not get any response, he can report it to the Governor.

Table-3.9 shows the percentage of recommendations made to the Governor under section 12 (1), (3) and (5).

Table 3.9

Table Showing the Percentage of Disposed Cases under Section 12(1), 12(3) and 12(5) from 1972 to 2001

Year	*Disposed Cases*	*Sec 12(1)*	*Sec 12(3)*	*Sec 12(5)*	*Total*	*%*
1972-73	594	0	0	0	0	0
1974	744	0	7	0	7	0.94
1975	776	0	7	0	7	0.90
1976	1087	0	7	0	7	0.64
1977	915	0	2	0	2	0.21
1978	1132	0	6	0	6	0.53
1979	1302	0	3	0	3	0.23
1980	2827	4	1	0	5	0.17
1981	1916	1	1	0	2	0.10
1982	1691	2	0	0	2	0.11
1983	2506	9	8	0	17	0.67
1984	3966	4	0	0	4	0.10

Year	*Disposed Cases*	*Sec 12(1)*	*Sec 12(3)*	*Sec 12(5)*	*Total*	*%*
1985	3775	3	1	0	4	0.10
1986	7530	2	1	0	3	0.03
1987	6652	0	14	0	14	0.21
1988	6460	2	9	1	12	0.18
1989	6562	6	3	0	9	0.13
1990	6263	77	2	0	79	1.26
1991	8436	16	0	4	20	0.23
1992	8142	6	0	1	7	0.08
1993	8942	64	0	10	74	0.82
1994	9267	32	5	6	43	0.46
1995	9486	3	3	5	11	0.11
1996	11041	9	0	0	9	0.08
1997	16534	39	2	3	44	0.26
1998	12299	28	0	3	31	0.25
1999	11531	94	1	17	112	0.97
2000	11137	139	0	69	208	1.87
2001	11323	126	3	79	208	1.84
2002	11631	122	2	63	187	1.61
2003	10179	54	2	15	71	0.7

Source: The Annual Consolidated Reports, The Lokayukta and Upa-Lokayukta.

The table shows the percentage of reports made to the Governor by Lokayukta. In the first 5 years, the percentage was increasing but was decreasing from 1975 to 1980. In 1983, it was 0. 67 and decreased in 1987. In 1990 it was 1.96%. Since 1999, it increased. The number of reporting to the Governor by the Lokayukta is nearly 1% during the last few years. The question arises whether the Governor has taken any action on Lokayukta's report? The answers received by the complainants through the questionnaires indicate that the

Governor does not respond to the reports by and large. The cases are not disposed for a long period after reporting to the Governor. (This issue is discussed in the fourth chapter in detail.) It signifies that the Executives neither interfere nor respond.

The Legislator does not show any interest in Lokayukta's functioning.

Table 3.10

Table Showing Dates and Discussions Made on Lokayukta's Report in the Legislature

Year	*Date of Submission to Hon'ble Governor*	*Date of Presentation before Legilative Assembly / Council by Governor*	*Whether Discussed? If Yes When?*
1972-73	17.11.1973	16.12. 1974	No
1974	30.11.1974	09.03.1976	No
1975	19.03.1976	27.10.1977	No
1976	28.04.1977	26.12.1980	No
1977	24.10.1977	26.12.1980	No
1978	19.09.1979	24.04.1982	No
1979	04.02.1980	24.04.1980	No
1980	17.02.1981	26.04.1982	No
1981	29.01.1982	20.03.1986	No
1982	11.03.1983	24.03.1986	No
1983	12.03.1986	27.11.1986	No
1984	14.05.1985	18.11.1987	No
1985	25.07.1986	11.04.1989	No
1986	05.10.1987	18.12.1990	No
1987	20.09.1988	02.04.1993	No
1988	20.09.1989	02.04.1993	No
1989	22.01.1991	02.04.1993	No
1990	04.06.1992	27.04.1993	No

Year	*Date of Submission to Hon'ble Governor*	*Date of Presentation before Legilative Assembly / Council by Governor*	*Whether Discussed? If Yes When?*
1991	25.05.1993	12.07.1996	No
1992	27.01.1994	12.07.1996	No
1993	15.10.1994	10.04.1997	No
1994	31.07.1995	10.04.1997	No
1995	29.06.1996	21.07.1997	No
1996	05.07.1997	02.04.1999	No
1997	21.09.1998	22.04.1999	No
1998	26.02.1999	22.03.2000	No
1999	25.04.2000	24.07.2001	No
2000	16.05.2001	23.04.2002	No
2001	07.05.2002	NOT YET	No

Source: The Annual Consolidated Reports, The Lokayukta and Upa-Lokayukta.

The last column of the table answers 'No' to all. The reports by the Lokayukta are never discussed in the Legislative Council or Assembly. Before 2001 the reports were kept in the House but were not discussed, between 2002 to 2004 were not kept or discussed and from 2005 onwards Lokayukta office did not prepared and kept the reports. It indicates that there is no support to say that the Executive or Legislator is interested in Lokayukta institution. There is no interference but there is no support as well.

One more aspect of working of Lokayukta is whether he can deal in the ministerial cases? In the first chapter, there is a wide discussion on corruption in politics. Indian politics is deeply rooted in the corrupt practices. If one wants to control corruption, the process must start from the politicians to eradicate it. Lokayukta has very limited powers in this regard.[34] The second limitation is that the people are used to complain against a politician- particularly the ministers.

The number of ministerial cases lodged with the Lokayukta is very small. Table 3.11 shows the number.

Table 3.11

Table showing Total Number of Ministerial Cases Lodged to the Lokayukta from 1972 to 2001

Year	*Total of Lodged Cases*	*Cases Lodged Against Ministers*	*Percentage*
1972-73	903	29	3.21
1974	1073	11	1.03
1975	1311	2	0.15
1976	1804	5	0.28
1977	2150	19	0.88
1978	2549	9	0.35
1979	2969	3	0.10
1980	3746	0	0.00
1981	2588	3	0.12
1982	2540	4	0.16
1983	4002	5	0.12
1984	5926	Nil	Nil
1985	7381	7	0.09
1986	10319	3	0.03
1987	8891	2	0.02
1988	8520	4	0.05
1989	9027	4	0.04
1990	9518	2	0.02
1991	12015	7	0.06
1992	12288	0	0.00
1993	13184	0	0.00
1994	13855	0	0.00
1995	14617	0	0.00
1996	17888	5	0.03

Year	*Total of Lodged Cases*	*Cases Lodged Against Ministers*	*Percentage*
1997	21198	1	0.00
1998	17664	1	0.01
1999	15608	4	0.03
2000	14877	5	0.03
2001	16021	7	0.04
Total	254432	52	0.02

Source: The Annual Consolidated Reports, The Lokayukta and Upa-Lokayukta.

Totally, 254432 cases have been lodged to the Lokayukta till 2001. Only 52 cover the complaints involving Ministers, which is negligible. Again those received most of them were not dealt with finally. Because, ex-ministers are not under Lokayukta's purview. Lokayukta has to leave these cases without enquiry. This is one more limitation of Lokayukta's jurisdiction.

3.11 CONCLUSIONS

Due to lack of jurisdiction, ignorance by the Executive and Legislature, the utility of the institution has limitations. In this atmosphere, can Lokayukta work impartially and independently; can it prove useful to a common man? This is the inference of this part of study based on the reports of the Lokayukta and Upa-Lokayukta office. Whether it is substantiated by the empirical reality will be discussed in the next chapter, which deals with the report of fieldwork; i.e. surveys and interviews.

REFERENCES

1. Ghosh S. K.—Indian Panorama: Truimphs and Tragedies— 939
2. Maharashtra Debates-33, 6 Sept. to 9 Oct. 1971— Discussion on Lokayukta Bill No. XIII of 1971— 938
3. Informal Dicussion Made with A Pueon – Lokayukta Office
4. The Maharashtra Lokayukta and Upa-Lokayukta Act,1971— Section 5 (a)—03

5. The Maharashtra Lokayukta and Upa-Lokayukta Act,1971—Rules, 1973—16
6. The Maharashtra Lokayukta and Upa-Lokayukta Act,1971-Rules, 1973-17
7. The Maharashtra Lokayukta and Upa-Lokayukta Act,1971-Rules, 1973—14
8. The Maharashtra Lokayukta and Upa-Lokayukta Act,1971——Rules, 1973—14
9. Interview- Mr. Jayyaram—Ex- Upa- Lokayukta
10. The Maharashtra Lokayukta and Upa-Lokayukta Act, 1971— 1
11. The Maharashtra Lokayukta and Upa-Lokayukta Act, 1971—4
12. Interview—Mr. Tipnis—Ex- Lokayukta
13. Interview—Mr. Iyer— Ex-Upa-Lokayukta
14. The Annul Consolidated Report, The Lokayukta and Upa-Lokayukta, 1972—32
15. The Annul Consolidated Report, The Lokayukta and Upa-Lokayukta, 1972—72
16. The Annual Consolidated Report, The Lokayukta and Upa-Lokayukta, 1972—30
17. Informal Discussion With The Registrar, Lokayukta on 30 Dec. 2003
18. The Annul Consolidated Report, The Lokayukta and Upa-Lokayukta, 2000—14
19. Interview—Mr. Iyer— Ex-Upa-Lokayukta
20. The Lokayukta and Upa-Lokayukta Act, 1971— Section 8(1) (b)- 8
21. The Lokayukta and Upa-Lokayukta Act, 1971 — Section 1(b)—3
22. The Annul Consolidated Report, The Lokayukta and Upa-Lokayukta, 1974 —22
23. *Ibid.*
24. The Lokayukta and Upa-Lokayukta Act, 1971—10
25. The Lokayukta and Upa-Lokayukta Act, 1971 Third Shedule—12
26. The Lokayukta and Upa-Lokayukta Act, 1971 Section 8(1) (b)—5
27. The Lokayukta and Upa-Lokayukta Act, 1971 Section 8(3)—5
28. The Lokayukta and Upa-Lokayukta Act, 1971 Section 8(5)—5

29. The Lokayukta And Upa-Lokayukta Act, 1971 Section 9(1) (a), (b)—5
30. Interview—Mr. Tipnis—Ex- Lokayukta December 29, 2003
31. The Lokayukta and Upa-Lokayukta Act, 1971 Section 12(1)—7
32. The Lokayukta and Upa-Lokayukta Act, 1971 Section 12(3)—7
33. The Lokayukta and Upa-Lokayukta Act, 1971 Section 12(5)—8
34. Interview—Mr. Tipnis—Ex- Lokayukta December 29, 2003

4

Report of Field Work

4.1 INTRODUCTION

The very purpose of introducing Ombudsman machinery is to curb corruption and maladministration. With this intension, the Government of Maharashtra passed 'The Maharashtra Lokayukta and Upa-Lokayukta Act, 1971'. In the preceding chapters, functioning of Lokayukta in Maharashtra was discussed with the help of the Act as well as the Annual Consolidated Reports submitted to the Maharashtra Legislature by the Lokayukta and Upa-Lokayukta. The functions, powers and role of the Lokayukta have been discussed there along with the limitations and drawbacks of the Lokayukta machinery. However, the Act is silent about several things, which are important in practice such as, disposal of cases, balance cases, vague or improper complaints, etc. The Annual Consolidated Reports highlight its working with statistics. Even though this statistics and information in the reports provide working of Lokayukta in Maharashtra, that doesn't serve the whole purpose of understanding the role played by him especially, his achievements to control corruption and maladministration. There are many things that do not find place in the reports. Therefore, it is necessary to read between the lines. Hence, an attempt was made to throw light on empirical reality in this study. And for this purpose, it is necessary to take into account the components that are directly concerned with the Lokayukta, namely:

(a) The complainants;

(b) The concerned departments;

(c) The functionaries in the Lokayukta office;

d) The persons those adorned the chair of Lokayukta and Upa-Lokayukta

In order to obtain the reactions of these components, with a view to understand and analyze the empirical reality, a survey method was adopted in this study. Accordingly, there were 2 questionnaires prepared for this purpose one each for—the complainants, the departmental authorities where the officials against whom these complaints were made.

Besides these two questionnaires, interviews were scheduled for the Lokayukta, Upa-Lokayukta and the functionaries in the Lokayukta office. Each structured questionnaire consisted of open-ended and close-ended questions. The questionnaires were administered through mail and personal contacts as and when feasible.

This chapter deals with the survey based on the questionnaires and interview schedules conducted. Thus, it is a report of fieldwork done. There are three sections of this report. The first section provides analysis of the responses of the complainants. In the second section, the responses of concerned authority as well as the functionaries in the Lokayukta office are discussed. The third section deals with the interviews of the present and Ex-Lokayukta and Upa-Lokayukta. Finally, a few conclusions are drawn from the data collected.

SECTION 1

ANALYSIS OF QUESTIONNAIRE TO THE COMPLAINANTS

4.1.1 Universe

According to the objectives and hypotheses of this study, a questionnaire for the complainants was prepared containing 19 questions. The foremost important difficulty was how to select the respondent complainants that is locating universe of survey. In order to search it, efforts were made to procure the comprehensive lists of complainants with their addresses for preceding 3 years from the office of the Lokayukta, Mumbai, with an intension to work out a random sample from the list. However, in spite of constant follow up in this regard, the officialdom could not be moved. The office of Lokayukta on the pretext of secrecy provision did not provide the information on the names and addresses of the complainants. To divulge such information, the Lokayukta office has expressed its inability to maintain secrecy as per section 10 (2) of the Lokayukta Act.

It says,

"Every investigation shall be conducted in private and in particular, the identity of the complainant and of the public servant affected by the investigation shall not be disclosed to the public or the press whether before, during or after the investigation."[1]

We tried to convince the functionaries as well as the Lokayukta to make available names and addresses strictly for academic, i.e. research purpose. They were also assured to keep the information in confidence and will be used only for research. However, our efforts were gone vain. The New Information Act, 2002 (which is replaced by Right to Information Act, 2005 of Government of India) has proved of no use in this regard.

Without names and addresses, it was not possible to reach to the complainants. It was not possible to work out a random sample for the universe. Therefore, the hope for any random sampling had to be given up. As a result, the only alternative left with us was to choose complainants, i.e., their names and addresses from the annual reports of the Lokayuktas. Fortunately, for our use the reports carry nearly 500 letters of thanks and some references of the cases with the names and addresses of the complainants. We took these names and addresses from the reports for the survey, which were spreaded over 8 years. It was really a tough exercise to procure names and addresses of the complainants from the reports. Because, there were a number of difficulties, such as:

1. The addresses were incomplete;
2. A year wise and department wise comprehensive list of the addresses was not provided in the reports.

3. We were not sure whether the complainant concerned was still residing on the address or not.
4. Out of 500 entries, only 108 addresses were complete and useful for us.

Thus, after the scrutiny 108 names were valid for our survey. This was also a sizable number considering the restrains and the odds that were faced to prepare a sample for investigation.

4.1.2 The Structure of the Questionnaire for the Complainants

The questionnaire for the complainants was prepared according to the hypotheses as given in the first chapter. Due consideration was also given on the objectives of this study laid down while framing the questions. The questionnaire has 2 sections. The first section is on the personal information of the respondents such as, name, occupation, and sex. It aimed at understanding as to which the Lokayukta is a helping hand. The second section focuses on the analyses of hypotheses of the study. It consists of 19 questions. These questions relate to:

1. Perception of the complainants on the institution of Lokayukta.
2. Procedural aspects of the office of Lokayukta such as affidavit, place of registration, documents attached with the complaints, etc.
3. The frequency of contacts with the Lokayukta including a place of investigation and details such as, physical presence at the time of the investigation of the complainant as well as concerned authority.
4. The treatment and response from the Lokayukta and Upa-Lokayukta in terms of disposal of complaint by primary investigation, detail investigation and investigation by other agencies such as CBI, CVC, etc.
5. The time incurred for the disposal of complaint which also includes the response and emphasis given by Lokayukta to complainant visa-vis opposite party.

6. Partiality, impartiality and favoritism on the part of Lokayukta office through

   [a] opinion about institution of Lokayukta;

   [b] perception of the complaints whether decision to approach Lokayukta was proper or not;

7. Relationship between Lokayukta and the departmental authorities including suggestions if any about working of Lokayukta.

During the personal inter-actions with some of the complainants at the Lokayukta office or in the departmental office, we asked them about the investigation system adopted by the Lokayukta and need for modification and improvement in it. Their responses are added to the given responses of the questionnaires. Thus, the questionnaire comprising 19 questions for the complainants was structured. (See, appendix No. I.)

The questionnaire was dispatched to 101 complainants by post. Out of these 101, we could get returned 27 questionnaires by post duly filled in by post from the concerned respondents. So far of the remaining respondents are concern a substantial number of them did not give any response. Thus, we could not get the questionnaire returned complete or incomplete from as many as 61 complainants. Besides, 10 were returned as address was not available and 3 as addressee dead. This is the break-up of 101 (27+61+10+03) respondents to whom the questionnaires were sent by post. Out of these 108 complainants, at the time of visits to the Lokayukta office, we could contact and serve questionnaires to 6 complainants. The remaining 7 complainants were contacted in person in the city Aurangabad. (See, appendix No. II)

Thus, we tried to contact totally 114 complainants.

These 114 complainants whom we tried to contact for our survey had lodged their complaints to different government departments and local government agencies in Maharashtra. Hence, we could not select the complainants as well as the government departments as per our plan. As we planned for this survey, we were to select the respondents on the basis of first 5 departments with the highest number of complaints in ascending order or first 5 departments which are generally described as corruption prone departments such as, police, revenue, PWD, etc. On the basis of these criteria, the efforts were made to obtain information including names and addresses of the complainants from the office of Lokayukta. However, it was a sorry state of affairs that we could not get the required information as per proposed survey design. As a result, we were forced to conduct survey of the complainants as per the addresses given in the reports of the Lokayukta.

Thus, out of 114 complainants, to whom the questionnaires were provided, 40 complainants had filled in their questionnaires. (27 by mail, 6 at Lokayukta office, 7 at city Aurangabad) The department-wise break-up of these 40 complainants is given below:

Table 4.1

Department wise break-up of the complainants

No.	*Name of department*	*No. of complaints*
1.	Revenue	11
2.	Irrigation	03
3.	PWD	03
4.	Home	01
5.	Tribal Development	01
6.	Education	06
7.	Health	01
8.	General Administration Department	01
9.	Co-operation	02
10.	Director of printing, Stationary and publications	01
11.	Director of Sports	01
12.	Local Self Government Agencies	09
	Total	40

ANALYSIS OF RESPONSES

We served the questionnaire to 114 complainants. Out of 114, 53 questionnaires came back. 61 complainants didn't respond. Out of 53 that came back, 40 sent the fulfilled questionnaire where as 13 were unable due to death or changes in the addresses.

Table 4.2

Table Showing the Complainants whom the Questionnaires were served for Survey

Returned Responses		*Responses Not Returned*	*Total*
Returned With Fulfilled Questionnaire	Returned With Out Questionnaire		
40	13		
53		61	114

Thus, analysis of 40 responses is made in this study.

It was not possible in given situation to select proportional male and female respondents proportionately. Even the reports of the Lokayukta also do not carry the break-up of complainants into male and female. However, in the first section of the questionnaire, we asked their name, occupation and sex. On that basis, the break-up of 40 respondents in our sample as male or female is given here:

Table 4.3

Table Showing the Percentage of Male and Female Respondents

	Male	*Female*	*Total*
Complainants	34	06	40
Percentage	85%	15%	

Graph-I

Male & Female Responce

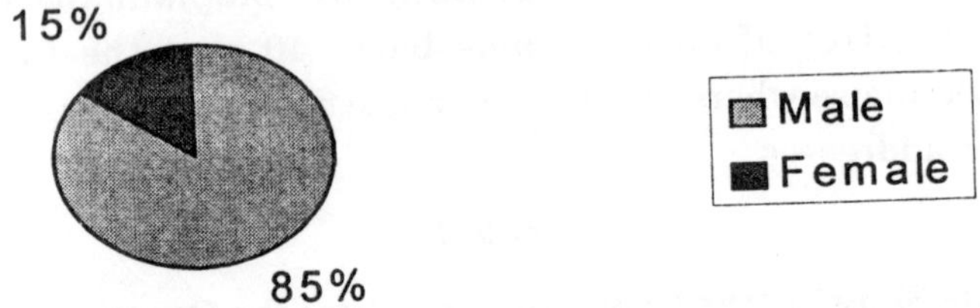

Totally, 15% of female lodged the complaints whereas the male complainants were 85%. To our surprise, the retired persons come to the Lokayukta in more than in-service personnel as shown in the Table-4.4.

Table 4.4

Table showing the Percentage of Persons go to Lokayukta after and before Retirement

	After Retirement	*Before Retirement*	*Other than Services*	*Total*
Complainants	18	14	08	40
Percentage	45 %	35 %	20 %	

Graph II

Persons Go to Lokayukta After and Before Retirement

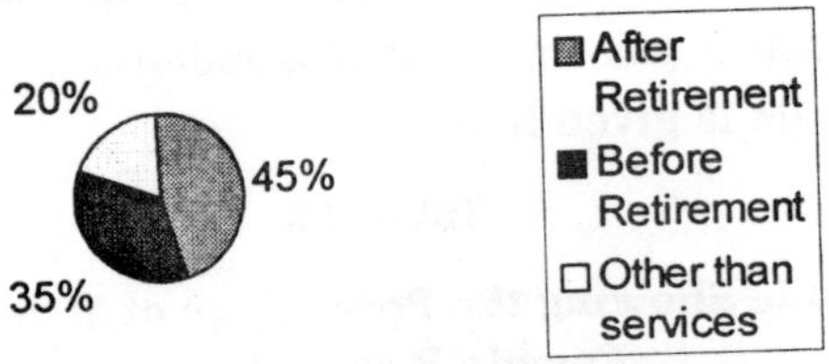

45 % complainants lodged the cases after retirement. It indicates two things- first, they have a fear in their mind about their seniors or leading uncertainty of the job and second, the large number of them rush to Lokayukta for retirement benefits.

As it is said earlier, the main purpose of Lokayukta is to curb corruption or control maladministration, it is expected that the cases of corruption and maladministration should constitute the majority. But it is not the fact. It is observed through the reports that a very small number of cases pertain to corruption. The cases which are included in this survey comprise of subjects like bribery or giving or taking black money fall under 'allegation' where as, favoritism, nepotism or misuse of power and post are covered under 'grievances' as per the section 2 (b) and (d) of the Act. In the second section of the questionnaire, we asked the complainants what were their complaints. We wanted to know what number of cases of allegation and grievance were lodged to the Lokayukta. This was an open-ended question. Answers given to the question show that only 2 cases of allegation and 38 of grievances were lodged out of 40. Table 4.5 shows the break-up of the cases of allegation and grievances:

Table 4.5

Table Showing Percentage of Allegations and Grievances

	Cases of Allegation	*Cases of Grievance*	*Total*
Complainants	02	38	40
Percentage	05%	95%	

Graph III

Allegation and Grievances

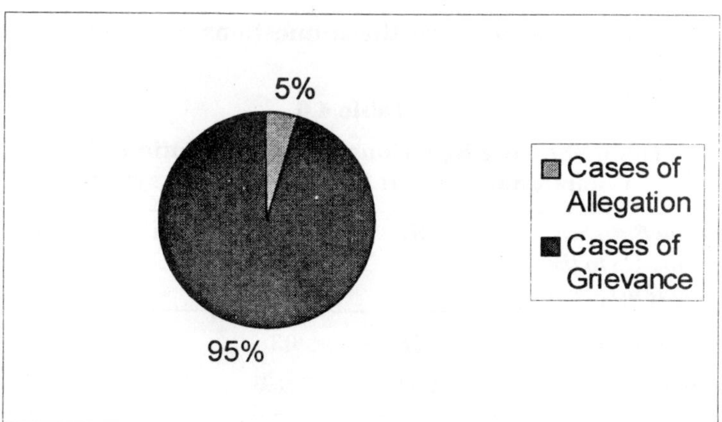

Thus, there are only 5% of cases about corruption. Mr. Mohni, the Ex-Upa-Lokayukta, during his interview told that per year only 3% of cases of corruption are filed with Lokaykuta. It is surprising to note that the break-up of the complaints in the survey is also supporting his statement. One of the hypotheses of the study is,

> "More the effective Lokayukta, greater is the possibility of reaching at the deep roots of corruption with a view to overcome the problem of corruption."

However, our findings show that even though, Lokayukta is effective in dealing with large number of other cases, the possibility of reaching at the deep roots of corruption through Lokayukta is remote. By and large, the Lokayukta is required to handle very few cases of corruption.

It can be concluded that institution of Lokayukta is effective so far as the sundry issues by way of grievances. However, to go to this hypothesis and perception about the Lokayukta, we tried to understand the perception of complainants about Lokayukta. Hence, we asked them the following questions.

1. Are you satisfied that you go to the Lokayukta? Why?
2. What is your opinion about Lokayukta institution?

The answers given to these questions are shown in the Table 4.6—

Table 4.6

Table Showing Reactions on the Perception of the Complainants about Approaching Lokayukta

Are You Satisfied that You Go to the Lokayukta?	*Yes*	*No*	*Nil*	*Total*
Complainants	36	03	01	40
Percentage	90 %	7.5 %	2.5 %	

The main purpose of the study was to know whether the institute satisfies the complainants or not. The table shows that

Graph IV

Perception of Complaints about Lokyukta

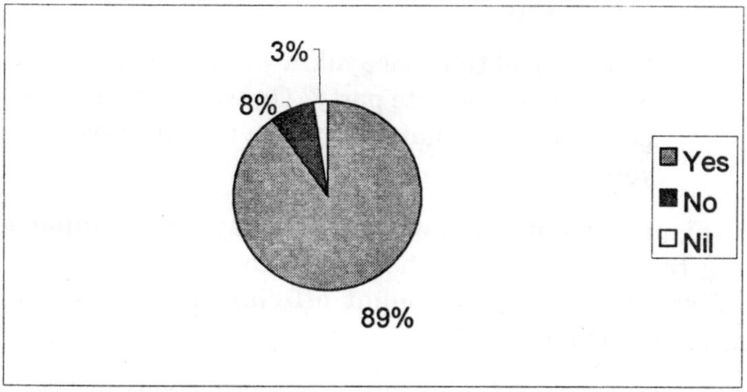

90% complainants answered positively to this question, 7.5% answered negatively and 2.5% kept mum. It means, the complainants that come to the Lokayukta are satisfied and found solace in approaching to Lokayukta. Hence, it can be inferred that so far ventilation of corruption, Lokayukta is not very effective; but to redress the grievances, it tries to prove effective. However, this is a very general perception about the Lokayukta, which is obviously expressed to a question of their satisfaction.

In order to substantiate their response in this regard, the respondents were asked to give reasons as to why they approached Lokayukta in an open-ended question. The answers given by the respondents to this question were as below:

1. Going to Lokayukta is not costly.
2. The access to Lokayukta machinery is easy especially as compared to the courts.
3. Disposal of cases is done in a reasonable time; i.e. much delay is not incurred.
4. They can get justice on a single post-card also. That is the procedural requirements are not complicated.

Our second hypothesis was about Lokayukta's impartiality. In order to know the equality of treatment as well as fairness and impartiality, we asked two questions to the respondents:

1. At the time of inquiry, did you feel that Lokayukta is partial with you?
2. Did you feel that Lokayukta was giving more weightage to your opposite party? Or, whether your opposite party thought that Lokayukta is more favourable to you?

It is important to know how far Lokayukta is impartial in giving treatment to both the parties in front of him, i.e. the complainant, the government official against whom the complaint was registered.

The responses of these questions are given in the Table 4.7 & 4.8.

Table 4.7

Table showing whether Lokayukta was Partial

At the Time of Inquiry, Did You Feel that Lokayukta is Partial With You?	*Yes*	*No*	*Nil*	*Total*
Complainants	03	31	06	40
Percentage	7.5 %	77.5 %	15 %	—

Graph V

Whether Lokayukta was Partial

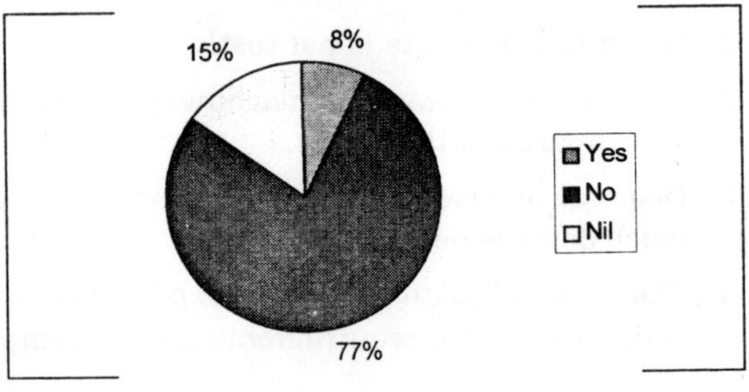

Table 4.8

Table Showing whether Lokayukta was Favorable to Opposite Party

Did you feel that Lokayukta was giving more waitage to your opposite party?	*Yes*	*No*	*Don't Know*	*Nil*	*Total*
Complainants	06	27	02	05	40
Percentage	15 %	67.5 %	5 %	12.5 %	

Graph VI

Whether Lokayukta was Favorable to Opposite Party

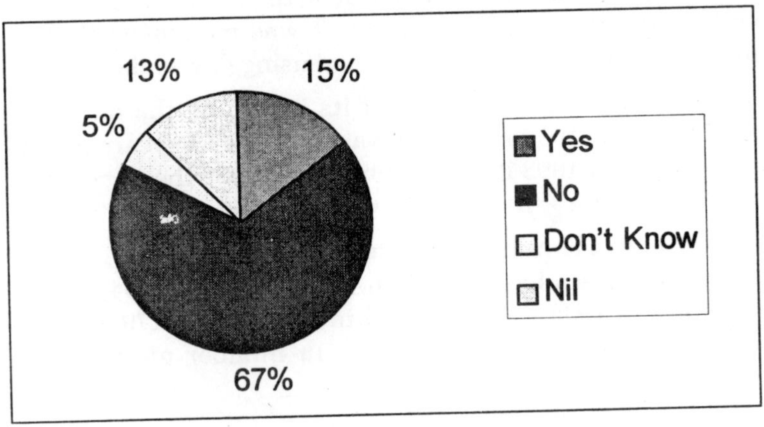

As per table- 4.8, 77.5 % complainants didn't feel that Lokayukta was partial. One of the respondents noted that Lokayukta gives protection to the wrong policies of the government. 67.5 % feel that Lokayukta didn't give any special importance to the opposite party; i.e. government. But, 7.5 % feel that it was partial and 15% feel that it gives more importance to the opposite party. We tried to know why some people think so. We also talked to them on telephone. By this conversation, we observed that Lokayukta forwarded a special report to the Governor stating that the concerned department did not give attention in many cases. In those cases the complainants felt that the Lokayukta was not favorable to them. So, overall conclusion is that the Lokayukta is neither favorable to government nor partial in its treatment.

The third hypothesis was the success of Lokayukta depends upon the availability of adequate investigating officers and response from the government in this regard. The matter of separate investigating officer is mainly related to the working of the office of Lokayukta and also provisions of the Act and not to the complainants. Therefore, this hypothesis can be tested by the interviews of the Lokayukta. Therefore, it is discussed later.

Our forth hypothesis is "the greater number of complaints lodged to the Lokayukta, fuller will be the utility of the office"—while going through the reports, it was mentioned that the number of complaints has been increasing day by day.

In 1972, in the first year of its inception, the number of cases lodged to the Lokayukta was 903. After 10 years in 1982, it was 2540; in 1992 it was 12288 and in 2002 the number was 15745.

Not only the number has increased but also the number of disposed cases has also risen. In 1972 it was 594, in 1982 was 1691' in 1992 was 8142 and in 2002 was 10179. Table IX shows this comparative increase in number after each 10 years:

Table 4.9

Table Showing the Comparative Increase in the Cases after 10 Years

Year	*No. of lodged cases*	*No. of disposed cases*	*No. of balanced cases*
1972	903	594	309
1982	2540	1691	849
1992	12288	8142	4146
2002	15745	10179	3555
Total	31476	20606	8859

During the period of last 30 years, totally 31,476 cases were lodged and 10,179 cases were disposed by the Lokayukta. It means the number is in a growing order. That proves its utility in the eyes of the Government and Lokayukta office and the complainants. The usefulness of the office to them can be understood in terms of how many complainants approach the Lokayukta and get themselves registered? Who advised them to go the Lokayukta? How long did their cases took to get dispose off? What time and money are required to spend to get justice from Lokayukta? How many times they were required to visit the Lokayukta office?

Thus, utility of Lokayukta to the complainants depend on these aspects. We asked the complainants a few questions as given below:

1. From where did you get information about Lokayukta?
2. Where was inquiry of your complaint conducted?
3. Was the hearing made in your presence?
4. How many times you visited the Mumbai office?
5. How long your case took to be disposed?
6. After which stage of inquiry, your case was disposed?

And the answers were:

Table 4.10

Table Showing The Sources of Complainants on Information about Lokayukta Institution

From where did you get information of Lokayukta office?	*Friends / Relatives*	*Familiar as Govt. Servant*	*Newspaper / Media*	*Unable to reply*	*Total*
Complainants	14	21	05	—	40
Percentage	35 %	52.5 %	12.5 %	—	

Graph VII

Source of complainants of information of Lokyukta

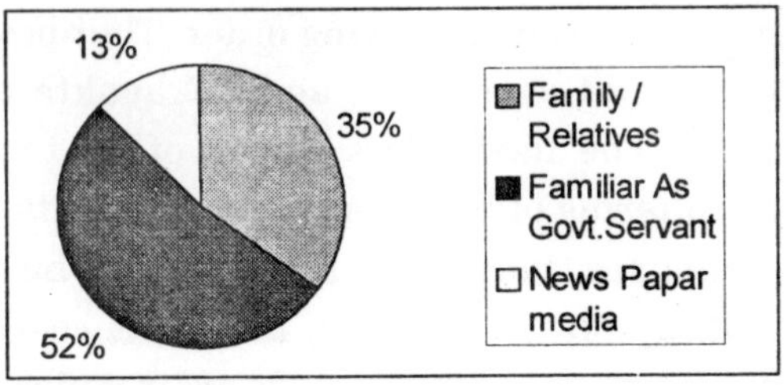

The table shows not only utility but also familiarity and popularity of the institute. 35 % complainants got information through their friends, relatives, colleagues, but 52.5 % knew themselves. It means, 52.5 % as Government Servant, knew on their own.

The institution of Lokayukta is of greater use to the people if they are able to approach it at divisional and district level and not always compelled to go to Mumbai office, of the head-quarter of Lokayukta. Therefore, we asked the complainants the question, where the case was conducted.

Table 4.11

Table Showing the Place of Case Inquiry

Where Was Case Inquiry Made?	*In the Office of Mumbai*	*At District Level*	*Total*
Complainants	24	16	40
Percentage	60%	40%	

Graph VIII

The Place of Case Inquiry

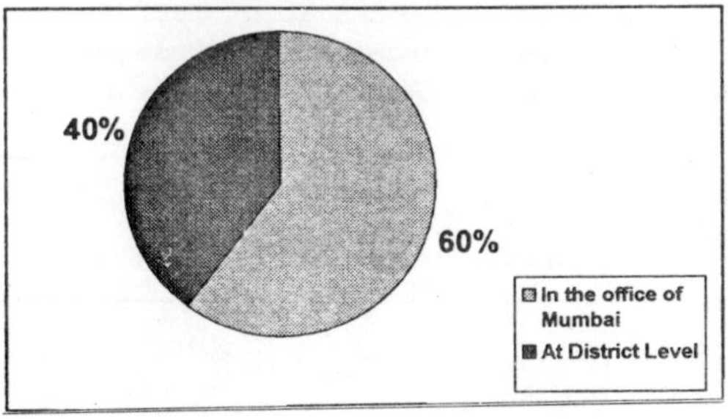

It shows that in 40% cases the inquiry was conducted at the district or divisional level, which was quite useful to the complainants. Time and money is not consumed or wasted due to this method of inquiry.

The third indicator of utility we observed through the reports is that a complainant doesn't require to attend a hearing in person compulsorily. It can be made in their absence also. We asked them whether the complainants were present to the hearing or not and the response to this question is stated in the Table 4.12.

Table 4.12

Table Showing the Presense of Complainant at Hearing

Was the hearing made in your presence?	*Yes*	*No*	*Can't answer*	*Total*
Complainants	15	22	03	40
Percentage	37. 5 %	55 %	7.5 %	

Graph IX

The Presense of Complainant at Hearing

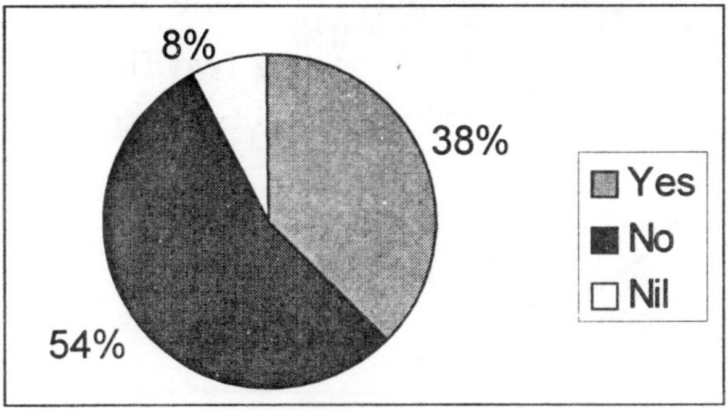

55% told that they were not present for the hearing. It means, the office doesn't require the presence of complainants for hearing. It is understood that in all cases it is not possible to conduct inquiry in the absence of the complainants. The question was how many times and how frequent they visited the Lokayukta office. In order to know it, we asked them a question how many times the complainants had visited the Lokayukta office and the response to this question are as following:

Table 4.13

Table Showing the Frequency of Visits to the Mumbai Office by the Complainants

How many times you visited to the Mumbai office?	*Once*	*Two Times*	*Several Times*	*Never*	*Nil*	*Total*
Complainants	02	05	03	25	05	40
Percentage	5%	12.5%	7.5%	62.5%	12.5%	100%

Graph X

The Frequency of Visits to the Mumbai Office by the Complainants

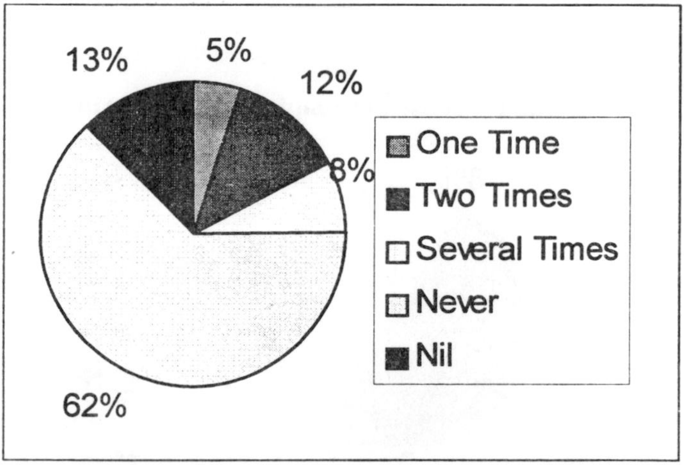

62.5% complainants had never seen the office of the Lokayukta. They lodged their complaints by correspondence. It means, the Lokayukta doesn't always need the people to go or to follow their cases in person. The office is prompt in this respect. Usually, as soon as the complaint is lodged, the people get response within 10 to 15 days.[2] Out of 40 people, only 3 complainants visited the office for a several times—but, they answered that they visited by their own, the office didn't required them to report.

The complainants didn't need to go to the office time and again, is one of the strong points. Another is their cases are disposed from the point of complainants without frequent visits within a reasonable time period. The answers to the question how much time their case took to dispose is as below:

Table 4.14

Table showing how Much Time the Cases took to be Disposed

How long time your case took to be disposed?	*Less than 6 Months*	*6 Months to 1 Yr.*	*1 Yr. to 2 Yr.*	*More than 2 Yrs.*	*Pending*	*Nil*	*Total*
Complainants	14	11	07	05	03	01	40
Percentage	35 %	27.5 %	17.5 %	12.5 %	7.5 %	2.5 %	100%

Graph XI

How Much Time the Cases Took to be Disposed

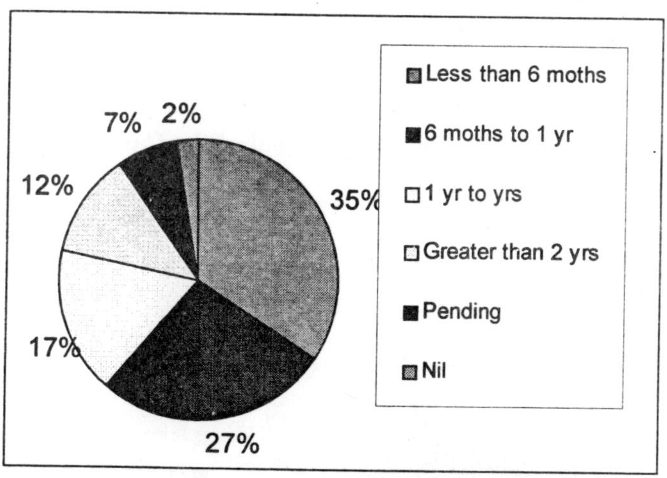

35% complainants got justice within a period of 6 months. Some of cases were disposed i.e. 27.5% in a period of 6 months to 1 year to dispose. Only 5 respondents i.e. 12.5% were required to wait for 2 years to get their cases settled.

Remaining only 7.5 % complainants answered that their cases were pending. In these pending cases, the Lokayukta reminded two or three times to the Governor, but no action was taken. It means, this part of pendency is due to the executive and not from the side of Lokayukta office. It also shows Lokayukta's helplessness after making a special report to the Governor. We asked Ex-Lokayuktas about this obstacle from the side of executive. (This point is discussed later.)

In order to probe further as to what stage the complainants could get their cases disposed we put them following question and the responses were as following:

After which stage of inquiry, your case was disposed?

The replies are noted below:

Table 4.15

Table showing the speedy Disposal of the Cases

After which stage of inquiry, your case was disposed?	*Primary Enquiry*	*Secondary Investigation*	*Detail Investigation*	*Don't Know*	*Total*
Complaimants	32	03	04	01	40
Percent	80 %	7. 5 %	10 %	2.5 %	100%

Graph XII

The Speedy Disposal of the Cases

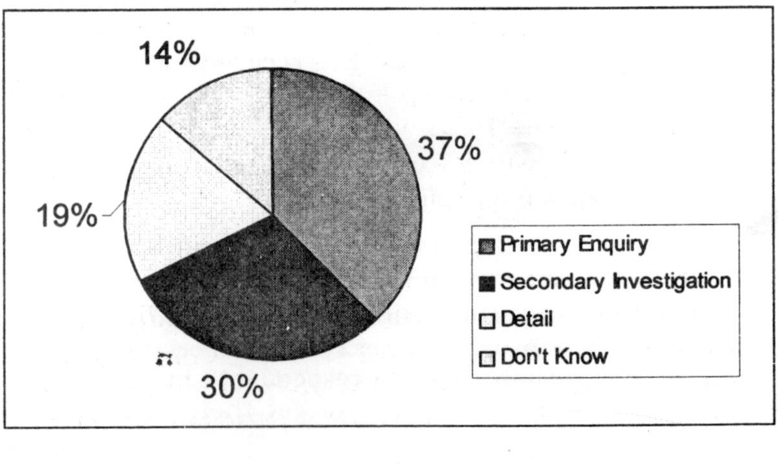

In a very large number, i.e. 80 % cases are disposed after a primary or nominal enquiry. It means, Lokayukta gives justice at primary stage as per as possible. In 7.5% cases, the complainants in which, the information by the concerned authority was not provided timely, and hence took the stage of secondary investigation. Only 10% cases needed in detail investigation, through the machineries such as CBI or CVC.

We can conclude by these responses that to the questions 1 to 6 stated above, the complainants are satisfied by and large. We asked the complainants the reason of their satisfaction and the reasons given by them are:

1. The cases are disposed without continuous record.
2. The complainant doesn't need to attend hearing. Many of the complainants had never seen the Lokayukta office and got justice through a single post card or single page application.
3. The complainant doesn't need advocate or mukhtyar to lodge a case. It doesn't need money. After complaining, the office make investigation through its own machinery and the complainant doesn't need to make any effort.
4. Finally, the people get justice speedily and without money.

These are the reasons that the Lokayukta effectively prove its utility and more and more people are lodging their complaints to the Lokayukta. This is one side of success of the Lokayukta. The Ex- Lokayuktas and Ex-Upa-Lokayuktas also supplemented this findings in their interview. The reports also add their voice that by these reasons, the Lokayukta is getting popularity among the common citizen.

But, some people are not satisfied towards the institute. Though, 80% said that they are satisfied, 7.5% are not satisfied and 2.5% avoided answering this question. We tried to go through this problem, that is why Lokayukta is not absolutely effective? Of course, every thing under the sky could not come to the Lokayukta. But, what are its exact limitations was our point of research. The maximum reports make an outcry that the government offices do not provide the document/ information on time. Hence, non-satisfaction of the people and pendency of the cases according to the reports is due to the fact that Government offices do not provide timely and adequate information to the Lokayukta office and also the government offices do not take action on the queries and special report by Lokayukta.

This is what Lokayukta reports say about the state of affairs on information and document. In order to understand the co-relation and effectiveness of Lokayukta and to supply adequate information and document by concerned departments, two questions were asked to the complainants—

1. In your case, did the concerned authority provide any necessary information/documents on time?
2. Was the concerned authority present at the time of hearing?

Answering the first question, the responses are as below:

Surprising to note that the findings of the responses of 40 complainants we surveyed do not confirm the assertion of the reports. Following table gives the break-up of the answers:

Table 4.16

Table Showing the Responses by the Government Offices to the Case Enquiry made by the Lokayukta

In your case, did the concerned authority provid any necessary information/documents on time?	*Yes*	*No*	*Don't Know*	*Nil*	*Total*
Complainants	23	04	08	05	40
Percentage	57.5%	10%	20%	12.5%	

Though, the reports of Lokayukta stated that the government offices do not provide documents on time, 57.5%

Graph XIII

The Responses by the Government Offices to the Case Enquiry made by the Lokayukta

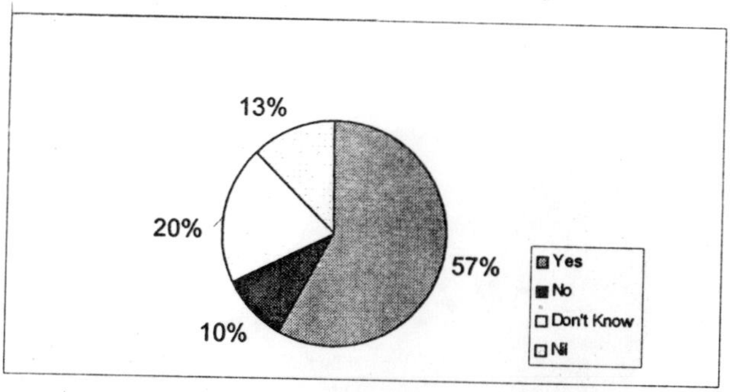

respondents told that in their cases, it was provided. Further, the Ex- Lokayuktas and Ex-Upa-Lokayuktas also supported this in their interviews to this researcher. We asked them about the discrepancy in the reports and the replies of the respondents in this regard. It is very clear that only 10% complainants faced difficulties in getting the documents from the concerned officer. They were not provided papers on time. As against this, 57.5% reported that they could get the documents regarding their complaints from the officers concerned on time. We asked the Lokayukta and Upa-Lokayukta about the discrepancies in the statements of reports and the responses of the complainants. But, our efforts had gone vain. The Lokayukta were sticking to the position taken in the reports. We asked the complainants whether the concerned were present at the time of inquiry and the answers was as follow:

Table 4.17
Table Showing the Presence of the Concerned Authority to the Hearing

Was the concerned authority present at the time of hearing?	*Yes*	*No*	*Nil*	*Total*
Complainants	22	15	03	40
Percentage	55%	37.5%	7.5%	100%

This shows that 55% of the concerned authorities were present at the time of hearing, whereas 37.5% were not present.

Graph XIV

The Presence of the Concerned Authority to the Hearing

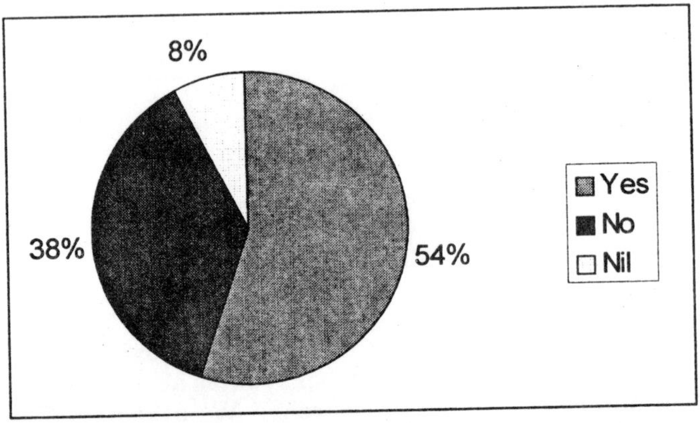

Finally, it was important to know the opinion of the complainants about Lokayukta. Hence, the question was asked—

What is your opinion about Lokayukta institution?

The question was open and the responses were as different as following:

1. Only due to Lokayukta I got justice.
2. Lokayukta is very good machinery.
3. Lokayukta helps people to solve their administrative difficulties.
4. It is a democratic device that controls administration.
5. It is the highest institute that gives justice within a lowest time.
6. Only Lokayukta can control unending corruption. The central level machinery must come up.
7. It is trustworthy, impartial, people oriented machinery.

8. It gives justice without spending our money and time.
9. It is a single helping hand of a common man.
10. It is a single non-corrupt government institute in the state.

These opinions about the institution of the Lokayukta are positive. Hence, it can be said that the institute could impress as many as 38 persons out of 40 were interviewed. However, 2 were not positive about the institute. The following are their impressions:

1. Lokayukta protects the government servants and wrong policies adopted by the government.
2. Lokayukta gives justice, but the result was not implemented and I am not justified yet.

Thus, Lokayukta's recommendations and thoughts aimed at wrong deeds are not fully and timely implemented.

We asked to the complainants to suggest some changes in the present Lokayukta system in Maharashtra. And there are a few suggestions of these respondents about the working of the Lokayukta:

1. Lokayukta's results must be binding on the government and non- government organizations.
2. There should be decentralization of Lokayukta's working. Lokayukta must work at district place.
3. Lokayukta must have more powers in implementing its recommendations.
4. Lokayukta institute must get more publicity.
5. There must be 2 Upa- Lokayuktas to help Lokayukta. One of them a retired District Judge and one Retired IAS so that it can dispose more and more cases.

These suggestions display that the people are not only familiar with the institute but also are conversant with its working. People give thought over the functioning of Lokayukta for the ventilation of their grievances.

Thus, the surveys of the complainants were made.

SECTION II

4.4 SURVEY OF THE CONCERNED AUTHORITIES

Besides the responses of the complainants, obtaining the opinion and reactions of the concerned officers involved in those particular cases were also our aim. For that purpose, we arranged the survey of the concerned authorities. But, unfortunately response to this survey was very dull.

At first we dispatched the questionnaires to all 114 government officers against whom 114 complaints were lodged. But not a single officer responded. Meanwhile, we got 40 responses by the complainants. So we decided to send the questionnaire once more to those 40 officers who were involved in 40 complaints so that we could cross-examine a minimum 40 of concerned persons. We served questionnaires to 9 officers personally. Out of those, besides, visiting 3 or 4 times, only 2 got filled. Remaining 7 from Amravati, Beed and Sholapur didn't send back the questionnaires. Remaining 31 questionnaires were provided by post; but we could not receive replies. We talked on telephone to some of the offices; but the response was not. It was not possible to go in person to all those 40 officers. Because, those were from all over Maharashtra. Second thing was we tried to contact the officers of Amravati, Sholapur and Beer in person; but because pessimistic response by those offices, we had to drop the idea. Consequently, we cancelled to go other cities also in person. Due to this difficulty, we couldn't get the opinion of the officers and conclude that government officers are lethargic and irresponsible in general about the functioning of Lokayukta. This apathy on the part of officers affects Lokayukta's working.

This questionnaire contained two sections. The first section was related to the particular cases, but could be filled by any predecessor of the office. Where as, the second section was expected to be fulfilled by that particular officer or the administrative wing of that department.

4.4 SURVEY OF THE FUNCTIONARIES IN THE LOKAYUKTA OFFICE

In addition to the complainants and government officers,

we interviewed the Lokayukta functionaries. It is because the procedure relating to deal with the cases was very much there in the Act. We wanted to know an actual procedure and working of Lokayukta in this regard.

Though, we didn't get chance of surveying the functionaries, we had informal discussions with them whenever we visited the Lokayukta office, Mumbai.

Through this informal discussion and on our observation of working of the staff, we could conclude that the functionaries in the Lokayukta office are efficient and helpful to the complainants or visitors of the Lokayukta. Efficient and co-operative staff in the Lokayukta office is one of the reasons of getting a speedy justice.

SECTION III

4.5 INTERVIEWS OF EX, SITTING LOKAYUKTAS AND UPA-LOKAYUKTAS

As perception of the complainants is important, so is the perception of the Ex- Lokayuktas and Ex-Upa-Lokayuktas because those are the actual functionaries at the helm of delivery system. They provide services to the people on their grievances. Therefore, we made frequent visits to Lokayukta office and interviewed the Ex- Lokayuktas and Ex-Upa-Lokayuktas. There are as many as 7 persons turn by turn those who adorned the chair of the Lokayukta. At the time of survey, three of them, Mr. Shimpi, Mr. Setalwad, Mr. Kotwal were not alive. Mr. Deshpande and Mr. Kamat were not available due to illness. Hence, we interviewed remaining 3 ex-persons. 6 persons have adorned the chair of the Upa-Lokayukta. Among those, Mr. Mohni, Mr. Jayaraman and Mr. Iyyer were available. Mr. Nadkarni and Mr. Bhave are not alive whereas, Mr. Shivramkrishnan was not available due to his ill health.

We approached these persons of the high offices with a view to discuss and obtain their clarification on some aspects of the functioning of the offcicce of the Lokayukta. Especially, we had in our mind the framework prepared for the complainants as well as the field offices. It was therefore, decided to know and understand their views and hence we raised these points during interviews with the Lokayuktas and Upa-Lokayuktas:

1. The difficulties they come across in the way of their functioning as successful Lokayuktas or Upa-Lokayuktas in respect of adequacy of staff and budget, intervention on the part of the government, the ministers and secretaries, etc.
2. Their views and opinions on jurisdiction of Lokayukta.
3. What is their stand on the methodology on enquiry of the cases? Are they satisfied with the present arrangement or subscribe to the view for separate investigating team?
4. What measures they have taken to improve over all system of Lokayukta?
5. Besides these points, efforts were also made to understand the winning contribution of individual respondent.

Table 4.18

Table Showing the list of Lokayuktas and Upa-lokayuktas Interviewed

No.	*Name*	*Post*	*Period*	*Date of Interview*
1	Justice P. S. Shah	Ex-Lokayukta	26 Oct. 1989-25 Oct. 1994	5 Nov. 2003
2	Justice H. H. Kantharia	Ex-Lokayukta	27 Oct. 1994-30 Nov. 1998	5 Nov. 2003
3	Justice V. P. Tipnis	Sitting-Lokayukta	1 Jan. 1999 - 31 Dec. 2003	30 Dec. 2003
4	Mr. S. P. Mohnı	Ex-Upa-Lokayukta	16 Nov. 1983-3 Feb. 1988	6 Nov. 2003
5	Mr. N. .Jayraman	Ex- Upa-Lokayukta	28 Feb. 1994-27 Feb. 1999	7 Nov. 2003
6	Mr. R. C. Iyyer	Sitting-Upa-Lokayukta	8 March 1999-31 March 2004	17 Nov. 2003

JUSTICE P.S. SHAH, EX-LOKAYUKTA

P. S. Shah noted that non-response on the side of government was a major difficulty in the functioning of Lokayukta. He is not satisfied in his tenure due to delay in implementing his recommendations by the government offices. He also voiced like Mr. Kantharia that the government never interrupted in his workings but was never interested with his working or implementing his recommendations. He added that the Lokayuktas have a very low budget. The reports say that the Lokayukta office has an inadequate staff, which is one of the reasons of pending cases. Mr. Shah didn't agree to it. We cross-questioned that their reports said that the staff was not adequate; but he answered that he got adjusted with the number of staff available. He expressed his opinion that Lokayukta must have power of implementing its own suggestions. "Extended powers and jurisdiction, adequate and experienced staff, incentives to staff, finality in powers will make Lokayukta more effective," he says. He also added that he could not justify one of the complaints. In that case, Ex-Minister was accused. But, as Ex-Minister is out of Lokayukta's purview and he was helpless. But, the complainant appealed in the High Court against Lokayukta's decision. Recently, the Court made it clear that the word 'Ex' does not matter. What is important that the person held the post at the time when it vented. Mr. Kantharia and Mr. Shah added that if Maharashtra Lokayukta will get its own investigating team and more powers like Karnataka Lokayukta, it can deal with the cases of maladministration to reduce it. At last, we questioned him about his measures to improve the Lokayukta system. He answered that his results only are his winning contribution.

JUSTICE H. H. KANTHARIA, EX-LOKAYUKTA

Justice Kantharia pointed out indifference on the part of the executive and the legislature as hurdle in the effective functioning of the Lokayukta. Due to this difficulty according to him, large number of cases are to be kept pending. He also faced odd position as incumbent of Lokayukta because of recommendatory and not mandatory status. He did not give any specific comment on pausity of budget. He told about adequacy of staff that it was good and adequate. We reminded him that the reports say that it was not; but he disagreed.

He is of the opinion that Chief Minister, Ex-Ministers, Ex-Secretaries must be brought under Lokayukta's purview. He was in favor of separate investigating team at the disposal of Lokayukta. Kantharia is a person who thinks that Lokayukta institute needs more publicity. His significant contribution as a Lokayukta is that he took initiative to publicize the institute, he delivered the speeches inside and outside the country in the public functions as well as on AIR. He also published articles on this issue. He tried to create trust among the citizens that Lokayukta is 'lokanche ayukta'. He never took remuneration while talking or writing on Lokayukta. Because, he thought that giving publicity to the institute was his duty. He also pinpointed that P. C. Alexander, as the then Governor supported him. But, he agreed that as a Lokayukta he couldn't reduce lethargy of the government. He called Lokayukta 'doot' i.e. god sent man. He expressed his expectation that Lokayukta must get more power. He explained that Lokayukta is not for controlling corruption only but also to get ventilation of public grievances.

MR. V. P. TIPNIS, SITTING-LOKAYUKTA

Mr. Tipnis told that the government offices many times didn't provide document on time. He used to fire them. He also added that he had a good rapport for the Governor. He told that he is happy with his staff, but added that there was need for more financial provisions from the government. On the question of jurisdiction of Lokayukta, he answered that it needs extension of the jurisdiction but present jurisdiction also makes him effective in functioning. He opined that if Lokayukta would get separate investigating team, it would be better- but the present system is also good for him. Totally, he is happy with the machinery. The measure he has taken to improve the system is that he made a record of special reports to the Governor. He submitted the special Reports to the Governor in large number and made him to think and act on Lokayukta's reports in some cases. The question arises how far of his reports were implemented. He answered that 60% were implemented till date. He was in oppose to give publicity to the institute and his opinion about that was that a learned man must know about such machinery and any one should come to it if known about the machinery. The notable thing about Mr. Tipnis is that he is the first Lokayukta who delegated his powers to the Registrar and Additional Registrar. He thought that it is necessary to give speedy justice to delegate and dispose the cases quickly and this is his wining contribution that he disposed more cases. He also decreased a large number of pendency. He disposed the cases that were pending since last 8 to 10 years which according to him was not large but disrespected the post of Lokayukta. He made it clear that Lokayukta machinery is not working against corruption only. Basically the idea of Ombudsman came up as a redressal of public grievances, it is the Lokayukta.

We asked the Upa-Lokayuktas first three questions. They answered as below-

MR. MOHNI S.P., EX- UPA-LOKAYUKTA

Mr. Mohni focused an ethical and philosophical difficulty that it is not fair that only the Ex-Judges are appointed as Lokayukta. In his opinion, Judges prefer evidences and judicial process that are not necessary for Lokayukta's function. "Judges are experienced and experts in law and judiciary; but sometimes they catch and realize administrative problems," is his opinion. He suggested an alternative that sometimes the Lokayukta must be from the civil services or that investigation must be beyond the law sometimes. He didn't agree that the inadequate staff, inadequate accommodation or finance is the limitations in Lokayukta's functioning. According to him, efficiency is never bothered by these limitations. He supported that the separate investigating team could make Maharashtra Lokayukta more effective. He subsequently provides example of Rajas than and Karnataka Lokayukta that they have a separate team and can work independently.

MR. N. JAYRAMAN, EX-UPA-LOKAYUKTA

Mr. Jay Raman told that the limited jurisdiction of Lokayuta was his main difficulty in working. He suggested that Ex-public servants, Ex-Ministers, Universities, Judges, Speaker, Election Commissioner must be brought under Lokayukta's purview. This will make them more effective. He supported separate investigating machinery. To a question about his views about Lokayukta system, he told that it is necessary in all the States as well as at the Center. He persuaded the Central Government to bring up Lokpal. For that purpose, he wrote to the Central Government many a times. He also published articles in the newspapers and magazines on the issue. He regretted that his efforts were in vain.

MR. R.C. IYYER, SITTING-UPA-LOKAYUKTA

Mr. Iyyer pinpointed that if the Anti Corruption Bureau of the State Government should be placed under the control of the Lokayukta, it would be more effective in controlling corruption. According to him, the basic problem is that in the cases of corruption, government tends to delay in taking a decision or circumvent the recommendation and the legislature is not alert enough to call government in question on that issue. He is satisfied with his staff but not with budget. He could not attend the International Ombudsman Conferences due to lack of budgetary provisions. He also could not arrange the timely divisional visits many times. he supported the separate investigating team. His view on the institution is that it is able to provide substantial relief to a large number of persons at very low cost.

Thus, the 6 persons opined their views on Lokayukta. Raveling here the gist of interviews, it can be said that the Lokayukta institute requires:

1. Chief Minister, Ex-Ministers, Ex-Public Servants under his purview,
2. Separate investigating team,
3. To work as a mandatory body,
4. To oblige the government office to provide a timely and adequate information/document.

5. Governor must recommend its special reports.
6. Legislature has to take interest in its working.

4.2 CONCLUSION

Lokayukta in Maharashtra is an important tool with the citizen to ensure smooth and corruption free administration. To sum up, the first section of this chapter, fortunately, very dignified persons adorned the chair of Lokayukta and tried their best to make the post effective and dignified. But there are a number of limitations to jurisdiction of Lokayukta. There is a continuous demand for the amendment in the Lokayukta Act. One more notable thing is that due lack of separate investigating team, Maharashtra Lokayuta could not work effectively. The second section of this chapter dealt with the direct functioning of the Maharashtra Lokayukta. Basically, due to lack of jurisdiction and separate investigating team, the Lokayukta could not be utilized fully by the citizen. Another thing is that the utility argued by the office stated in the first section is not absolute. The figure given by the office is considered either solved or disposed under various sections but this disposal is largely on the side of the office and not on the side of citizens. Office says that the cases are disposed but the complainant is not justified. In this chapter, tables of interest taken by ministry with the Lokayukta's working are also given. Legislature never discussed the report of Lokayukta, which shows a very poor response to the Lokayukta office from the side of Legislature. One more aspect is that there is very less number of ministerial cases lodged to Lokayukta. All these facts about the Lokayukta office shows that it need to amend some sections of the Lokayukta Act. What is important is that the Chief Minister should come under Lokayukta's purview. In the next chapter, survey and interviews in this regard are discussed.

REFERENCES

1. The Maharashtra Lokayukta and Upa-Lokayukta Act, 1971, Government Printing, Stationary and Publications, Maharashtra State, Mumbai—1973 —8
2. The Annual Consolidated Report, The Maharashtra Lokayukta and Upa-Lokayukta, 2001— Published by Government Press, Mumbai.—45

5

Conclusion

The modern society is complex. Therefore, the role of the state in the management of the public affairs is pivotal. Bureaucracy is an apparatus of a state. It exercises the powers of the state. In democratic political system, the politicians and the bureaucrats are the two power centers. These power centers take decisions, prepare policies and execute them. Obviously, the administration influences every aspect of the common man's life, such as drinking water, sanitation, food grains, housing, roads, electricity, health, education, employment, etc. The common man encounters number of difficulties in getting the goods and services from the long chain of bureaucracy. Delays, non-execution, indifferent attitude, insensibility, ill treatment, sense of insecurity are the matters of daily experiences of the people. Thus, the citizens who are constitutionally the custodians of democratic set up, are at the mercy of huge the bureaucratic syndrome. There is a dire need of effective machinery to redress the grievances of the citizens. To add to these grievances is the phenomenon of corruption. Both the politicians and bureaucrats make use of the lever power in their hands for individual benefits and hence indulge in large-scale corruption, irregularities and bribes. Especially, when the nexus is between the two there is always the multiplication of corrupt practices. However to curb the rising corruption is the big issue of the civilized society.

The system of Ombudsman i.e. Lokpal at the Centre and of Lokayukta at the States, are engaged in the process of redressing the grievances of the citizens and eliminating the corruption. To understand and to analyze the functioning of Maharashtra Lokayukta is the main object of this study.

There are number of devices to control corruption. A comprehensive review of the legal measures, organizational set up, the special establishments, committees and commissions to cope up with the problem of corruption in general and in the events of big scandals in particular was made in the first chapter of the study. The main object was to understand the inherent limitation of all these exercises in the absence of an independent and impartial regular machinery to deal with rising corruption were experienced for very long time. Against this background, the idea of introducing Ombudsman like institution emerged in India in the sixties. A detailed description of the evolution of proposed Lokpal at national level is highlighted in the second chapter of this study. It is a matter of sorry state of affairs that the country is badly in need of Lokpal whereas the politicians are determined not to have one. A step by step account of Lokpal Bill is given in the second chapter which reveals that there is lot of confusion about the jurisdiction of Lokpal. A section of politicians and thinkers are of the opinion that some positions such as the Prime Minister, the Chief Election Commissioner, etc. are sacrosanct and hence should not come within the purview of Lokpal. They plead for the privileged status of these posts. But they forget that the absence of privileges is the core of democracy. The study points out the lack of consensus about the jurisdiction of proposed Lokpal. The deeper analysis also reveals the reluctance on the part of those who are at the helm of affairs to give serious thought to the very concept of Ombudsman as the watchdog of the citizen. The way in which the Lokpal bill is withdrawn, lingered with select committee, allowed to be killed due to dissolution of the House. etc. clearly indicates the callous neglect of citizens' agony by not providing timely instrument of ombudsman to them. Thus it seems that there is no political will behind the formation of Lokpal at national level. The will of the people is equally not strong to compel the government to act upon the measure in this regard. There are agitations in this country on flimsy issues. Some of them are really concerned about the sufferings of the citizens. But we could not hear during our study a bold voice of citizens and agitations for the establishment of Lokpal. Therefore, it can be concluded that the overall environment in the country is not conducive to the emergence of Lokpal and its effective functioning at the national level. The first chapter gives the worldwide experience of the system of Ombudsman. Comparatively, high position of the countries with Ombudsman in terms of their ranks in corruption prone countries has proved the utility of the office of Ombudsman. The remarkable thing we could point out through this study is whereas we are not in position to set up Lokpal at the national level in spite of our efforts in this direction for more than thirty years, the other countries are far ahead and successful, in building up network of ombudsman in different fields of social life, public and private, commercial and service-oriented sector, etc. Thus, non-seriousness about Lokpal is the critical area of our political and administrative culture especially, when the concepts such as good governance and citizens' charter are gathering momentum. Our observation is all related to the components, i. e. the complainants the government-i. e. the Governor, the Legislature, the Cabinet, the officials of departments, the NGOs are responsible for this state of affairs.

Effectiveness of Lokayukta in Maharashtra

The object of this study is to understand how far Lokayukta is effective in Maharashtra. The number of complaints is the indicator to prove it. According to the Reports of Lokayukta, the office received 903 complaints in the first year of its formation and the number reached up to 15,745 by 2002. This fact reveals that the people are used to approach Lokayukta for their grievances. The effectiveness is also reflected in the disposed number of cases. It can also be supported by decreasing number of pending cases compared with the number of lodged cases; the number of disposed cases are, 309 in 1972, 849 in 1982, 4146 in 1992, and 3555 in 2002. During our discussion with the Lokayukta we confirmed its effectiveness in quantitative terms also.

Role of Lokayukta to Control Corruption

Lokayukta is viewed as an independent and an impartial device to control corruption. Therefore, to what extent the

Lokayukta in Maharashtra has been in a position to control the corruption is a moot question. This can be tested by the cases of corruption handled by Lokayukta. The Lokayukta's yearly reports as well as the responses of the complainants we analyzed reveal that the large number of complaints the office of the Lokayukta deal with are other than the allegations of corruption. We pointed out that out of the total cases, only 3% cases were on corruption. Our conclusion in this regard is whereas Lokayukta in Maharashtra is quite effective in redressing the grievances of the citizens; it could not reach the deep roots of corruption. It has proved its utility in the ventilation of grievances and not dealing with the allegations of corruption. When we proceed to probe the role of Lokayukta a little further, we come to know that there is a lack of clarity and consensus on this issue on the part incumbent at the office of Lokayukta and Upa-Lokayukta. We observed that some of them emphasized the need of the ventilation of grievances by Lokayukta. Ventilation of grievances by Lokayukta, as if the task of controlling corruption, is not relevant to its functioning. This is the perspective of some of the interviewees. What is the approach of the government in this regard? The Lokayukta submits yearly reports to the government so as to place it in the House. We could not find any efforts taken on the part of the government to study the findings of the report with a view to eliminating corruption. Neither the Legislature nor the Cabinet in any way considered the reports seriously and tried to know how far the institution of Lokayukta has been successful in wiping out corruption. The house seldom discusses the reports in detail. It can be said that there is wide gap in the perception of western model of Ombudsman as a crusader against corruption and the Indian model wherein the Lokayukta has not so far occupied any space in the battle against corruption.

Impartiality of Lokayukta

There is a strong point in the whole system of Lokayukta in Maharashtra, and that is those who occupied the position of Lokayuktas are the High Court Judges and the men of integrity. We experienced courteous and amicable treatment in the Lokayukta office as well as full co-operation of the interviewee Lokayuktas during our visits. As compared to the other machineries such as the Election Commission, the Union and State Public Service Commissions, etc. The machineries with focus on impartiality, prompt and straightforward working the image of Lokayuktas has been unquestionable. In respect of other machineries referred above both people of integrity and impartiality as well as those with doubtful integrity occupied them. However, the graph of the Lokayuktas in this regard has been constantly high. In our survey, 90% of the respondents expressed their satisfaction of approaching Lokayukta. They were also treated well. To the specific question whether Lokayukta was impartial to them in dealing with the complainant or against? Was he favorable to government side? The respondents without any hesitation stated- impartiality. The purpose of the Lokayukta of ventilating grievances, therefore, has been fulfilled.

Methodology of Functioning of Lokayukta

The success, utility of any institution or organization largely depends on the methodology of its working. As the Lokayukta is concerned with the complaints of the citizens, the grievances and the irregularities as well as corruption, there is an urgent need of full-fledged investigating machinery under his control. But to our surprise, this element of the institution finds very little place in its organizational set up. Firstly, there is no uniform method adopted in all the States. In the states like Karnataka and Rajasthan, there is investigating machinery at the disposal of Lokayukta. However, in Maharashtra, the Lokayukta has to depend on the Police, CBI, etc. for investigation. The concerned departments also are entrusted with work of investigation. This arrangement creates obstacle in its working. Secondly, all the Lokayuktas, who were interviewed, were not very keen on investigating machinery. Some of them insisted upon the need of it. A few pointed out with separate or no separate investigating machinery they could investigate the complaint. Thirdly, the government over a period of long working of Lokayuktas did not care to review the methodology of enquiry. No new technology is being equipped with the Lokayukta for speedy investigation.

About the procedure of disposing complaints for investigation there are certain lacunae in the Act, the rule as well as in the practice. Thus, the cases, which were not investigated due to some reason or the other were also treated and shown in the report as the disposed cases. Table 4.5 and 4.6 of the chapter IV show such cases. There is no mention of actual redressal of complaints that are supposed to be disposed cases. However, the reports include vague, improper, anonymous cases as disposed cases. It is very difficult to assess the performance of the Lokayukta due to mixing of investigated and non- investigated cases.

Lokayukta and the Government Departments

Much depends on the healthy relation and interaction between the office of the Lokayukta and the government departments. The Lokayukta receives complaints against the officials of different departments. But, our study reveals that the officers of the department do not co-operate and supply information on the complainants regularly and fail to follow the rule as per the Lokayukta Act. This results into delay in the disposal of complaints. All the interviewees had the same feeling. We also experienced the indifference on the part of the officials. Our survey indicated that not a single respondent official replied and returned our questionnaire duly filled in.

Positive Features of Lokayukta in Maharashtra

In nutshell the Lokayukta in Maharashtra has positive and strong features as given below:

1. Any person can lodge a complaint to the Lokayukta and can get justice within a short period of time.
2. The number of the people approaching the Lokayukta is increasing.
3. The percentage of disposal of cases and grievance redressal has increased from inception.

4. Lokayukta is free from any Executive, political or governmental control.
5. The persons of dignity and integrity have adorned a chair of the Lokayukta.
6. There is no interference in Lokayukta's working from the side of the government or executive.
7. Lokayukta can deal with any matter of citizens' grievances.
8. Lokayukta deals with the governmental matters. In the private sectors, Ombudsman is necessary to control the uncertainty of jobs.

Weaknesses of Maharashtra Lokayukta

The Lokayukta in Maharashtra has some weaknesses:

1. The cases are disposed but grievances are not absolutely redressed.
2. There is a lack of immediate response by the government departments in providing evidences as well as implementing recommendations.
3. Lokayukta does not have its separate investigating machinery.
4. The Executive and Legislature are not so far interested in Lokayukta's working.
5. NGOs and media do not take notice of the Lokayukta's working in a significant way.
6. Lokayukta as per the Act, can take a cognizance by its own on any matter but, normally he avoids it. There are a very few cases in which it did so.

These positive features and weaknesses of Lokayukta in Maharashtra shows that though it is a very good institution, it needs to be strengthened. The institute needs more prestige and popularity. It needs administrative reforms.

Suggestions

Some suggestions are made here on the basis of observations on the working of Lokayukta and interactions with incumbents on the one hand and complainants on the other:

1. There should be discussion, exchange of views, and dialogues on the role of Lokayukta. The model guidelines of such processes will be of immense help in this regard.
2. A high level committee should be appointed to study and recommend amendments to the Lokayukta Act including the reform measures to make Lokayukta more effective to control corruption.
3. A periodical review be undertaken on the Annual Consolidated Reports of Lokayukta regarding his performance on reducing corruption. Instead of leaving the Annual Consolidated Reports undiscussed, there should be some methodology to be evolved so that attention will be given to the findings of the reports. It can be suggested that there shall be the Cabinet Committee to review and comment on the report with action taken on it. Further, the committee of the House appointed for the purpose should also consider the reports along with comments of the Cabinet.
4. It is necessary to give a serious thought to provide independent investigating machinery to the Lokayukta.
5. Stringent actions should be taken on those officials with an entry into their Confidential Reports who do not give co-operation to the Lokayukta.
6. There should be more transparency in the working of Lokayukta. The secrecy clause, if possible could be removed. This will help to gain confidence about the machinery of Lokayukta.
7. The Lokayuktas, be oriented to initiate the cases and process them without waiting for complainants as and when possible. Thus, tradition of sue-motto be cultivated in line with judicial activism.
8. It is suggested that search for mechanism and modality be undertaken to make the findings of Lokayukta be binding and mandatory instead of recommendatory at present.

9. In the era of privatization, the private sectors should come under Lokayukta's purview. There should be the separate Ombudsman in the private, especially in the co-operative sector so far Maharashtra is concerned..
10. In the days of comparative and inter-disciplinary studies, Lokayukta should compulsorily attend the All India Lokayuktas and Upa-Lokayuktas Parishads as well as International Ombudsman Conferences so that it could helpful to compare and reduce the weakness of the Maharashtra Lokayukta.

In short the focus of this study, as far as the future course of Lokayukta is concerned, is on strengthening the link between the phenomenon of rising corruption and Lokayukta as a friend, philosopher and a guide of citizenry as corrective measure in an atmosphere of larger complaints of bribery, corruption, irregularities and favoritism handed over to Lokayukta who will come out with punishment and will pave the way for corruption free democratic society.

Appendices

APPENDIX-I

The members of International Ombudsman Institute are:

(source: A website developed by IOI updated on May 12, 2002)

AFRICA:

Office of the Ombudsman, Korea

Commission Against Corruption, Macao

AUSTRALIA AND PACIFIC:

Office of the Ombudsman, Hong Kong

State Comptroller and Commissioner For Complaints From The Public, Israel

Northern Ireland Assembly Ombudsman and Commissioner for Complaints

Center For Human Rights, Moldova

De Nationale Ombudsman, The Netherlands

Parliamentary Ombudsman, Norway

Provedor de Justica, Portugal

Office of the ombudsman, Romania

Defensor del Pueblo, Spain (Regional)

Defensor del Pueblo, Andaluz, Spain (Regional)

Arareko Pays Vasco, Spain (Regional)

Parliamentary Commissioner For Administration and Commissioner For Complaints, Northern Ireland

Office of the Ombudsman, Slovenia

Riksdagens Ombudsman, Sweden

Parliamentary Commissioner For Administration and Health Service, United Kingdom

Commission for Local Administration in England, London

Commission for Local Administration in Wales

Office of The Ombudsman, Uzbekistan

British and Irish Ombudsman Association

NORTH AMERICA:

Office of The Ombudsman, Alberta

Office of The Ombudsman, British Columbia

Office of The Ombudsman, Manitoba

Office of The Ombudsman, Ontario

Office of The Commissioner of Official Languages

Le Protector Du Citoyen, Quebec

Office of The Ombudsman, Alaska

Citizen's Aide Ombudsman, Arizona

Office of The Citizen's Aide Ombudsman, Iowa

Joint Office of Citizen's Complaints, Ohio

Commonwealth Ombudsman, Puerto Rico

King County Office Of Citizen's Complaints, Seattle, Washington

Office of The Ombudsman, New Zealand

Office of The Commonwealth Ombudsman and Defense Force Ombudsman, Federal

Office of The Ombudsman, New South Wales

Ombudsman and Commissioner-Health and Community Services Complaints Commission, Northern Territory

Office of The Ombudsman, South Australia

Office of The Control Yuan, Taiwan

Office of The Ombudsman, Tasmania

Office of The Ombudsman, Victoria

Parliamentary Commissioner For Administrative Investigations, Western Australia

CARIBEAN AND LATIN AMERICA:

Defensor Del Pueblo De La Republica, Argentina

Office of The National Ombudsman, Barbados

Defensor De Ios Habitants, Costa Rica

Comisionado Nacional de Protection De Los Derechos Humanos, Honduras

Comision Nacional de Derechos Humanos, De Jaliso, Mexico

Comision Estatal de Derechos Humanos Del Estado De Veracruz, Mexico

Defensoria de Pueblo, Peru

Panama Defensoria De Pueblo, Peru

EUROPE:

Volksanwaltschaft, Austria

Office of The Federal Ombudsman, Belgium

Mediateur de La Region Wallonne, Belgium

Folketings Ombudsman, Denmark

Office of The Parliamentary Ombudsman, Finland

Office of The Chancellor of Justice, Finland

Mediateur de La Republic, France

Ombudsman of The European Union

Public Defender Georgia

Petitions Committee of The German Bundestag, Germany

Office of The Ombudsman, Gibraltor

Office of The Ombudsman, Greece

National Ombudsman, Israel

APPENDIX-II

Abbreviations

CBI	Central Bureaue of Investigation
CEO	Chief Executive Officer
CM	Chief Minister
CVC	Central Vigilance Commission
EOI	European Ombudsman Institute
IGP	Inspector General of Police
IOI	International Ombudsman Institute
JSC	Joint Select Committee
MP	Member of Parliament
NGO	Non-Governmental Organization
NRI	Non-Residence of India
PIL	Public Interest Litigation
PM	Prime Minister
PMO	Prime Minister's Office
PWD	Public Works Department
RBI	Reserve Bank of India
RTI	Right To Information

Bibliography

BOOKS

1.	Agrawal B. R.	Our Judiciary—National Book Trust, India—1996 Ist Ed. 1993
2.	Altas Syed Husain	Corruption and Density of Asia—Simon & Schuster (Asia) Pvt. Ltd., Singapore—1999
3.	Anderson Stanley V.	The California Commission on Judicial Qualification—Prentice Hall, London—1968
4.	Barnabas A. P.	Citizens' Grievances and Administration—Indian Institute of Public Administration, New Delhi—Sept. 1969
5.	Berthwal C. P.	Public Administration in India—Ashish Publishing House, New Delhi—1993
6.	Chandra Ramesh & Dr. Shrivastava R. C.	Development of Judicial System in India—April 1971
7.	Dadabhai Naoriji	Poverty and Un-British Rule in India—Ministry of Information and Broadcasting, Government of India, May 1996- Ist Ed. July 1962

8.	Dhawan R. K.	Public Grievances and Lokpal –Allied Publishers Pvt. Ltd., New Delhi—1981
9.	Dr. Acharya Nandkishor	The Polity in Sukranitisara Vagdevi Prakasan, Bikaner-1987
10.	Dr. Altekar A. S.	State and Government in Ancient India—Motilal Banarsidas, Delhi-7—1972—Ist Ed. 1958
11.	Dr. Awasthi A.	Aspects of Administration—Allied Publisher Pvt. Ltd., New Delhi—1964
12.	Dr. Bhatia K. L.	Judicial Activism and Social Change—Deep & Deep Publications, New Delhi—1990
13.	Dr. P. N. Mathur	The Gazetteer of India, New Delhi—1978
14.	Dr. Saxena D.R. & Mehra K.P.	Ombudsman- Deep & Deep Publications, New Delhi—1990
15.	Singhvi L.M. (Ed.)	Lokpal: Ombudsman in India—The Institute of Constitutional and Parliamentary Studies, New Delhi
16.	Verindra Grover & L. Arora Rajan (Ed.)	India: 50 years of Independence— Deep & Deep Publications, New Delhi—1997
17.	N. Narayan Swamy, M. P. Boraian, M.A. Jeyaraju (Ed.)	Corruption at Grassroots—Concept Publishing Co., New Delhi—1997

18.	Gelhorn Walter	Ombudsman and Others—Harvard University Press, London—1967
19.	Gerhart Eugene C	Quite It! – Universal Law Publishing Co. Pvt. Ltd., 1998
20.	Ghosh S. K.	Indian Panorama: Triumphs and Tragedies—Vol. III—A. P. H. Publishing Corporation, New Delhi—1999
21.	Golembiewski T. Robert	Public Administration As A Developing Discipline Marcle Dekker Inc, London—1
22.	Grover Verinder	Political System in India—Deep & Deep Publications, New Delhi—1989
23.	Haj Mohamedullah Bin	The Administration of Justice of Muslim Law—Law Department, University of Allahabad, Allahabad—1934
24.	Hood Christopher C.	The Limits of Administration—John Wiley & Sons, London—1976 Ist Ed. 1952
25.	Husain Wahed	Administrative Justice During The Muslim Rule in India — University of Calcutta, Calcutta—1934
26.	Jagannadhaman V. & Makhija H. R.	Citizen, Administration and Lokpal—S. Chand & Co., New Delhi—1969
27.	Jain M. P.	Outlines if Indian Legal History—N. M. Tripathi

		Pvt. Ltd., Bombay—1976 Ist Ed. 1952
28.	Jain M.P.	Lokpal (Ombudsman) in India- I.C. P. S. Publication, New Delhi-1970
29.	Jain R.B.	Public Administration in India: 21st Century Challenges for Good Governance— Deep & Deep Publications, New Delhi—1987
30.	Jaiswal K. P.	Hindu Polity –The Banglore Publishing Co. Ltd., Banglore—1967
31.	Jonson Buttoph Janet & Joslyn A. Richard	Political Science Research Methods—Prentice Hall in India Pvt. Ltd., New Delhi—1987
32.	Kalam Abdul A.P.J.	India 2020- Penguin Books, New Delhi—1998
33.	Lal Bhure	Corruption- Functional Anarchy in Governance—Siddharth Publications, New Delhi—2002
34.	Lewis Norman & S. S. Singh	Ombudsman— Indian Institute of Public Administration, New Delhi—Sept. 1995
35.	M. Hallaya	Emergency: A War on Corruption—S. Chand & Co. (Pvt.) Ltd., New Delhi—Sept. 1975
36.	Mahajan V.D.	India Since 1526— S. Chand & Co. (Pvt.) Ltd.,

		New Delhi-1996—Ist Ed. 1978
37.	Maheshwari S. R.	The Administrative Reforms Commission—Laxmi Narayan Agrawal, Agra—1972
38.	Mansukhani H. L.	Corruption and Public Servants—Vikas Publishing House Ltd., New Delhi—1979
39.	Mc'nil H. William & Jean W. Sedlar	Reading in World History Classical India-4 –Oxford University Press, London—1978- Ist Ed. 1967
40.	Monterio B. John	Corruption: Control of Maladministration—P.C. Mankatlal & Sons, London—1966
41.	Motiwala O. P.	Administrative Justice in India
42.	Palkiwala N. A.	A Judiciary Made To Measure—M. P. Rai, Bombay—1973
43.	Parmar Mary	Lokayukta—Reliance Publishing House, New Delhi—2000
44.	Pattanayak Raimann	Bureaucracy, Politics and Administrative Change—Anmol Publishing Pvt. Ltd. New Delhi
45.	Prakash Rai	Constitution, Fundamental Rights & Judicial Activism in India—Mangal Deep Publications, Jaipur—1997

46.	Prasad Vishnu	Administrative Tribunals in Action—Oxford & IBH Publishing House Co. New Delhi—1974
47.	Ramkrishna P. V.	A Treatise on Anti-Corruption Laws in India—S. Gogia & Com., Hyderabad, 1996—Ist Ed. 1969
48.	Rao B. Guru Rajah	Ancient Hindu Judicature—Ganesh & Co., Madras—1910
49.	Ray S. N.	Modern Comparative Politics: Approaches, Methods and Issues—Prentice Hall of India Pvt. Ltd., New Delhi, 1999
50.	Rowat Donald	The Ombudsman: Citizen's Defender—George Allen & Urwin Ltd., 1965
51.	Sathe S. P.	Administrative Law—Butterworths India, New Delhi, 1999—Ist Ed. 1976
52.	Sharma S. P.	Reading in Kautilya's Arthashastra—Agam Prakashan, Delhi—1976
53.	Sharma Giridhar	Implementation of Ombudsman Plan in India—Ashish Publishing House, New Delhi, 1981
54.	Shukla K. S. & Singh S. S.	Lokayukta—Indian Institute of Public Administration, New Delhi—1988
55.	Singh Bakshish	The Supreme Court of India: As An Instrument of

		Social Justice—Sterling Publishers Pvt. Ltd., New Delhi,—1976
56.	Singh M. M.	Justice By Tribunals—The World Press Pvt. Ltd., Calcutta, 1973
57.	Singhvi Nita	Administration & Citizen—Somaiya Publication, Pvt. Ltd., Bombay, 1977
58.	Shrivastava Chandra	Development of Judicial System in India
59.	Stacy Frank	The British Ombudsman—Clarwndon Press—1971
60.	The Banking Ombudasman Scheme	Reserve Bank of India, Central Office, Mumbai—2002
61.	Vajpayee Atal Behari	Four Decades in Parliament—Ed/ N/M/ Chatate—Sahara Publications, Delhi-1998—Ist Ed. 1996
62.	Williams David	Maladministration: Remedies for Injustice—Oyez Publishing Ltd., London, 1976
63.	Wyner J Allen	Executive Ombudsman in India—1973
64.	Zaidi A. M.	The Annual Register of Indian Political Parties—1981—S. Chand & Com. Ltd., New Delhi—1982

ENCYCLOPAEDIA

1. Collier's Encyclopedia-18—William Halsey—Macmillian Education Company, New York—1950

2. 21st Century Universal Encyclopedia-21—L. Collinghood—Regency Publishing, New Delhi—1983-1996
3. Encyclopedic Dictionary of Public Administration-2 – S. K. Das, Sarup & Sons, New Delhi—1996
4. Encyclopedia Americana-8—Americana Corporation, New York—1829

JOURNALS

1. Administrative Change 22(2), Jan.-Jun., 1995—Ed. A. B. Mathur, Jaipur
2. Australian Journal of Public Administration 48(2) Jun. 1989—Pub. By Royal Australian Institute of Public Administration—Ed. Roger Scott & Roger Wettenhall
3. CBI Bulletin- Vol. IV(1) Jun. 1996—Pub. By CBI Publications, New Delhi—Ed. Rajendra Kaul
4. Indian Journal of Public Administration, Jan–Mar 1985(1); Apr-Jun 1988(34); Jan–Mar 1989(1); Apr-Jun 1990(36); Apr-Jun 1991(37); Oct- Dec. 1993(35); Jan–Mar1995(43); Apr-Jun 1997(30); Jul-Sept 1997(13) Pub. By Indian Institute of Public Administration, Ed.: T. N. Chaturvedi
5. International Review of Administrative Science 50(3) 1984
6. Journal of National Academy of Administrative Science, Mussorie, Vol. XV (2&3) 1970 Pub. By National Academy of Administrative Science, Mussorie.
7. Kurukshetra –April 2001
8. Management in Government 21(1-3) Apr-Dec. 1989. Pub. By Cabinet Secretariate, New Delhi
9. One India, One People- Feb. 2000
10. Political Science Review- Vol. 3(1) May 1964 Pub. By Dept. of Political Science, University of Rajasthan, Jaipur
11. Canadian Journal of Public Administration, Jun 1976

12. Southern Economist- Vol. 41(11) Oct. 2002 Ed. Sushila Subrahamanyam
13. The Radical Humanist- 60(10) Jan 1997 62(12) Mar 1999 Pub. By Navchetan Publishers
14. The Calcutta Journal of Political Studies- Pub. By Dept. of Political Science, Calcutta University.

ACTS

1. Prevention of Corruption Act, 1947- 4th Edition—1996 S. Gogia & Com., Hyderabad
2. Prevention of Corruption Act, 1988-13th Edition—1999- Eastern Book Com., Lalbagh, Lucknow
3. Lokpal & Lokayukta Bill, 1996- Pub. By The Secretariat, Loksabha, New Delhi
4. The Maharashtra Lokayukta & Upa- Lokayukta Act, 1971—Government Printing, Stationary & Publications, Maharashtra State, Mumbai—1973

NEWSPAPERS

1. Indian Express—12 Oct. 1999, 12 Oct. 2002, 16 Oct. 2002
2. The Times of India— 22 March 2001, 3 Aug. 2001, 27 Feb 2002, 3 Sept. 2002, 24 July 2002, 7 Dec. 2002, 17 Aug 2002, 18 May 2003, 6 June 2003, 13 June 2003, 22 Dec 2003, 14 Jan 2005
3. The Hindu—8 Aug 2002, 2 Dec 2002, 4 Dec. 2002, 10 Dec 2002, 12 Dec 2002, 13 Dec 2002, 20 Dec. 2002
4. Dainik Loksatta—6 June 2003, 7 june 2003, 22 Aug 2003, 26 Aug 2003, 14 Jan 2005
5. Dainik Samna—7 June 2003, 20 Aug. 2003, 23 Dec. 2003
6. Dainik Lokmat—2 July 2003, 7 July 2003
7. Dainik Maharashtra Times—20 Aug. 2003, 22 Aug. 2003
8. The Asian Age—24 Sept. 2003
9. The Mumbai Age— 25 Sept. 2003
11. Dainik Sakal—1 Oct. 2004, 10 Oct. 2004, 16 Dec. 2004

REPORTS

1. Committee on Prevention of Corruption, 1962 – Pub. by Govt. Press, Mumbai.
2. The Annual Consolidated Report—The Maharashtra Lokayukta & Upa- Lokayukta – 1972-73 to 2003 Pub. by Govt. Press, Mumbai.
3. Public Administration in India—A Report of Survey—May 1953—Paul Applbee—Govt. of India, Cabinet Secretariat, New Delhi.
4. Joint Committee on The Lokpal and Lokayukta Bill, 1968—Pub. by Cabinet Secretariat, New Delhi.
5. Report of Administrative Reforms Commission, Aug 1966— Pub. by Cabinet Secretariat, New Delhi.
6. Information Bulletin- Lokpal for India—Nov 1996—Pub. by Cabinet Secretariat, New Delhi.
7. Budget—2002-03—General Administration Department— Pub. by Cabinet Secretariat, New Delhi.
8. Loksabha Debates—1969, 1971, 1985, 1989, 1996, 2001, 2003.
9. Maharashtra Debates—33—1971— Pub. by Mantralaya, Mumbai.

WEBPAGES

1. http://www.eduskunta.fi.efkta/eoa/.
2. http://www.synigorus.gr/en-who-is-in.ca.
3. http://www.ombudsmen.govt.nz/laying.htm.
4. http://www.colorado.edu.ombuds/index/htm/
5. http://www.unichicago.edu/student/ombudsperson/html.
6. http://www.unichicago.edu.student person/html.
7. http://www.falcon.cc.ku.edu/~ombuds.index/html
8. http://www.colostate.edu.
9. http://www.cvo-gov.sate/us/.

10. http://www.ombudsman.ci.detroit.us
11. http://www.milelegislativecouncilortg.ioc/contact.htm
12. http://www.lic.ombudsman.htm.
13. http://www.nr.state.ky.us/nrecp/dep/smbizair/index/html.
14. http://www.policeombudsman.org.main/htm
15. http://www.homeoffice.gov/uk/ppoweb/index.missionhtm.html/
16. http://www.go.org.uik/html/
17. http://www.fos.dorcon.co.uk/ombudsman
18. http://www.theiob.or.uk/
19. http://www.oea.co.uk/htm
20. http://www.pensions-ombudsman.org.uk/html.
21. http://www.cvo-gov.state/us.
22. http://www.cao.org.au/campaign/mining/ombudsman/2001.index/html
23. http://www.bo.se
24. http://www.ombudsman.ro.kr/history/on/htm/
25. http://www.corp.com/customer-rights.html/
26. http://www.tirol-hph.highway.telecom.
27. http://www.irlgov.ie./okombudsman/speeches.co
28. http://www.ombud.gov.bc.ca/publications
29. http://www.bjp.org/html
30. http://www.alfa.nic.in.isdeb.is11/ses2/20130996.htm
31. http://www.expressindia.comnews/weather.htm.
32. http://www.apnapanjub.com/txplanning/taxplanningindex.htm
33. http://www.indiainfo.com
34. http://www.unitedbankofindia.com/open.htm
35. http://www.transparency.org/documants/cpi/bps.html
36. http://www.worldbank.org/
37. http://www.corruptindia.com/rewards.htm

38. http://www.ioiacc.org/programme.html
39. http://www.abc.net.au/concon.school/eduo/html
40. http://www.ombudsman.or.kr/history/ombudsman
41. http://www.law.ualberta.com
42. http://www.ombudsman.govt.nz/laying.htm
43. http://www.adobe.com/products
44. http://www.odin.dep.no/odin
45. http://www.ombudsman.org.ukl/htm
46. http://www.ombudsmen.manitoba.mb.ca
47. http://www.ombudsman.yk.ca/omb-mainwhite.html.
48. http://www.kentlaw.edu.com
49. http://www.ombudsman.ni/index/html.
50. http://www.obo.org.uk/1/html.
51. http://www.falcon.cc.ku.edu~ombuds.index/html
52. http://www.colostate.edu
53. http://www.rene.pixelsight.com/ps/html
54. http://www.hlinote.k12.hi.us/state/boe/ombudsman.nsf.complaint
55. http://www.cao.org.au/campaigns/mining/ombudsman/2001.index.
56. http://www.slso.org.ukl
57. http://www.tdjc.state.tx.u/adminrvw/home/htm
58. http://www.dental-omkbud/sa/html
59. http://www.prison-ombudsman.uk/html.
60. http://www.elec/ombudsman.org.

Index